The GUIDE to BOOK PUBLISHERS 2002

The complete guide to book publishers in the UK & Ireland

- 5th Edition -

© Writers' Bookshop 2001
ISBN 1 902713 12 5

First published by Writers' Bookshop
Remus House, Coltsfoot Drive,
Woodston, Peterborough PE2 9JX

All rights reserved
Edited by James Feeke and Liz Stokes

From the publisher

This is the fifth edition of this guide to book publishers in the UK and Ireland. The information it contains has been supplied by the publishers and editors themselves, and is current at time of going to press.

We hope to continually improve the book's usefulness to writers and other users, and welcome any comments or suggestions for future editions.

Introduction — by Sally Spedding

'There are just too many books...' bemoaned a leading literary agent I met recently. She then more hopefully went on to list what publishers and agents are looking for in what is strictly a business world, and an overcrowded one at that.

The buzz word is PASSION. Books which have heart and soul, written with a distinctive voice *will* be noticed and rise from the slush piles to knock the editor or agent between the eyes.

How can you as a writer achieve this in an ever competitive field where everyone seems to be writing? Although my experience lies totally with fiction that word has to be the common denominator for non-fiction too. For potential novelists, however, I would suggest they begin with reading and writing poetry. By responding in words to emotions, relationships, events of the past/present/future, you are selecting what is more than merely of interest. You are tapping into your psyche, which is unique. It is this big 'I' which will be crucial to your fiction.

Poetry teaches us to construct, to discard, to polish what is left of the poem. To develop an awareness of the sounds of words, to use their richness and search for the best, least clichéd way of expression. To achieve musicality through the rhythm of each word, line and stanza using devices such as assonances and alliterations to name but a few.

Likewise the short story. Here again, your passion, obsession if you like, can fuel your writing. The germ of an idea developed here may well provide fruit for a longer work of fiction. But neither poetry nor the short story should be viewed as the easy option. A necessary stepping stone, yes, whose shape is more readily seen than a complex work of four hundred pages.

A short story should engage the reader immediately, with a beginning crafted to draw him or her in - to want to know more, just as in a novel. Consider place, weather, viewpoint and how much of your character/s and story can be developed through effective dialogue. The ending too, should be convincing and not the contrived 'twist in the tale' which all too often appears...

By paying great attention to the big 'I' and dealing with ideas which may disturb you, terrify you or bring you intense joy, then asking yourself, 'what if?' This can trigger some interesting ideas. Here you can tap into deepest fears/anxieties. ie: a missing child. A home which is no longer there etc etc... Thus making your work more immediate and distinctive.

You should read as much as you can of contemporary fiction, but not with the intention of copying themes or styles. The biggest turn-off to any publisher or agent is when they receive a letter such as:

> Dear John Brown,
>
> I write exactly like Catherine Cookson, so I'm sure you'll be interested in my novel...

I would also suggest to the would-be novelist that they accrue a track record of competition wins/commendations, inclusion in anthologies/magazines etc. Not only does success build up your confidence but shows editors and agents that you are a serious writer.

So now ask yourself *why* would you even consider writing a novel? The answer will have to sustain you through months, even years of research, writing and re-writing. If it's merely because 'I've always wanted to write' then maybe you should try something else. If your response is something like, 'I'm absorbed by people's propensity for great good and the profoundest evil...' etc etc. Or, 'I want to explore what might happen when two complete strangers in a strange country, far from home, suddenly meet and fall in love...' Just two small examples, yet each pregnant with possibilities.

However, as a novelist, you will have to go much further than this. You must consider the novel's genre - ie: historical/crime/horror/saga/science/fiction/fantasy etc. It is easier to place your work if it falls within a specific genre, so why put obstacles in the way? Also think global. America is a huge market.

You'll need to create a plot outline but as your characters begin to live and breathe through your intimate knowledge of them, they may well end up driving the narrative. Try and make your characters memorable, by researching each one fully, making them human, warts and all. Ask yourself what lies behind them? (Their pasts) What lies above them? (Their goals) What is preventing them from achieving these goals?

Remember not to make your main protagonist more sinned against than sinning, and show your reader courtesy by now killing them off too early! Unless of course, your main character has already died at the start, and has left a mystery behind...

I've already mentioned *place*, and you only have to read Daphne du Maurier or Annie Proulx to see how this can almost become the main character! Dredge from your own experiences and try and visit where your work is set. No more boring holidays! I travelled to the Vosges to research one of my books and found a palpable sense of danger there, which I certainly wouldn't have picked up on just from travel guides.

Word length. Rumour has it that books are getting slimmer. However, a good average is 80,000 words for a novel. Unlike the short story, this gives you more scope for foreshadowing, flashbacks, multiple viewpoints, the use of diaries, letters, faxes, emails etc. In one recently published American ghost story, 'House of Leaves', the pages are themselves a labyrinth of different fonts with bizarre footnotes to draw the reader deeper into the mystery.

Minette Walters used maps and photographs in her 'The Shape of Snakes' which helps create a certain verisimilitude. In my own 'Wringland' there's an old woman's illustrated 'journal' to add to the atmosphere.

I would also urge you as writers to experience as much of the outside world as possible. Giving up the day job to write isn't generally a good move. You need to hear people, observe everything, and, true to Parkinson's Law, if time is precious you'll probably do more anyhow. It is a rare published writer who can afford to live comfortably on royalties and the annual PLR cheque.

Constantly read your work aloud to yourself. You'll soon pick up overwriting, repetitions etc. If you belong to a writers' group the feedback can be very useful, for one can get too close too one's work. Attend any events where editors and agents are actively seeking new talent. The Annual Writers' Conference held at Winchester at the end of each June is an excellent example where you can also enter competitions and get noticed.

So you've finished. What next? If this is your first novel then have a plot outline and blurb (50-100 words) for a second before you approach any editors or agents. No-one wants a one-book writer. You must be seen to have 'legs!' The prospect of having to repay a publisher's advance is the stuff of nightmares! Be prepared.

Ensure your work is as polished as it can be. No grammatical errors or inaccuracies. Check time sequences and make each chapter ending make the reader want to turn the page. Remember, many editors these days don't have the time to spend on massive editorial changes, so give yourself the best chance before your work leaves you.

This Guide to Book Publishers will be invaluable in your search for a publisher, and, having targeted which ones to try, (obviously don't send fantasy to one who clearly doesn't handle that genre) make sure your work is presented to a professional standard. Double spaced, in a readable font (ie: Arial 12) with good ink quality. Never send dog-eared pages. First impressions are crucial, as is your covering letter.

I personally always had two approaches. If the publisher accepts unsolicited manuscripts: Either a) Simply send off the synopsis, blurb plus your letter and the first three chapters and return postage. Make sure you spell the editor's name correctly.

Or b) Telephone first. Ask to speak to the editor who deals with your genre. Then you can briefly give him/her the novel's blurb, a bit about yourself and, all being well, you'll be asked to send in the synopsis etc and first three chapters.

It's a pushy world out there, believe me, and this saves you the expense of postage if for example the firm is not taking any more MSS say for another three months. If the answer is an unequivocal no then keep trying elsewhere. Never give up!

Your covering letter should be no more than one page long. State the genre straight away. Sell yourself. Mention any writing successes however modest, any unusual jobs. Why you feel you work will sell and who your readership will be. Don't say 'Aunty Doris loved it.' That's the kiss of death!

Some publishers who haven't merged are more independent and are looking for the unusual, the sort of book which *doesn't* fit a genre. I suggest that if you've been published in any way, however small, you invest in membership of The Society of Authors and they'll help you in your search as well as providing interesting and useful meetings. Some publishers like Headline deal more with commercial fiction. Check out your library and booksellers to see who is publishing what. Read the dedications - often they reveal an editor or agent's name.

You can read elsewhere on the intricacies of the publishing process, royalties, translation and PLR rights. (ie: Michael Legat's 'An Author's Guide to Publishing.' - Pub. by Robert Hale.) My angle here is as a fiction writer who never gave up. I believed in what I was trying to say, because fiction can show us deep truths about the human condition and the world we inhabit. Truths, because they are formed by each encounter, each experience we have. And, if we truly are writers, then nothing is wasted. I also believe that publishers don't really know what they're looking for until they see it. So, do use this Guide, and may it bring you good luck.

AA Publishing

Britain's leading publisher of road atlases and world travel guides. The range includes atlases of Britain, Europe and the USA. The World Travel Guide range includes 7 major series of illustrated guides with maps. These cover all the world's major travel destinations. AA Publishing is also well known for its high quality range of illustrated guides to Britain, France and many other topics.

Editor(s): Michael Buttler - Editorial Director, John Howard - Managing Director, Stephen Mesquita - International Sales and Marketing Manager
Address: Fanum House, Basingstoke, Hampshire RG21 4EA
Telephone: 01256 491573
Fax: 01256 491974
Email: michael.buttler@theaa.com
Website: www.theaa.co.uk
Imprints: AA Publishing
Parent Company: The Automobile Association
Payment Details: Overall fee in most cases
Unsolicited Manuscripts: No

AAVO

Specialises in books about television. On Camera and Directing On Camera are classic how-to handbooks about TV production and direction, both written by Harris Watts, a former Senior Instructor at the BBC's production training school. In April 1999 AAVO published 'Better than Working - Life Behind The Camera' by Richard Hakin, an entertaining behind-the-scenes account of life in a camera crew with an introduction by David Puttnam CBE, producer of 'Chariots of Fire', 'The Killing Fields' etc. A new On Camera handbook will be published later this year or early in 2002.

Editor(s): Harris Watts
Address: 8 Edis Street, London NW1 8LG
Telephone: 020 7722 9243
Fax: Same as phone
Email: tottatv@aol.com
Unsolicited Manuscripts: Yes, if about television

Ab-Libris

Ab-libris is an e-book publisher which specialises in academic texts with an emphasis on computing. Our range of titles cover a wide spectrum of publishing from travel and walking guides, biography to science fiction. We are interested in publishing work that has a defined, if niche, demand.

Our system allows the reader to print the book, transfer from one computer to another, with a security mechanism that prevents the e-book from being able to be read on more than one machine.

Editor(s): Martin Ellis
Address: 10 Burnside, East Boldon, Tyne & Wear, NE36 0LS
Telephone: 0709 209 1131
Email: editor@ablibris.com
Website: www.ablibris.com
Payment Details: 25%
Unsolicited Manuscripts: No, please e-mail synopsis

ABC-CLIO Ltd

ABC-CLIO publishes general A-Z style encyclopedias and reference works on high interest topics in several areas of study including: world history; politics; international relations; society; biography; sport; folklore and mythology; and science and technology.

Editor(s): Robert G Neville, Simon Mason & Tony Sloggett
Address: 35A Great Clarendon Street, Oxford OX2 6AT
Telephone: 01865 311350
Fax: 01865 311358
Email: bneville@abc-clio.ltd.uk
Parent Company: ABC-CLIO Inc, Santa Barbara, California USA
Payment Details: By negotiation
Unsolicited Manuscripts: Yes

ABG Professional Information

ABG Professional Information is the publishing arm of the Institute of Chartered Accountants in England and Wales. Providing support for the professionals in both practice and industry, we publish over 300 key titles covering the breadth of accounting, tax, auditing, company law, financial management and IT.

Address: 40 Bernard Street, London WC1N 1LD
Telephone: 020 7920 8991
Fax: 020 7920 8992
Email: abgbooks@icaew.co.uk
Website: www.abgweb.com
Parent Company: ICAEW

Abson Books London

Language/dialect glossaries, history.

Editor(s): Michael Ellison, Sharon Wright
Address: 5 Sidney Square, London E1 2EY
Telephone: 020 7790 4737
Fax: 020 7790 7346
Email: absonbooks@aol.com
Unsolicited Manuscripts: Yes

Council Of Academic And Professional Publishers

Trade association for academic and professional publishers.

Address: 1 Kingsway, London WC2B 6XD
Telephone: 020 7565 7474
Fax: 020 7836 4543
Email: mail@publishers.org.uk
Website: www.publishers.org.uk
Parent Company: The Publishers Association
Unsolicited Manuscripts: No

Acair Ltd

Scottish Highlands and Islands, modern and historical, Gaelic and English, children's Gaelic, educational, music, poetry and song, learners of Gaelic.

Editor(s): Norma MacLeod
Address: 7 James Street, Stornoway, Isle of Lewis HS1 2QN
Telephone: 01851 703020
Fax: 01851 703294
Email: acair@sol.co.uk
Website: www.acairbooks.com
Imprints: Acair
Payment Details: Payment by arrangement if published
Unsolicited Manuscripts: Yes

Act 3 Publishing

A book publisher, established in 1985, with one book at present in print: Hypnosis in Psychotherapy - Understand Yourself, and Resolve Your Emotional Problems. Now considering potential best-selling fiction and non-fiction for publication.

Address: 67 Upper Berkeley Street, London W1H 7QX
Telephone: 020 7402 5321
Payment Details: No advances, payment negotiable
Unsolicited Manuscripts: In the first instance send only a one-page resumé with SAE

Adam Hart (Publishers) Ltd

Founded as independent publishing company in 1992 to publish research on Christopher Marlowe, Elizabethan poet-dramatist, by historian A D Wraight. Publications to date: In Search Of Christopher Marlowe by A D Wraight and Virginia F Stern (1993) pb. re-issue of publication by Macdonald for Marlowe's 1964 quartercentenary of his birth, and by Vanguard Press in New York, 1965. Acclaimed as the definitive biography of Marlowe. Valued by students as their 'bible'. Lavishly illustrated. Other books by A D Wraight: Christopher Marlowe & Edward Alleyn (1993). Research on Alleyn Papers. The Story That The Sonnets Tell (1995) The 'Riddle' of Shakespeare's Sonnets resolved. Shakespeare: New Evidence (1997) Research in Lambeth Palace Library on documentary evidence discovering Marlowe's brief return to England as a secret agent in 1595 to work for the Earl of Essex on a survey of Italy where he lived in exile since his supposed 'death' in 1593. Not yet published: The Legend of Hiram, documentary evidence revealing that the First Folio was a Masonic publication. Christopher Marlowe & the Armada. Evidence of his participation in the English navy in the campaign against the Spanish Armada.

Editor(s): A D Walker-Wraight, Y M Hart
Address: Adam Hart (Publishers) Ltd, The Rose, 10 Idmiston Road, London SE27 9HG
Telephone: 020 8670 5182
Fax: 020 8670 5182
Email: 100126.3574@compuserve.com
Website: www.author.co.uk/marlowe/

African Books Collective Ltd

Founded in 1989, ABC is a major self-help initiative by a group of African publishers to promote their books in Europe, North America and Commonwealth countries outside Africa. It is collectively owned by its founder-member publishers. ABC is a donor organisation supported and non-profitmaking on its own behalf, and because of this, is in a position to offer its members more favourable terms than are normally available under conventional commercial distribution agreements. Titles in English and children's in Swahili are stocked. Membership has grown to 58 publishers in 12 African countries. Over 1500 titles are now stocked in ABC's UK warehouse.

Address: The Jam Factory, 27 Park End Street, Oxford OX1 1HU
Telephone: +44 (0)1865 726686
Fax: +44 (0)1865 793298
Email: abc@africanbookscollective.com
Website: www.africanbookscollective.com
Unsolicited Manuscripts: No

Age Concern Books

Age Concern Books (the publishing wing of Age Concern England) produces a range of practical handbooks aimed at older people and their carers. The range includes personal finance and benefits guides, retirement titles, as well as series produced for both professional and family carers. We publish approximately 18 new titles each year, with annual sales exceeding 110,000 copies.

Editor(s): Publisher: Richard Holloway
Address: Age Concern Books, Age Concern England, Astral House, 1268 London Road, London SW16 4ER
Telephone: 020 8765 7200
Fax: 020 8765 7211
Email: hollowr@ace.org.uk
Website: http://www.ageconcern.org.uk
Parent Company: Age Concern England (registered charity)
Payment Details: Normal royalty terms offered to authors
Unsolicited Manuscripts: Very rarely accepted

Agenda Ltd

Agenda publish books on popular music. The musicians covered in our books are considered intellectual or have academic influences within their music. Our books are ideal for basic ground work for thesis dissertations for colleges and universities. We hope to upgrade our Captain Beefheart book and publish investigations of the music of The Doors, Sun Ra and The Residents, adding to our existing catalogue which includes... Leonard Cohen, Arthur Lee, Joni Mitchell, Mike Bloomfield, Al Kooper, Scott Walker, Van Morrison, Bob Dylan, Tom Waits, Tim Buckey, Nick Drake, Frank Zappa, Jim Morrison, Jack Kerouac, Thin Lizzy and The Incredible String Band.

Editor(s): Tony Coleman and Ken Brooks
Address: Units 1-2 Ludgershall Business Park, New Drove, Ludgershall SP11 9RN
Telephone: 01264 335388
Fax: 01264 335270
Email: Paul@dmac.co.uk
Website: http://www.dmac.co.uk/agenda.html
Imprints: 12
Payment Details: As negotiated
Unsolicited Manuscripts: No

Air Research Publications

Publishers of specialist (non-fiction) aviation books. Especially World War 2 and military aviation history.

Editor(s): Simon Parry
Address: PO Box 223, Walton-on-Thames, Surrey KT12 3YQ
Telephone: 01932 243165
Fax: Same as phone
Email: books@airresearch.co.uk
Website: www.airresearch.co.uk
Payment Details: Royalty on sales
Unsolicited Manuscripts: Yes, and returned

Airlife Publishing Ltd

Two non-fiction imprints. Airlife: military aviation; civil aviation; military and naval history; military and naval biography; books for pilots. Sweet Lake: environment, maritime history and art, and earth sciences.

Editor(s): Peter Coles
Address: 101 Longden Road, Shrewsbury SY3 9EB
Telephone: 01743 235651
Fax: 01743 232944
Email: airlife@airlifebooks.com
Website: www.airlifebooks.com
Imprints: Airlife, Sweet Lake
Payment Details: Royalty
Unsolicited Manuscripts: Yes

Albrighton Publications

Two publications on education of minority groups in Britain: Language, Race And Education (1988); Equality And Education (1992).

Editor(s): Author for these publications: Gurbachan Singh
Address: 53 The Hollow, Littleover, Derby DE23 6GH
Telephone: 01332 764064

Ian Allan Publishing Ltd

Transport, aviation, military, sport and leisure. No fiction, poetry, children's titles, books of memories, biographies or autobiographies.

Editor(s): Peter Waller
Address: Riverdene Business Park, Molesey Road, Hersham, Surrey KT12 4RG
Telephone: 01932 266600
Fax: 01932 266601
Email: info@ianallanpub.co.uk
Website: http://www.ianallanpub.co.uk
Imprints: Ian Allan Publishing, Dial House, OPC, Midland Publishing
Parent Company: Ian Allan Group Ltd
Payment Details: Subject to contract terms agreed
Unsolicited Manuscripts: No

J A Allen & Co Ltd

An imprint of Robert Hale Limited. Equine and equestrian publishers - non-fiction titles on any area of horse-related subjects. Prefer authoritative works by established experts in their fields. Broad academic base, also publishing some commercial titles and have a junior list which does include fiction.

Editor(s): Publisher, Caroline Burt
Address: Clerkenwell House, 45-47 Clerkenwell Green, London EC1R 0HT
Telephone: 020 7251 2661
Fax: 020 7490 4958
Email: allen@halebooks.com
Website: http://www.halebooks.com
Parent Company: Robert Hale Ltd
Payment Details: Royalties paid twice-yearly
Unsolicited Manuscripts: No. Submissions by email will be considered

Allison & Busby

Publishes literary fiction, crime fiction, literary biography and writers' guides.

Editor(s): David Shelley
Address: 111 Bon Marche Centre, 241 Ferndale Road, London, SW9 8BJ
Telephone: 020 7738 7888
Fax: 020 7323 2023
Email: all@allisonbusby.co.uk
Website: www.allisonandbusbyltd.uk
Parent Company: Editorial Prensa Iberica, SA, Barcelona
Unsolicited Manuscripts: Sample text and synopsis, plus SAE

Alternative Medicine.com

Publisher of a discrete list of alternative medicine definitive guides on a wide range of topics including arthritis, cancer, chronic fatigue, heart disease, and weight control, plus the landmark publication - a 1,100 page reference entitled 'Alternative Medicine: The Definitive Guide' first published in 1994 and which has now sold over 650,000 copies.

Editor(s): John Anderson
Address: C/o Roundhouse Publishing Ltd, Millstone, Limers Lane, Northam, Devon, EX39 2RG
Telephone: 01237 474474
Fax: 01237 474774
Email: round.house@fsbdial.co.uk
Website: www.roundhouse.net
Payment Details: Royalties twice yearly
Unsolicited Manuscripts: No

Alun Books/Goldleaf Publishing

Small press, limited resources, specialising in books by Welsh authors/about Welsh subjects - mostly in English.

Editor(s): S Jones
Address: 3 Crown Street, Port Talbot, West Glamorgan SA13 1BG Wales
Telephone: 01639 886186
Imprints: Alun Books (literature: poetry and fiction), Goldleaf (local history), Barn Owl (children's)
Parent Company: Alun Books (founded 1977)
Payment Details: 10% royalty
Unsolicited Manuscripts: No

Amber Lane Press

Original modern play scripts - only plays that have been staged professionally will be considered; books on theatre and modern drama.

Editor(s): Judith Scott
Address: Church Street, Charlbury, Oxon OX7 3PR
Telephone: 01608 810024
Fax: Same as phone
Email: Jamberlane@aol.com
Payment Details: Formal author's contract with advance and percentage royalty
Unsolicited Manuscripts: No

Amberwood Publishing Ltd

Introducing - Amberwood Publishing, founded in 1991 with the object of publishing affordable books on natural health care. All titles are commissioned from authors who are chosen for their expertise. Each book is presented in a format suitable for the general public and students alike. All at Amberwood care about the information we publish. Our aim is to market factual scientifically-based literature for the benefit of the growing number of people wanting to use natural medicine, such as aromatherapy, herbal medicine and nutritional therapy.

Editor(s): June Crisp, Victor Perfitt
Address: Suite 4, Alpha House, Laser Quay, Culpeper Close, Medway City Estate, Rochester, Kent ME2 4HU
Telephone: 01634 290115
Fax: 01634 290761
Email: books@amberwoodpublishing.com
Website: www.amberwoodpublishing.com
Payment Details: Percentage of retail sales
Unsolicited Manuscripts: Yes

AMCD (Publishers) Ltd

AMCD specialises in European and Far Eastern books, especially China. We would be interested to look at children's books as well as European history and business books. Short summaries with S.A.E only please.

Editor(s): J S Adams
Address: PO Box 182, Altrincham, Cheshire WA15 9UA
Telephone: 0161 434 5105
Fax: As phone
Email: j.s.adams@amcd.co.uk
Website: www.amcd.co.uk
Imprints: AMCD, Jensen Books
Parent Company: AMCD
Payment Details: Half-yearly
Unsolicited Manuscripts: Summary and short chapter. SAE for return

Amnesty International Publications

Amnesty International is a worldwide voluntary human rights movement that campaigns for the release of prisoners of conscience, fair trials for political prisoners and an end to torture, 'disappearances', political killings and the death penalty. Amnesty International works impartially to promote all human rights enshrined in the Universal Declaration of Human Rights and other international standards. The organisation publishes books relating to this work, and produces short specialist reports on human rights abuse issues, which are available on the World Wide Web. It publishes an annual country-by-country report on human rights.

Address: 99-119 Rosebery Avenue, London EC1R 4RE
Telephone: 020 7814 6000
Email: info@amnesty.org.uk
Website: www.amnesty.org.uk
Parent Company: Amnesty International UK
Unsolicited Manuscripts: No

Amolibros

Amolibros manages a number of imprints which are usually distributed by Gazelle Book Services. It specialises in assisting small or private publishers to produce and market their books. Popular titles managed include Outrageous Fortune by Terence Frisby (author of There's A Girl In My Soup) and Thoth, published by Edfu Books. The Turquoise Conspiracy by Bilge Nevzat, the inside story on Asil Nadir.

Editor(s): Jane Tatam
Address: 5 Saxon Close, Watchet, Somerset TA23 0BN
Telephone: 01984 633713
Fax: Same as phone
Email: amolibros@aol.com
Website: www.amolibros.co.uk
Unsolicited Manuscripts: No

Anchor Books

A small poetry imprint, with the aim of getting lesser known poets into print.

Editor(s): Managing Editor: Sarah Andrew; Editor: Neil Day
Address: Remus House, Coltsfoot Drive, Woodston, Peterborough PE2 9JX
Telephone: 01733 898102
Fax: 01733 313524
Email: anchorbooks@forwardpress.co.uk
Website: www.forwardpress.co.uk
Parent Company: Forward Press Limited
Payment Details: Top 100 Poets of the Year share a cash prize (£3,000 first prize)
Unsolicited Manuscripts: For anthologies: poems up to 30 lines any subject, any form

Andersen Press Ltd

Founded in 1976 by Klaus Flugge, Andersen Press publishes quality picture books and fiction for children. Main authors and artists on the list are David McKee, Tony Ross, Michael Foreman, Ruth and Ken Brown, Susan Varley, Colin McNaughton, Max Velthuijs, Emma Chichester Clark and Melvin Burgess. Specialises in selling foreign co-editions. Bestselling titles: Badger's Parting Gifts (Susan Varley), Elmer (David McKee), Junk (Melvin Burgess).

Editor(s): Editorial Director: Janice Thomson; Editor: Audrey Adams (Fiction)
Address: 20 Vauxhall Bridge Road, London SW1V 2SA
Telephone: 020 7840 8703
Fax: 020 7233 6263
Website: www.andersenpress.co.uk
Imprints: Tigers, Andersen Young Readers' Library, Andersen Press Paperback Picture Books, Andersen Giants
Payment Details: Royalties twice-yearly
Unsolicited Manuscripts: With SAE; 3 sample chapters and synopsis for novels

Anderson Rand

Publisher of 'The European Book World' the authoritative book trade directory, providing trade professionals with up-to-date business contact details from listings of over 25,000 publishing organistions, 63,000 libraries and 50,000 booksellers in East and West Europe and former Soviet Europe. Over 150 indexes include: 4000 subject specialities, named staff, library and bookseller types, telephone/fax, market types, non book stock and organisation size.

Editor(s): Dr Robin Anderson
Address: 10 Willow Walk, Cambridge CB1 1LA
Telephone: 01646 683203
Fax: 01223 566643
Email: ar.info@dial.pipex.com
Website: http://www.anderson-rand.com
Unsolicited Manuscripts: N/A

Anglia Publishing

Specialist in metal detecting and amateur archaeology. Most titles which Anglia has published relate to the identification of small metallic finds. The scope is large because metal detecting turns up a very wide variety of material: Bronze Age axes to Butlin's holiday camp enamel badges! The buyers of Anglia's titles also come from a wide spectrum, not just metal detectorists and amateur archaeologists but also museum staff, professional archaeologists and, of course, collectors. The possibilities to add to Anglia's growing lists are large indeed. New titles are eagerly sought: books and booklets, which can be as short as 10,000 words. Would someone like to write little books about pipe tampers through the ages, shotgun cartridges and bullets? Get the idea?

Editor(s): Derek Rowland
Address: Unit T, Dodnash Priory Farm, Hazel Shrub, Bentley, Ipswich IP9 2DF
Telephone: 01473 311138
Fax: 01473 312288
Email: DR@angliabooks.com
Website: www.angliabooks.com
Imprints: Anglia Publishing, Anglia Shoe-Box Library
Payment Details: Royalty negotiable, payable quarterly
Unsolicited Manuscripts: No - a synopsis first or a telephone call

Anglia Young Books

Cross-curricular stories for primary schools, specialising in historical fiction with support material for the literacy hour.

Editor(s): Rosemary Hayes
Address: Durhams Farmhouse, Butcher's Hill, Ickleton, Saffron Walden CB10 1SR
Telephone: 01799 531192
Fax: Same as phone
Email: r.hayes@btinternet.com
Website: www.btinternet.com/~R.Hayes/
Imprints: Anglia Young Books
Unsolicited Manuscripts: No

Angling Publications Ltd

Angling Publications was founded in 1988, we publish two monthly magazines which are dedicated to carp fishing. The titled 'Carpworld' and 'Crafty Carper', and Tim Paisley is the editor of both publications. Carpworld is a full colour publication with a minimum of 200 pages, Crafty Carper is also full colour, 128 page publication. Both magazines run monthly competitions and contain articles on all aspects of carp fishing, tackle, tactics, waters, news, letters, bait, shops, stories etc.

Editor(s): Tim Paisley
Address: 272a London Road, Highfields, Sheffield, South Yorkshire S2 4NA
Telephone: 0114 2580812
Fax: 0114 2582728
Email: info@carpworld.uk.com
Website: www.carpworld.uk.com

Anness Publishing Ltd

Publisher of illustrated non-fiction titles. Subjects include: food and drink, gardening, crafts, interiors, reference, health, new age, children's.

Address: Anness Publishing Ltd, Hermes House, 88-89 Blackfriars Road, London SE1 8HA
Telephone: 020 7401 2077
Fax: 020 7633 9499
Email: info@anness.com
Imprints: Lorenz Books, Aquamarine, Hermes House, Southwater and Peony Press
Parent Company: Anness Publishing Limited
Unsolicited Manuscripts: Yes - occasionally

Antique Collectors' Club

Publishers of books on art, antiques, gardening and children's classics. We also publish a magazine - ten issues a year of articles on art, antiques and collectables.

Editor(s): Mark Eastment
Address: 5 Church Street, Woodbridge, Suffolk IP12 1DS
Telephone: 01394 385501
Fax: 01394 384434
Email: sales@antique-acc.com
Website: http://www.antique-acc.com
Imprints: Garden Art Press, ACC Children's Classics
Payment Details: Negotiable
Unsolicited Manuscripts: No

Anvil Press Poetry Ltd

Poetry, poetry in translation.

Editor(s): Peter Jay
Address: Neptune House, 70 Royal Hill, London SE10 8RF
Payment Details: To be negotiated if work accepted
Unsolicited Manuscripts: Yes must include SAE

The Appletree Press Ltd

A wide range of internationally renowned giftbooks developed with the tourist market specifically in mind. Our range of over 400 titles cover the following areas: The Celtic Collection, English, Irish, Scots and Welsh Interest, Cookbook Collections featuring the cuisines of over 50 countries and regions, Yearbooks and Diaries, Travel Guides, Literature, Reference, Foreign Language editions (French, German, Spanish, Italian) of our most popular titles are available along with a full range of POS.

Editor(s): Paul Harrow
Address: The Appletree Press Ltd, The Old Potato Station, 14 Howard Street South, Belfast BT7 1AP
Telephone: 028 9024 3074
Fax: 028 9024 6756
Email: reception@appletree.ie
Website: www.appletree.ie
Imprints: Appletree Press
Payment Details: On selection and final approval
Unsolicited Manuscripts: The Manager, Creative Department

Applied Rural Alternatives (ARA)

ARA exists for the charitable purpose of advancing the education of the general public in rural development in an environmentally sensitive manner with particular reference to under-developed countries. ARA arranges visits/leatures, etc, in the UK on organic husbandry, environmental problems in farming and appropriate technologies. Details of the current programme are available on receipt of an SAE. Publications available are 'The Pace of Change in Farming - the organic option' (£2 remainder) and 'Cheap Food - can we afford it?' (£2.50 remainder). Cheques to 'ARA (SEBUNA)' with order.

Editor(s): D Cussens, D Stafford
Address: ARA, 10 Highfield Close, Wokingham, Berkshire RG40 1DG
Telephone: 0118 962 7797
Parent Company: ARA
Unsolicited Manuscripts: None, please

Arc Publications

Arc Publications is not only committed to publishing works by new British writers, but actively seeks to promote work by internationally significant poets higherto neglected in the UK, whether in their original English or in translation. Poets submitting work should be familiar with the type of work we publish.

Editor(s): Tony Ward
Address: Nanholme Mill, Shaw Wood Road, Todmorden, Lancashire OL14 6DA
Imprints: Arc Publications
Unsolicited Manuscripts: Send representative selection, no reply without SAE

Arcadia Books Ltd

Arcadia Books is an independent literary publishing house established in 1996. We publish in the areas of fiction, biography, and autobiography, travel writing, gay and gender studies. We specialise in translated fiction: fully 40% of our 2000 list is devoted to fiction in translation. Recent successes include The Last Kabbalist of Lisbon by Richard Zimler (30,000 copies sold), The Twins by Tessa de Loo, Easter by Michael Arditti and The Hite Report on Shere Hite by Shere Hite. Our EuroCrime series features the writing of Richard Zimler and Nicolas Freeling as well as crime writing from France, Norway and other European countries.

Editor(s): Gary Pulsifer
Address: 15-16 Nassau Street, London W1W 7AB
Telephone: 020 7436 9898
Fax: 020 7637 7357
Email: info@arcadiabooks.co.uk
Website: www.arcadiabooks.co.uk
Unsolicited Manuscripts: No

Architectural Association Publications

Books on architecture and related disciplines, generated by the activities and debates of an international school of architecture.

Editor(s): Pamela Johnston
Address: 36 Bedford Square, London WC1B 3ES
Telephone: 020 7887 4021
Fax: 020 7414 0782
Email: publications@aaschool.ac.uk
Website: www.aaschool.ac.uk
Imprints: AA Publications
Parent Company: Architectural Association
Unsolicited Manuscripts: No

Archive Editions

Publishers of historical documents, in facsimile, on the Middle East, Asia and conflict zones in Europe.

Address: 7 Ashley House, The Broadway, Farnham Common, Slough SL2 3PQ
Telephone: 01753 646633
Fax: 01753 646746
Email: ArchiveEdn@aol.com
Website: www.archiveeditions.co.uk
Imprints: Archive Editions
Payment Details: Available on request

Aris & Phillips Ltd

Archaeology - Egyptology, classical (Greek and Latin) texts, Hispanic classics (Spanish and Portuguese).

Editor(s): A A Phillips, L M Phillips
Address: Teddington House, Church Street, Warminster, Wilts BA12 8PQ
Telephone: 01985 213409
Fax: 01985 212910
Email: aris.phillips@btinternet.com
Website: www.arisandphillips.com
Imprints: Aris & Phillips
Unsolicited Manuscripts: Yes

Art Sales Index Ltd

Art Sales Index Ltd records 140,00 entries of fine art sold at auction worldwide every year. This information is on hard copy, CD ROM, online and on the web.

The database with over 2.2 million entries by 185,000 artists covers over forty years of fine art auctions
Editor(s): Duncan Hislop
Address: 194 Thorpe Lea Road, Egham, Surrey
Telephone: 01784 451145
Fax: 01784 451144
Email: asi@art-sales-index.com
Website: www.art-sales-index.com
Unsolicited Manuscripts: No

Arthritis Research Campaign (ARC)

A national charity which exists to raise funds for research into arthritis and rheumatism. It produces a range of booklets and leaflets on arthritis, as well as publications for medical professionals and students.

Address: ARC Trading Ltd (Supplies), Brunel Drive, Northern Road Industrial Estate, Newark NG24 2DE
Telephone: 01636 673054
Fax: 01636 708714
Website: www.arc.org.uk
Parent Company: Arthritis Research Campaign, Copeman House, St Mary's Court, St Mary's Gate, Chesterfield S41 7TD

Articles Of Faith Ltd

Specialises in short print runs of religious books for the schools educational market.

Editor(s): C Howard
Address: Resource House, Kay Street, Bury BL9 6BU
Telephone: 0161 763 6232
Fax: 0161 763 5366
Email: ArticlesFaith@cs.com
Website: www.articlesoffaith.co.uk
Unsolicited Manuscripts: Yes

Ashgate Publishing Limited

Ashgate Publishing is one of the world's leading publishers of academic research in the social sciences and humanities, and of professional practice in the management of business and public services. It has two main imprints: Ashgate for academic research and Gower for business practice. As an independent, privately owned company, Ashgate Publishing plans for the long term but acts quickly in the short term. Publishing decisions are made swiftly, but in the context of a long terms strategy to develop the company's capabilities for the benefit of authors, readers and librarians. Ashgate Publishing has its own marketing distribution and editorial facilities in Europe, the USA, East Asia and Australia. This enables the company to issue and distribute all its titles simultaneously in the major international academic and professional markets and to attend books fairs and academic conventions across the developed and developing countries of the world.

Editor(s): Various
Address: Gower House, Croft Road, Aldershot, Hampshire GU11 5HR
Telephone: 01252 331551
Fax: 01252 317446
Email: info@ashgatepub.co.uk
Website: www.ashgate.com
Imprints: Gower Publishing, Lund Humphries, Variorum
Payment Details: Information on application
Unsolicited Manuscripts: Yes

Ashley Drake Publishing Ltd

Established in 1994, the company publishes under its various imprints and has worldwide sales, marketing and distribution capabilities.

We publish scholarly books under the Welsh Academic Press imprint, trade titles under the St David's Press whilst Morgan Publishing produces titles with the financial contribution of authors.

Whatever type of book you have written, we can help you get it published and marketed worldwide.

Editor(s): Ashley Drake
Address: PO Box 733, Cardiff, CF14 2YX
Telephone: 029 2056 0343
Fax: 029 2056 1631
Email: post@ashleydrake.com
Website: www.ashleydrake.com
Imprints: Welsh Academic Press, St David's Press, Morean Publishing
Payment Details: Yes, standard rates.
Unsolicited Manuscripts: Yes, but only chapters 1 & 2, contents & synopsis.

Ashmolean Museum

The Ashmolean Museum, established in 1683, contains the University of Oxford's collections of art and antiquities, ranging in time from the earliest implements of man some two million years ago to twentieth century works of art.

Its most famous treasures are the drawings of Michelangelo and Raphael, the Alfred Jewel, the Egyptian antiquities, Greek vases, Uccello's painting The Hunt in the Forest, the collections of Greek and Roman coins and the Chinese stoneware and porcelain.

The Museum publishes catalogues of temporary exhibitions as well as catalogues and books about the Museum's permanent collections. They include a wide range of books and booklets, mostly illustrated in full colour, teacher resource packs and academic volumes, meeting the needs of the general visitor and schools and colleges, as well as those of the University's academics.

Editor(s): Ian Charlton
Address: Beaumont Street, Oxford, OX1 2PH
Telephone: 01865 278010
Fax: 01865 278018
Email: publications@ashmus.ox.ac.uk
Website: www.ashmol.ox.ac.uk
Imprints: Ashmolean Museum, University of Oxford; Griffith Institute
Parent Company: University of Oxford (Registered Charity)
Unsolicited Manuscripts: No

Aspire Publishing

Fiction (all genres), autobiography and biography. Founded 1997. Also non-fiction especially political or controversial issues. No unsolicited MSS. Send SAE for guidelines. Publications printed and produced in UK as a matter of policy. Trade clients include all major bookshop chains, wholesalers and library suppliers.

Editor(s): Senior Editor: Patricia Hawkes
Address: 8 Betony Rise, Exeter EX2 5RR or 9 Wimpole Street, London W1M 8LB
Telephone: 01392 252516
Fax: 01392 252517
Email: aspire@centrex.force9.net
Imprints: Aspire Publishing, Greenzone Publishing
Parent Company: XcentreX Ltd
Payment Details: None
Unsolicited Manuscripts: No

ASR Resources (trading as G M Hibbs Associates)

Design, management, psychological and educational - with a cybernetic perspective.

Editor(s): Genevieve M Hibbs PhD
Address: 465 Twickenham Road, Isleworth TW7 7DZ
Telephone: 020 8892 1933
Imprints: Resources Occasional Papers, SCOHNE Papers
Unsolicited Manuscripts: No

Association For Scottish Literary Studies

The ASLS is an educational charity promoting the languages and literature of Scotland. We publish works of Scottish literature which have either been neglected or which merit a fresh presentation to a modern audience; essays, monographs and journals on the literature and languages of Scotland; and Scotnotes, a series of comprehensive study guides to major Scottish writers. We also produce New Writing Scotland, an annual anthology of contemporary poetry and prose in English, Gaelic and Scots from writers resident in Scotland or Scots by birth or upbringing.

Editor(s): Duncan Jones (Managing Editor, New Writing Scotland)
Address: ASLS, c/o Department of Scottish History, 9 University Gardens, University of Glasgow, Glasgow G12 8QH Scotland
Telephone: 0141 330 5309
Fax: Same as phone
Email: d.jones@scothist.arts.gla.ac.uk
Website: http://www.asls.org.uk
Payment Details: £10 per page (New Writing Scotland only)
Unsolicited Manuscripts: For New Writing Scotland only

Aurelian Information Ltd

Internet books for beginners and office users in business and the charity sector. National charities database: the 7,500 leading national charities (and UK-based international charities) available for rental on electronic disks - floppy and CD-ROM.

Editor(s): Paul Petzold; Julia Kaufmann OBE
Address: Aurelian Information Ltd Research Unit, 4a Alexandra Mansions, West End Lane, London NW6 1LU
Telephone: 020 7794 8609 (books) 020 7407 5987 (data)
Fax: Same as phone (books) 020 7407 6294 (data)
Email: aurelian@dircon.co.uk
Website: www@dircon.co.uk/aurelian
Imprints: Internet-For-All Books (books), National Charities Database (database information)
Unsolicited Manuscripts: No - proposals only, by letter

A
Aureus Publishing Limited

Primarily a leisure-driven company, Aureus Publishing specialises in sports books, music (all types) and other leisure titles. Aureus is a dynamic company with an international outlook.

Editor(s): Director: Meuryn Hughes
Address: 24 Mafeking Road, Cardiff CF23 5DQ Wales
Telephone: 029 2045 5200
Fax: Same as phone
Email: meuryn.hughes@aureus.co.uk
Website: www.aureus.co.uk
Imprints: Aureus
Unsolicited Manuscripts: Synopsis only please, typed. SAE required for reply

Aurum Press

General illustrated non-fiction: film, music, art and design, craft, sport, military history, biography. Practical photography titles published under Argentum Press imprint. Lifestyle titles published under Jacqui Small imprint.

Editor(s): Piers Burnett, Graham Coster, Jacqui Small
Address: 25 Bedford Avenue, London WC1B 3AT
Telephone: 020 7637 3225
Fax: 020 7580 2469
Email: sales@aurumpress.co.uk
Unsolicited Manuscripts: Yes

Author - Publisher Network

The network shares information on the business and technology of writing and publishing: main publication is 'Write to Publish!' newsletter with special issues of book reviews, or guidelines, or selected back issues as a collected works of 'The best of Write to Publish!' from 1992 to 2000.

Editor(s): David Bosworth, John Dawes (consultant)
Address: c/o SKS, Saint Aldhelm, 20 Paul Street, Frome, Somerset BA11 1DX
Telephone: 01373 451777
Email: (Editor) gsse@zoo.co.uk
Imprints: Write to Publish! (newsletter)
Parent Company: A-PN
Payment Details: All contributions are voluntary as information is shared by network
Unsolicited Manuscripts: No

Authors Online Ltd

Publishes both e-books and 'Print on Demand' titles - all genre. Please send submissions in e-format only but please download submission instructions from the website first.

The UK's premier e-bookshop with over 120 authors and now 200 titles. Established 1998.

Editor(s): Richard Fitt
Address: Adams Yard, Maidenhead Street, Hertford, SG14 1DR
Telephone: 01992 503151
Fax: 01992 535424
Email: theeditor@authorsonline.co.uk
Website: www.authorsonline.co.uk
Payment Details: 60% (Net) retail price
Unsolicited Manuscripts: Yes

Autumn Publishing Ltd

Children's publisher of quality mass-market activity books. These include 'Fun to Learn' sticker books and wall charts.

Address: Autumn Publishing Ltd, North Barn, Appledram Barns, Birdham Road, Chichester PO20 7EQ

Avon Books

Works on the basis of shared responsibility between author and publisher. This involves a payment or subsidy by the author as a contribution towards the cost of publishing his or her work.

Editor(s): Robin Salkia
Address: 1 Dovedale Studios, 465 Battersea Park Road, London SW11 4LR
Telephone: 020 7978 4825
Fax: 020 7924 2979
Email: enquiries@avonbooks
Website: www.avonbooks.co.uk
Payment Details: Negotiable
Unsolicited Manuscripts: Yes

AvonAngliA

Innovative publisher covering not only books, pamphlets and leaflets but postcards, posters and 'talking books' as well. Specialising in guidebooks, local history, business and transport subjects, it also owns Kingsmead Press, which concentrates on art books, Bath history and historical reprints. Small-run reprints and special productions for special opportunities include anniversaries and company histories; the full range of facilities exist including a writing service for those with a subject but no material.

Editor(s): Ian Body, Margaret Leitch
Address: 74 Ryder Street, Pontcanna, Cardiff CF11 9BU Wales
Telephone: 029 2040 7336
Fax: 029 2040 7476
Email: ian.body@avonanglia.com
Imprints: AvonAngliA, Kingsmead Press
Parent Company: AvonAngliA Publications and Services
Unsolicited Manuscripts: Accepted on most subjects - particularly transport, business and commerce, local history

Azure Books

Publishers of books in the broad subject area of human spirituality, such as you might find in the 'mind, body, spirit' section of a bookshop. Lively and entertaining, these books explore what it means to be a spiritual person in the early 21st century, taking in how we relate to ourselves, others and the world around us.

Editor(s): Alison Barr
Address: 1 Marylebone Road, London NW1 4DU
Telephone: 020 7643 0382
Fax: 020 7643 0391
Email: abarr@spck.org.uk
Imprints: Azure Books
Payment Details: By negotiation
Unsolicited Manuscripts: Please send synopsis and sample chapter

B
Bernard Babani (Publishing) Ltd

Established for nearly sixty years, we publish books only on radio, electronics and computing subjects aimed at the hobbyist, enthusiast and people needing help understanding computing in the workplace. Very good value for money.

Editor(s): M.H. Babani
Address: The Grampians, Shepherds Bush Road, London W6 7NF
Telephone: 020 7603 2581, 020 7603 7296
Fax: 020 7603 8203
Website: www.babanibooks.com
Unsolicited Manuscripts: Yes

M & M Baldwin

Publishers of books on local history, second world war codebreaking, and inland waterways (including The Working Waterways series and the Historical Canal Maps series).

Editor(s): Mark Baldwin
Address: 24 High Street, Cleobury Mortimer, Kidderminster DY14 8BY
Telephone: 01299 270110
Fax: Same as phone
Email: mmb@mbaldwin.free-online.co.uk
Imprints: M & M Baldwin
Payment Details: Annual royalty on sales
Unsolicited Manuscripts: Yes

Ballinakella Press

Small publishing house (circa 30 books to date), we now limit our works to in-series books. Our County House books are comprehensive architectural and historical records of the houses and families associated with them, of each Irish county. Our People And Places series of Irish family names are small but fairly comprehensive records of major Irish families or clans. We also have biographical records of characterful or historic Irish citizens or people of Irish descent. We occasionally consider books with a family history bent.

Editor(s): Dr Hugh W L Weir (Senior), Hon Mrs Grania Weir
Address: Whitegate, Co Clare, Ireland
Telephone: 35361 927030
Fax: 35361 927418
Email: info@ballinakella.com
Payment Details: By arrangement
Unsolicited Manuscripts: Only for Irish topographical and historical books in series

The Banton Press

Makes reprints of esoteric and occult titles from the 4th to 20th century. Subject areas include alchemy, astrology, autobiography, biography, Celts, druids, Egypt, folklore, history, kabbala, tarot, witchcraft, religion, philosophy, symbolism and sex worship. The books are perfect bound facsimile reprints with card covers and the title page as front cover. Also some titles on the Isle of Arran. New titles are added on an irregular basis.

Editor(s): Mark Brown
Address: Dippin Cottage, Kildonan, Isle of Arran KA27 8SB
Telephone: 01770 820231
Fax: Same as phone
Email: banton.press@btinternet.com
Imprints: Banton
Unsolicited Manuscripts: To Editor

B

Barefoot Books Ltd

Children's full-colour picture books: traditional myths, legends and fairytales, with a strong cross-cultural focus.

Editor(s): Publisher: Tessa Strickland
Address: 124 Walcot Street, Bath, BA1 5BG
Email: info@barefootbooks.com
Website: www.barefootbooks.com
Imprints: Barefoot Beginners, Barefoot Books, Barefoot Collections, Barefoot Poetry Collections
Payment Details: Advance against royalty
Unsolicited Manuscripts: No

Barny Books

We are a small, non profit making group working mainly with new writers or groups such as schools. We offer a readership and advisory service at a fee of £25 (£10 if less than 40 pages), editing by negotiation. No restriction on type of work published but insist on high quality english and writing.

Editor(s): Molly Burkett, Ben Cann
Address: Hough-On-The-Hill, Grantham NG32 2BB
Telephone: 01400 250246
Fax: Same as phone
Email: tcann@compuserve.co.uk
Website: www.tucann.co.uk
Imprints: Barny Books
Parent Company: Tucann, 19 High Street, Heighington LN4 1RG
Payment Details: 50/50 on profits
Unsolicited Manuscripts: Yes

Basic Skills Agency

Publish teaching and learning material to help children, young people and adults improve their basic skills, which we define as 'the ability to read, write and speak in English/Welsh and use mathematics at a level necessary to function and progress at work and in society in general.' We are a not-for-profit publisher. Our publications range from readers' packs, advice and material for teachers to some multimedia products. We also work with some commercial publishers. As well as publishing teaching and learning material, we also commission and publish research into the level of need, the cause of basic skills difficulties and the effectiveness of basic skills programmes.

Address: Commonwealth House, 1-19 New Oxford Street, London WC1A 1NU
Telephone: 020 7405 4017
Fax: 020 7440 6626
Email: enquiries@basic-skills.co.uk
Website: www.basic-skills.co.uk
Unsolicited Manuscripts: No

B
Batsford Books

Batsford publish authoritative non-fiction books in the following subject areas: film and entertainment; chess; bridge; embroidery; lace; art techniques; gardening; woodwork; fashion; practical crafts; heritage and design.

Brassey's publish military titles for the specialist market. Naval and aviation books are published under the Conway Maritime Press and Putnam Aeronautical imprints respective.

Salamander publish general interest books and cover subjects including cookery, crafts and interiors, gardening, American interest, transport, sport and health and military aviation.

Editor(s): R Huggins (Director), Tina Persaud (Batsford) / Caroline Bolton (Brassey's) / John Lee (Conway/Putnam) / Charlotte Davis (Salamander)
Address: 9 Blenheim Court, Brewery Road, London N7 9NT
Telephone: 020 7700 7611
Fax: 020 7700 4552
Email: btbatsford@chrysalisbooks.co.uk / brasseys@chrysalisbooks.co.uk / salamander@chrysalisbooks.co.uk
Website: www.chrysalisbooks.co.uk
Imprints: Batsford; Brassey's; Salamander; Robson
Parent Company: Chrysalis Books Ltd
Unsolicited Manuscripts: Yes

Beaconsfield Publishers Ltd

An owner-run small company publishing in medicine, nursing and patient care. Part of the list comprises professional quality books in homeopathic medicine.

Editor(s): John Churchill
Address: 20 Chiltern Hills Road, Beaconsfield, Buckinghamshire HP9 1PL
Telephone: 01494 672118
Fax: Same as phone
Email: books@beaconsfield-publishers.co.uk
Website: www.beaconsfield-publishers.co.uk
Imprints: Beaconsfield
Payment Details: Royalty
Unsolicited Manuscripts: No

Ruth Bean Publishers

Needlecrafts: lace-making, embroidery (practical and historical). Costume and costume history and anthropology related to textiles.

Editor(s): N W and R Bean
Address: Victoria Farmhouse, Carlton, Bedford MK43 7LP
Telephone: 01234 720356
Fax: 01234 720590
Email: ruthbean@cwcom.net
Payment Details: Negotiable
Unsolicited Manuscripts: Yes

B
Belitha Press

Belitha Press publishes high quality illustrated non-fiction books for children in the 3-13 age range. Subject areas include: art; environment issues; geography; history; literacy; music; natural history; numeracy; personal and social education; reference; science; technology.

Editor(s): Chester Fisher, Publishing Director
Address: 64 Brewery Road London N7 9NT
Telephone: 02076 973 000
Fax: 02076 973 3003
Imprints: Belitha Press, Big Fish, Learning World
Parent Company: C & B Media Group PLC

David Bennett Books Ltd

Books for babies, toddler play books, novelty books.

Editor(s): Helen Mortimer
Address: Kiln House, 210 New Kings Road, London SW6 4NZ
Telephone: 020 7731 6444
Fax: 020 7731 6554
Parent Company: Collins & Brown
Payment Details: Advance plus royalty or flat fee
Unsolicited Manuscripts: No

The Berean Publishing Trust

Small Christian publishing trust promoting the truth of God's Word Rightly Divided. See 2 Tim 2:15. The publications are the writings of our own authors.

Editor(s): Principal: Alan Schofield
Address: The Chapel of the Opened Book, 52a Wilson Street, London EC2A 2ER
Telephone: 020 7247 1467
Email: bptsales@compuserve.com
Website: www.bereanonline.org
Parent Company: The Berean Forward Movement
Unsolicited Manuscripts: No

Berg Publishers

Berg Publishers is an academic press specialising in anthropology, material culture, European History and politics and fashion and dress studies. We also publish an academic journal Fashion Theory. Submission guidelines are available upon request. We do not return unsolicited manuscripts.

Editor(s): Kathryn Earle, Editorial Director
Address: 150 Cowley Road, Oxford OX4 1JJ
Telephone: 01865 245104
Fax: 01865 791165
Email: enquiry@berg.demon.co.uk
Website: www.bergpublishers.com
Imprints: Oswald Wolff
Parent Company: Oxford International Publishers Ltd
Payment Details: Royalties paid annually
Unsolicited Manuscripts: No

B
Berghahn Books

Berghahn Books publish scholarly books broadly within the humanities and social sciences, with an emphasis on anthropology and European studies, especially German-American relations. We publish approximately 50 books and 10 journals a year in history, cultural studies, anthropology and sociology, politics and economics, Jewish studies, media and film studies, women's studies and military and war.

Editor(s): Commissioning Editors: Marion Berghahn and Sean Kingston (Anthropology)
Address: 3 Newtec Place, Magdalen Road, Oxford OX4 1RE
Telephone: 01865 250011
Fax: 01865 250056
Email: info@berghahnbooks.com
Website: www.berghahnbooks.com
Payment Details: Royalties paid once a year
Unsolicited Manuscripts: No

Berlitz Publishing Co Ltd

Publishers of self-teach language materials, pocket guides, phrase books and language travel products for children.

Address: Suite 120 24-25 Nutsford Place London W1H 5YN
Telephone: 0207 569 3160
Email: roger.kirkpatrick@berlitz.ie
Website: http://www.berlitz.com
Imprints: Berlitz
Parent Company: Berlitz International Inc
Unsolicited Manuscripts: No

Bible Reading Fellowship

The Bible Reading Fellowship (BRF) publishes resources for Bible reading and study, for Lent and Advent, for prayer and spirituality, for individual and group use. BRF also publishes resources for children under the age of 11 (Barnabas imprint), encouraging them to a stronger commitment to build foundations to last a lifetime and beyond.

Editor(s): Sue Doggett, Naomi Starkey
Address: First Floor, Elsfield Hall, 15-17 Elsfield Way, Oxford OX2 8FG
Telephone: 01865 319700
Fax: 01865 319701
Email: enquiries@brf.org.uk
Website: www.brf.org.uk
Imprints: Barnabas
Unsolicited Manuscripts: No

Bibliagora

Subject areas: contract bridge, philosophy and snooker. Publishers and international out-of-print book tracers.

Editor(s): David Rex-Taylor
Address: PO Box 77, Feltham, Middlesex TW14 8JF
Telephone: 020 8898 1234 / hotline: 07000 BIBLIO
Fax: 020 8844 1777
Email: biblio@bibliagora.com
Website: www.bibliagora.com
Payment Details: Negotiated
Unsolicited Manuscripts: No

BILD Publications
(British Institute Of Learning Disabilities)

The British Institute of Learning Disabilities (BILD) publishes a range of materials for anyone with an interest in learning disabilities. BILD publications include: textbooks aimed at professionals and students in the field; workshop training materials and independent study materials designed and tested by leading experts and aimed at front-line staff and carers; accessible publications on a wide range of topics designed for independent use by people with learning disabilities or with support from carers or family members.

Address: Wolverhampton Road, Kidderminster DY10 3PP
Telephone: 01562 850251
Fax: 01562 851970
Email: bild@bild.demon.co.uk
Website: www.bild.org.uk
Payment Details: By negotiation
Unsolicited Manuscripts: No

BIOS Scientific Publishers Ltd

Life sciences and medicine; particularly molecular biology, biochemistry, genetics, cell biology, plant biology, microscopy, anaesthesia and obstetrics and gynaecology. We publish textbooks, practical handbooks, high intensive care level review volumes and revision guides on all the above subjects.

Editor(s): J Ray, N Farrar
Address: 9 Newtec Place, Magdalen Road, Oxford OX4 1RE
Telephone: 01865 726286
Fax: 01865 200386
Email: jonathan.ray@bios.co.uk, nigel.farrar@bios.co.uk
Website: www.bios.co.uk
Payment Details: Royalties and advances (discussed on a book to book basis)
Unsolicited Manuscripts: Yes

Birlinn Limited And John Donald Publishers Limited

Scottish non-fiction (especially Highlands and Western Isles); military history; adventure and exploration; academic (mainly Scottish Studies).

Editor(s): Hugh Andrew
Address: West Newintton House 10 Newintton Road Edinburgh EH9 1QS
Telephone: 0131 668 4371
Fax: 0131 668 4466
Email: info@birlinn.co.uk
Website: http://www.birlinn.co.uk
Imprints: John Donald
Payment Details: Royalties and advances
Unsolicited Manuscripts: Yes - send registered, hard copy only

Black & White Publishing Ltd

Publish general fiction and non-fiction including classics, food and drink, humour, sport, biography and autobiography, photography and quiz books.

Address: 99 Giles Street, Edinburgh, EH6 6BZ
Telephone: 0131 625 4500
Fax: 0131 625 4501
Email: mail@blackandwhitepublishing.com
Website: www.blackandwhitepublishing.com
Imprints: B & W Publishing
Payment Details: Twice a year
Unsolicited Manuscripts: No, synopsis and sample chapters only - no material returned without SAE

Black Ace Books

We are only interested in completed full-length books. Bright ideas, proposals in synopsis form, work in progress and so on are not of interest. As far as our own list is concerned, some of the categories we definitely do not require include children's, DIY, poetry, religion, short stories. Relatively few of our books are non-fiction. Occasionally, for a really exceptional book, and provided we can devise a suitable budget, we may offer to publish work in such categories as biography, history, philosophy and psychology. Most of our output is high-quality literary fiction. Works likely to excite us would include an oustanding first novel from a new author with a fresh perspective and distinctive voice.

Address: PO Box 6557, Forfar DD8 2YS
Website: www.blackacebooks.com
Unsolicited Manuscripts: Write for guidelines with SAE. We do not respond to cold-calls or faxes

Black Spring Press Ltd

A small, independent publisher specialising in modern literary fiction as well as non-fiction reflecting contemporary culture. Titles include: Charles Jackson's The Lost Weekend, Roland Topor's The Tenant and Orson Welles's The Big Brass Ring.

Editor(s): Robert Hastings
Address: Burbage House, 83-85 Curtain Road, London, EC2A 3BS
Telephone: 020 7613 3066
Fax: 020 7613 0028
Email: bsp@blackspring.demon.co.uk
Payment Details: 10/12% Net receipts
Unsolicited Manuscripts: No

A & C Black

Children's educational books for 3-15 years (preliminary enquiry appreciated - fiction guidelines available on request), ceramics, art & craft, music, drama (New Mermaid Series), ornithology (Christopher Helm incorporating Pica Press), reference (Who's Who, Black's Veterinary and Medical Dictionaries), sport, theatre, travel (Blue Guides), books for writers.

Editor(s): Directors: Jill Coleman, Charles Black (non exec), Colin Adams, Oscar Heini, Paul Langridge, Janet Murphy, Terry Rovelett, Kathy Rooney
Address: Alderman House, 37 Soho Square, London, W1D 3QZ
Telephone: 020 7758 0200
Fax: 020 7758 0222
Email: enquiries@acblack.com
Website: Under construction
Imprints: Adlard Coles Nautical, Christopher Helm, The Herbert Press
Parent Company: Subsidiary of Bloomsbury Publishing plc
Unsolicited Manuscripts: No

Blackhat

Independent small-press publisher, specialising in contemporary open-field poetry. Interested in poetry and prose that test the boundaries of language and structure, while still having something actual to say. Not interested in poetry found on a newspaper reader's page. Approach at manuscript stage made by publisher to author, not other way around. Suggest writers save cost of postage, unless invited by editor. Small one-off print-runs only.

Editor(s): Lloyd Robson
Address: 40 Ruby Street, Cardiff CF24 1LN
Imprints: Canarant (audio tapes)
Payment Details: Variable
Unsolicited Manuscripts: No. Any received not guaranteed a reply

B

Blackstaff Press Ltd

Blackstaff has published over 700 titles, mainly of Irish (especially Northern Irish) interest, but covering a range of categories including history, politics, poetry, fiction and humour.

Editor(s): Anne Tannahill
Address: Blackstaff House, Wildflower Way, Apollo Road, Belfast BT12 6TA
Telephone: 028 9066 8074
Fax: 028 9066 8207
Email: info@blackstaffpress.com
Parent Company: W & G Baird
Unsolicited Manuscripts: Yes

Blake Publishing Ltd

Founded 1991 and rapidly expanding. Publishes mass-market non-fiction. No children's, or fiction. 50 titles in 2000. No unsolicited mss; synopsis and ideas welcome. Please enclose SAE.

Address: 3 Bramber Court, 2 Bramber Road, London W14 9PB
Telephone: 0207 381 0666
Fax: 0207 381 6868
Email: words@blake.co.uk
Payment Details: Royalties paid twice yearly
Unsolicited Manuscripts: Synopsis first please

B

Bloodaxe Books

Contemporary poetry. Note to prospective authors and agents: when submitting work to Bloodaxe, please enclose SAE or International Reply Coupons. If your work is not accepted for publication, we will not be able to return it to you unless you have sent return postage. While we are pleased to consider unsolicited submissions, we cannot accept any responsibility for loss or damage to manuscripts or artwork. Please also note the following: * If you want a quick response, send a sample selection of up to a dozen poems rather than a full-length collection. If you want us to consider something other than poetry, please send a preliminary letter and synopsis rather than the book itself. * We are not publishing any more fiction. * If you do not read any contemporary poetry, we are unlikely to be interested in your work. * It is usually advisable to submit poems to magazines before thinking about putting a book together. * We regret that we aren't able to offer detailed criticism of poetry submitted for publication (we currently receive about 100 books to consider each week). There are specialist organisations offering critical services, writers' workshops and courses.

Editor(s): Neil Astley
Address: Highgreen, Tarset, Northumberland, NE48 1RP
Telephone: 01434 240500
Fax: 01434 240505
Email: editor@bloodaxebooks.demon.co.uk
Website: www.bloodaxebooks.demon.co.uk
Unsolicited Manuscripts: See description

Bloomsbury Publishing

Literary fiction, biography, illustrated, reference, travel in hardcover; children's, trade paperback and mass market paperback.

Editor(s): Liz Calder, Rosemary Davidson, Kathy Rooney, Sarah Oedina, Emma Matthewson, Bill Swainson, Alexandra Pringle and Mike Jones
Address: 38 Soho Square, London W1D 3HB
Telephone: 020 7494 2111
Fax: 020 7494 0151
Website: www.bloomsburymagazine.com

BMJ Books

BMJ Books was established as a division of the BMJ Publishing Group at the beginning of 1997. The publisher is John Hudson and the Editorial section is headed by Mary Banks. The team publish 40 titles and new editions annually, mostly books but with some items on CD-ROM, Video and Diskette. Recently, online updating of major texts has been established and several of the books are carried with full text on the eBMJ site. Best-known of the output is the ABC series, originally published as articles in the BMJ and collated to become the first books from the BMJ.

Apart from the ABCs, BMJ Books also publish titles on Accident and Emergency/ Trauma, Anaesthesia, Cardiology, Evidence Based Medicine, Medical Writing and Research, Ophthalmology, Paediatrics and Statistics. The British National Formulary, co-published with the Royal Pharmaceutical Society, is another famous BMJ product.

Address: BMA House, Tavistock Square, London WC1H 9JR
Telephone: 020 7383 6185
Fax: 020 7383 6662
Email: orders@bmjbooks.com
Website: www.bmjbooks.com
Parent Company: BMJ Publishing Group

Bodmin Books, The Cornish Capital Publishers

Founded in 1972 to promote Cornish history, tradition, and present attractions, Bodmin Books pioneered attention to Bodmin Moor ('72), the Bodmin Riding custom ('74), and the delights of Kynance on the Lizard in West Cornwall ('76); and still holds the only definitive study of a nationally-known murder mystery Charlotte Dymond 1844 ('78). The occasionals imprint Cotterill & Munn was launched in 1997 with the publication of the words/music pamphlet The Ballad Of '97 commemorating the 500th anniversary of the Cornish Rising, and the annual Bodmin Community Christmas Day Party tabloid. 1998 saw a re-launch of the Bodmin Map with historical notes and placename references; and, in 1999, came Whit's End, a verse play to mark the 450th Prayer Book Rising anniversary. Bodmin Books will continue with academic studies, in 2001 arranging ISBN and copyright deposit of "Bodmin 1901-2000, A Century Of Memories"; and publishing a collection of articles on Bodmin's Parish Church with a first-ever date-list of 1500 years of events. Both imprints are voluntary co-operative hobbies, with authors contributing printing costs, and the company its storage space, production and promotional experience, and orders facilitation. If/when books sell, authors may be reimbursed some or all of their contribution.

Editor(s): Mrs P I Munn
Address: 4 Turf Street, Bodmin, Cornwall PL31 2DH
Imprints: Cotterill & Munn
Parent Company: Bodmin Books, The Cornish Capital Publishers
Payment Details: None
Unsolicited Manuscripts: No

The Book Castle

Publishes non-fiction of local interest (Bedfordshire, Hertfordshire, Buckinghamshire, Oxfordshire, the Chilterns), 6 titles a year. About 70 titles in print, eg Chiltern Walks series, The Hill Of The Martyr, Journeys Into Buckinghamshire, Changes In Our Landscape.

Editor(s): Paul Bowes, Sally Siddons
Address: 12 Church Street, Dunstable, Beds LU5 4RU
Telephone: 01582 605670
Fax: 01582 662431
Email: bc@book-castle.co.uk
Website: http://www.book-castle.co.uk/
Payment Details: Royalty
Unsolicited Manuscripts: Yes

The Book Guild Ltd

Founded in 1982, we are a small, independent general publishing house. We carry a diverse list which includes sponsored books, fiction, autobiographies, biographies, military histories, human interest titles and children's titles. Also have an expanding mainstream list. Approximately 80 titles a year.

Editor(s): Carol Biss - Managing Director
Address: Temple House, 25 High Street, Lewes, East Sussex BN7 2LU
Telephone: 01273 472534
Fax: 01273 476472
Email: info@bookguild.co.uk
Website: www.bookguild.co.uk
Payment Details: Royalties paid twice-yearly
Unsolicited Manuscripts: No

Borthwick Institute Publications

The Institute publishes a series of studies concerned with the ecclesiastical history of the north of England and other aspects of the history or historiography of Yorkshire. Also concentrates on issuing editions and catalogues of its deposited archives and providing guides to the handwriting and contents of records.

Editor(s): Editorial board
Address: St Anthony's Hall, Peasholme Green, York YO1 7PW
Telephone: 01904 642315
Fax: 01904 633284
Website: www.york.ac.uk/inst/bihr
Imprints: Borthwick Papers, Borthwick Texts and Calendars, Borthwick Lists and Indexes, Borthwick Studies In History, Borthwick Wallets, Monastic Research Bulletin
Parent Company: University of York

Marion Boyars Publishers Ltd

An established literary imprint (since 1960) with specialisations in fiction, fiction in translation, cinema and avant-garde music. Famous authors include Ken Kesey, Hubert Selby Jnr, Gilbert Sorrentino, Michael Ondaatje, Yevgeny Yevtushenko, Kenzaburo Oe, Pauline Kael, Robert Creeley, Julio Cortazar, John Cage, Ingmar Bergman, Georges Bataille and Carlo Gebler.

Submissions through literary agencies only.

Editor(s): Ken Hollings
Address: 24 Lacy Road, London SW15 1NL
Telephone: 020 8788 9522
Fax: 020 8789 8122
Email: marion.boyars@talk21.com
Website: www.marionboyars.co.uk
Unsolicited Manuscripts: Accepted for literary standard works (as against mass-market) with return p&p

B
BPS Books (The British Psychological Society)

BPS Books the imprint of The British Psychological Society, has a wide ranging list of titles both for academics and practitioners, not only in mainstream psychology but also in related fields such as health and social care, education, management and psychometrics. As well as books, we also publish a number of training packs for occupational settings and we have entered the multimedia arena with our CD ROM: Introduction to Statistics. Our books are well received internationally and we have currently translated into 25 languages.

Editor(s): Joyce Collins
Address: The British Psychological Society, 48 Princess Road East, Leicester LE1 7DR
Telephone: 0116 254 9568
Fax: 0116 247 0787
Email: joycol@bps.org.uk
Website: www.bps.org.uk
Payment Details: On request
Unsolicited Manuscripts: Yes

Barry Bracewell-Milnes

Economic policy, tax policy, tax avoidance and evasion.

Editor(s): Barry Bracewell-Milnes
Address: 26 Lancaster Court, Banstead, Surrey SM7 1RR
Telephone: 01737 350736
Imprints: Panopticum
Unsolicited Manuscripts: Write first

Bradford Libraries

Books of local interest.

Address: Central Library, Prince's Way, Bradford BD1 1NN
Telephone: 01274 753600
Fax: 01274 395108
Email: public.libraries@bradford.gov.uk
Parent Company: City of Bradford Metropolitan Council
Unsolicited Manuscripts: No

Bradt Travel Guides

Bradt Travel Guides have been meeting the needs of independent and environmentally conscious travellers for over 25 years. All our guides have the Bradt hallmark of hard information to ensure trouble-free and rewarding travel to new and unusual destinations. Our range includes Country guides, Backpackers manuals, Hiking guides, Wildlife guides and a by Rail series. Highly readable and personal travel writing is combined with well-researched, up-to-date information, user-friendly maps and straight-forward town plans.

Editor(s): Tricia Hayne
Address: 19 High Street, Chalfont St Peter, Bucks SL9 9QE
Telephone: 01753 893444
Fax: 01753 892333
Email: info@bradt-travelguides.com
Website: www.bradt-travelguides.com
Payment Details: Royalties
Unsolicited Manuscripts: No

Nicholas Brealey Publishing

We are publishers of leading-edge books for business that inform, inspire, enable and entertain. We also focus on personal development, the international and intercultural fields and topical bestsellers that go beyond the traditional business book to look at the global picture.

Editor(s): Nicholas Brealey
Address: 36 John Street, London WC1N 2AT
Telephone: 020 7430 0224
Fax: 020 7404 8311
Email: nicholas.commissioning@nbrealey-books.com
Unsolicited Manuscripts: Yes

Breedon Books Publishing Co Ltd

Local history, archive photography, sport, motor sport, biography and autobiographies by sports personalities.

Editor(s): Anton Rippon, Fiona Courtenay-Thompson
Address: The Parker Centre, Derby DE21 5SZ
Telephone: 01332 384235
Fax: 01332 292755
Email: anton@breedonbooks.co.uk
Imprints: Breedon Sport, Breedon Heritage
Payment Details: By arrangement
Unsolicited Manuscripts: Yes if accompanied by return postage

Brewin Books

Midland regional history topics. Biographies. Transport history: railways, buses, aircraft and canals. Joint publications with trusts, local authorities etc (non-fiction topics).

Editor(s): Alan Brewin
Address: Doric House, 56 Alcester Road, Studley, Warwickshire B80 7LG
Telephone: 01527 854228
Fax: 01527 852746
Email: alan@brewinbooks.com
Website: www.brewinbooks.com
Imprints: Brewin Books, Alton Douglas Books
Parent Company: Brewin Books Ltd
Payment Details: Usual royalties payable six-monthly
Unsolicited Manuscripts: No. But preliminary letter with synopsis acceptable

The Bridgeman Art Library

The Bridgeman Art Library is the world's most comprehensive source of fine art images for publication. It currently represents over 1000 museums, galleries, private collections and artists from the smallest private collections to prestigious national institutions such as the British Library in London, the National Museum of Sweden and the State Russian Museum, St Petersburg. The archive is unmatched in its breadth and depth. Every subject, period and style is covered from ancient history to the classics of the Renaissance and through to contemporary art, including design, architecture, antiques, manuscripts and historical artefacts. New images are added to collection daily and a team of specialist picture researchers, all art historians, are on hand to offer advice and research assistance. Searching is simple and enjoyable; images are fully catalogued and cross-referenced with keywords and may also be viewed and ordered conveniently online at www.bridgeman.co.uk.

Address: 17-19 Garway Road, London W2 4PH
Telephone: 020 7727 4065
Fax: 020 7792 8509
Email: info@bridgeman.co.uk
Website: www.bridgeman.co.uk
Unsolicited Manuscripts: No

B
Brilliant Publications

Brilliant Publications publishes books for teachers, parents and others interested in the education of children 0-13 years olds. The books are primarily resource books and activity sheets for use in classrooms, rather than stories for children. Potential authors are invited to phone or write for a catalogue so they can see the type of books we publish prior to sending in a proposal.

Editor(s): Priscilla Hannaford
Address: The Old School Yard, Leighton Road, Northall, Dunstable, Bedfordshire LU6 2HA
Telephone: 01525 222844
Fax: 01525 221250
Email: sales@brilliantpublications.co.uk
Website: www.brilliantpublications.co.uk
Imprints: Brilliants Publications
Payment Details: Royalties, payable twice-yearly
Unsolicited Manuscripts: We are always happy to receive contributions from new authors but would prefer to receive a proposal and sample chapter initially, rather than a complete manuscript. Authors should supply an SAE

British Cement Association

Cement, concrete, civil and structural engineering, construction, materials science and standards.

Editor(s): Martin Clarke
Address: Century House, Telford Avenue, Crowthorne, Berks RG45 6YS
Email: library@bca.org.uk
Website: www.bca.org.uk
Payment Details: Negotiable
Unsolicited Manuscripts: Yes

British Library Publications

The British Library has a flourishing publishing programme of approximately 40 titles per year and over 600 titles in print. The majority of the titles are academic works; however there is also an expanding list of general and illustrated books, based primarily on the Library's extensive historic connections.

Editor(s): David Way, Lara Speicher
Address: 96 Euston Road, London NW1 2DB
Telephone: 020 7412 7704
Fax: 020 7412 7768
Email: blpublications@bl.uk
Website: www.bl.uk
Imprints: British Library Publications
Parent Company: The British Library

British Museum Press

Subect areas: History and archaeology, Art History, Decorative Arts and Collecting, Numismatics, Ethnnography. Types of publications: Titles for the general reader, educational fiction and non-fiction books for children, Academic titles and Occasional Papers. Postcard sets and gift sets for adults and children.

Editor(s): Ms T Francis - Managing Editor (adults), Ms C Jones - Senior Editor (Childrens)
Address: 46 Bloomsbury Street, London WC1B 3QQ
Telephone: 020 7323 1234
Fax: 020 7436 7315
Email: sales.books@bmcompany.co.uk
Website: www.bmcompany.co.uk
Parent Company: British Museum Company Ltd
Payment Details: Variable
Unsolicited Manuscripts: Synopsis rather than manuscript

Andrew Brodie Publications

Andrew Brodie Publications produce a fast-growing range of educational books, providing valuable materials for parents to use at home with their children as well as resource books for teachers to use in school. Educational experts ensure that the books reflect the latest standards required of schools, while preserving traditional skills in handwriting, spelling and mathematics.

Editor(s): Andrew Brodie
Address: PO Box 23, Wellington, Somerset, TA21 8YX
Telephone: 01823 665493
Fax: 01823 665345
Email: andrew@andrewbrodie.co.uk
Website: www.andrewbrodie.co.uk
Imprints: Andrew Brodie Publications
Unsolicited Manuscripts: No

Brooklands Books Ltd

The Brooklands Books road test series provide an unparalleled source of motoring reference literature. The series includes the new Ultimate Portfolio series, as well as the popular Gold Portfolios, Performance/Muscle Portfolios and Limited Editions. New for 1999 is a series entitled 'Take on the Competition' which focuses on individual models. The Gold Portfolio and Performance Portfolio series now cover motor cycle marques. Our Motor Racing series, with collected contemporary race reports, summaries and results, cover some of the greatest motor races in the world. Brooklands Books also publish official technical literature fo MG, Land Rover, Jaguar, Triumph and Austin Healey, as well as their specially commissioned Owners Workshop Manuals.

Address: PO Box 146, Cobham, Surrey KT11 1LG
Telephone: 01932 865051
Fax: 01932 868803
Email: sales@brooklands-books.com
Website: www.brooklands-books.com

Brown, Son & Ferguson Ltd

Nautical and navigation both technical and non-technical (not biographical).

Editor(s): L Ingram-Brown
Address: 4/10 Darnley Street, Glasgow G41 2SD
Telephone: 0141 429 1234
Fax: 0141 420 1694
Email: info@skipper.co.uk
Website: www.skipper.co.uk
Payment Details: Standard royalty agreement
Unsolicited Manuscripts: Yes

Bryntirion Press

Bryntirion Press is the publishing branch of the Evangelical Movement of Wales. The press publishes books and evangelistic materials which bear witness to the historic evangelical faith of the Christian Church and in particular encourages publications which reflect a Welsh Evangelical ethos. Gwasg (GWASG) Bryntinon publishes material in the Welsh language.

Editor(s): Press Manager: Huw Kinsey
Address: Bryntirion, Bridgend CF31 4DX
Telephone: 01656 655886
Fax: 01656 665919
Email: evanmvt@draco.co.uk
Website: www.evangelicalmvt-wales.org
Parent Company: Evangelical Movement of Wales
Payment Details: Royalty payments 10%
Unsolicited Manuscripts: No

B
Burall Floraprint Ltd

Publish good-value gardening titles, from eminent horticultural authors, featuring vibrant pictures and thoroughly helpful text, all at very reasonable prices. Examples include the 128-page Shrubs For Everyone by Peter Seabrook and Clematis For Everyone by Raymond Evison. Most of the photographs in the books come from the extensive International Floramedia plant picture library. The same company (Burall Floraprint Ltd) is the UK's leading supplier of pictorial plant labels, as used to label plants in the majority of UK garden centres and horticultural retailers.

Address: Oldfield Lane, Wisbech PE13 2TH
Telephone: 01945 461165
Fax: 01945 474396
Email: floraprint@burall.com
Website: www.burall.com
Imprints: Floraprint, Floramedia
Parent Company: Burall Ltd
Unsolicited Manuscripts: No

John Burgess Publications

Writer and publisher of history books, local, regional and national interest, guide books to Britain, and of Law books.

Address: 28 Holme Fauld, Scotby, Carlisle CA4 8BL
Telephone: 01228 513173

B

Edmund Burke Publisher

Specialises in fine historical publications and limited editions.

Editor(s): Eamonn de Burca
Address: Cloonagashel, 27 Priory Drive, Blackrock, Co Dublin, Ireland
Telephone: 003531 2882159
Fax: 003531 2834080
Email: deburca@indigo.ie
Website: www.deburcararebooks.com
Imprints: Edmund Burke Publisher, Caislean Burc, De Burca

Business Education Publishers Ltd

Since 1979 Business Education Publishers have maintained a strong portfolio of traditional publications. An independant publisher, BEP specialise predominantly in the publication of teaching and learning material in the fields of business, leisure, information technology, computing, education, travel and tourism and local history.

BEP publishes a range of academic textbooks which are widely adopted by Schools, Colleges and Universities in the UK and abroad.

The University of Sunderland Press (UoSP) is a joint venture between Business Education Publishers. The UoSP was established in 1997 to enable the publication of refereed academic works in learning and teaching, literature, research, conference proceedings, and popular treatments of academic subjects.

An excellent understanding of the book industry allows us to strike the best deals with all industry parties, maximising exposure with minimum overheads in often small specialist markets. An experienced tight-knit team works very closely with authors, providing a full and reassuring service throughout.

Address: The Solar Building, Doxford International, Sunderland, SR3 3XW
Telephone: 0191 525 2410
Fax: 0191 520 1815
Email: info@bepl.com
Website: www.bepl.com

B
Butterworth Tolley

Butterworths serves the legal, accountancy and allied professions by publishing timely and acurate legal information in a variety of formats, including textbooks, journals, newsletters, law reports, loose-leafs, encyclopaedias, CD-ROMs and on-line services.

Butterworths Tolley's objective is to continue to provide solutions that anticipate and fulfil the changing needs of the profession. As we move into the next millennium, our exciting portfolio of electronic products and online services is set to maintain and enhance our special relationship with the profession.

Address: Halsbury House, 35 Chancery Lane, London WC2A 1EL
Telephone: 020 7400 2500
Fax: 020 7400 2842
Email: customer_services@butterworths.co.uk
Website: http://www.butterworths.com
Imprints: Butterworths, Tolley, Lexis
Parent Company: Reed Elsevier

Cairns Publications

Books and cards unfolding afresh prayers and meditations from the Christian spiritual heritage. Reflections on contemporary issues in the light of that inheritance.

Address: Orders: 47 Firth Park Avenue, Sheffield S5 6HF Enquiries: Jim Cotter, 1 Groes Nwydd, Llandecwyn, Gwynedd, LL47 6YR
Telephone: 0114 243 1182
Email: office@cottercairns.co.uk

Caister Academic Press

Publishers of academc journals and books on science. Publishes 'Current Issues in Molecular Biology' 'Molecular Biology Today'.

Address: 32 Hewitts Lane, Wymondham, Norfolk NR18 0JA
Telephone: 0870 3213681
Fax: 0870 3213682
Email: mail@caister.com
Website: www.caister.com
Unsolicited Manuscripts: Yes

Calder Publications Ltd

One of the remaining independent publishers, established in 1949. publishers of international modern fiction and drama with 18 Noble Prize winners for literature on the list. Authors include: Samual Beckett, Antonin Artaud, Howard Barker, L F Celine, Margeurite Duras, Robert Menasse and Frank Wedekind.

Editor(s): John Calder
Address: 51 The Cut, London SE1 8LF
Telephone: 020 7633 0599
Fax: 020 7633 0599
Email: info@calderpub.demon.co.uk
Website: http://www.calderpublications.com
Imprints: Calder Publications Ltd, John Calder Publisher, Riverrun Press (USA), New Paris Editions, ENO Opera Guides, Calderbooks, The Scottish Library, French Surrealism, German Expressionism, Opera Library
Payment Details: The Calder Educational Trust

C

Cambridge University Press

Primary and secondary school books. English language teaching. Academic publishing embraces just about every subject seriously studied in the English speaking university world.

Editor(s): Many subject specialists
Address: The Edinburgh Building, Shaftesbury Road, Cambridge CB2 2RU
Imprints: Distribute worldwide: Stanford University Press, MacKeith Press
Parent Company: University of Cambridge
Payment Details: Varies according to the nature and level of the individual book
Unsolicited Manuscripts: Send outline proposal

Canongate Books Ltd

High quality adult general fiction, English language and world literature in translation, Canongate Classics, Canongate International, Mojo Books, Pocket Canons, art, autobiography and biography, mountaineering, music, travel.

Payback Press (imprint). Writing focussing on Black culture, autobiography and biography, fiction and non-fiction, music, poetry.

Please phone before submission and ensure familiarity with lists by requesting a catalogue in advance or by checking the website. For practical and security reasons submissions by fax, email or on disk cannot be accepted, except by special arrangement. Please ensure the appropriate return postage is enclosed and allow 6-8 weeks for a response.

Editor(s): Publisher, Jamie Byng
Address: 14 High Street, Edinburgh EH1 1TE
Telephone: 0131 557 5111
Fax: 0131 557 5211
Email: info@canongate.co.uk
Website: http://www.canongate.net
Imprints: Canongate International, Payback Press, Mojo, Canongate Classics, Canongate Times

Capall Bann Publishing

Mind body spirit, women's studies, personal development, nautical, environmental, gardening, occult, folklore, animals, mediumship, crystals, astrology, tarot, alternative health.

Editor(s): Julia Day, Jon Day
Address: Freshfields, Chieveley, Berks RG20 8TF
Telephone: 01635 248711(editorial) / 01635 247050 (sales)
Email: capallbann1@virginbiz.com
Website: www.capallbann.co.uk
Imprints: Capall Bann
Payment Details: 10% quarterly
Unsolicited Manuscripts: Yes - but send synopsis first and sample section

Carcanet Press Ltd

'Everything an independent publisher should be' Willian Boyd. Since 1969, Carcanet has grown from an undergraduate hobby into one of the most prestigious 'small' publishers today. Strong Anglo-European, Anglo-Commonwealth and more local links ensure a quality and variety of publication from poetry, biography, translation and academic titles to its sturdy 'Fyfield' imprint, Carcanet is the market leader of its field. PN Review, its sister magazine showcases new writing and provides some of the best criticisms, reviews and articles around.

Editor(s): Michael Schmidt
Address: 4th Floor, Conavon Court, 12-16 Blackfriars Street, Manchester M3 5BQ
Telephone: 0161 834 8730
Fax: 0161 832 0084
Email: pnr@carcanet.u-net.com
Website: www.carcanet.co.uk
Imprints: Fyfield, Oxford Poets (1999)
Parent Company: Folio Holdings
Payment Details: Varies
Unsolicited Manuscripts: Brief synopsis (poetry preferred) to 'The Editor'

Cardiff Academic Press

Cardiff Academic Press is an independent academic publisher with particular interest in Religious Studies, Women's Studies and topics relating to Wales. Publishes under Cardiff Academic Press and Plantin imprints and distributes academic texts for overseas publishers Tuns Press, ILSI, ECW and Garamond.

Address: St Fagans Road, Fairwater, Cardiff CF5 3AE
Telephone: 02920 560333
Fax: 02920 554909
Email: E-bost:drakegroup@btinternet.com
Imprints: Plantins, ISLI, Tuns Press
Parent Company: The Drake Group Ltd
Payment Details: Pro-forma
Unsolicited Manuscripts: Yes but only biographical details and qualifications, brief synopsis, extent and target audience

Carlton Publishing Group

The Carlton Publishing Group includes the Carlton Books, Andre Deutsch, Granada Media, Manchester United Books and Liverpool FC Books imprints. Publishers of leading entertainment titles including TV and film tie-ins and sports titles from branded ITV Formula One to Official football team publishing. We also publish a huge variety of lifestyle, interiors, design, fashion and health titles including Cosmopolitan, New Woman and Vogue branded books.

Editor(s): Piers Murray Hill - Publishing Director, Martin Conteel - Sport, Venetia Penfold - Lifestyle, Penny Simpson - Leisure Reference, Nicky Pams - Granada Media
Address: 20 Mortimer Street, London, W1T 3JW
Telephone: 020 7612 0400
Fax: 020 7612 0401
Email: enquiries@carltonbooks,co.uk
Website: www.carlton.com
Imprints: Carlton Books, Andre Deutsch, Granada Media, Manchester United Books, Liverpool FC Books
Parent Company: Carlton Communications
Unsolicited Manuscripts: No

Jon Carpenter Publishing

Environment, sustainable economics and development, Green politics, social issues and health. Local history, especially Oxfordshire and Cotswolds. Authors should send for our author information sheet before submitting any other material.

Editor(s): Jon Carpenter
Address: Alder House, Market Street, Charlbury OX7 3PH
Telephone: 01608 811969
Fax: Same as phone
Email: carpenter@oxfree.com
Imprints: Jon Carpenter, The Wychwood Press
Payment Details: Royalties
Unsolicited Manuscripts: No

Casdec Print & Design Centre

Publishers and printers of educational non-fiction books, training materials for various bodies, and writers of open/distance learning materials. Specialise in publishing training and learning materials for universities, colleges, financial and other bodies. Publisher of the nationally-recognised Your Business Success bookkeeping and financial control system. Over 200,000 book keeping systems supplied to a national financial institution for use by clients.

Editor(s): T Moffat
Address: 21-22 Harraton Terrace, Birtley, Chester-le-Street, Co Durham DH3 2QG
Telephone: 0191 410 5556
Fax: 0191 410 0229
Email: cshotton@casdec.co.uk

C
Frank Cass & Co Ltd

Publisher of academic books and journals on Middle Eastern Studies, Militaria, Intelligence, History, Politics, Sports Studies, Business Studies and Legislative Studies.

Editor(s): Andrew Humphrys
Address: Crown House, 47 Chase Side, Southgate, London, N14 5BP
Telephone: 020 8920 2100
Fax: 020 8447 8548
Email: info@frankcass.com
Website: www.frankcass.com
Imprints: Frank Cass, Woburn Press
Payment Details: Royalties
Unsolicited Manuscripts: Yes

Cassell and Co.

Publishers of natural history, health, crafts, home decorating, interiors, spiritual, cookery, woodcrafts, gardening, personal development and science and military.

Editor(s): Ian Drury, Michael Dour, Richard Millbank, Nick Cheetham, Mark Smith
Address: Wellington House, 125 The Strand, London WC2R 0BB
Telephone: 020 7420 5555
Fax: 020 7420 7261
Website: www.cassell.co.uk
Imprints: Cassell Illustrators, Military, Paperback, Reference and Guides
Parent Company: Orion Publishing Group
Unsolicited Manuscripts: Yes

Kyle Cathie Ltd

An independent company founded in 1990, publishing illustrated non-fiction, prize-winning titles to high standards of design, specialising in cookery, gardening, health and beauty, design, style, reference. Bestsellers in 2000 include Natural Healing for Animals, Natural Alternative to HRT Cookbook, One Pot Wonders, The Wine Experience, Get the Look and Fantastic Flowers.

Editor(s): Caroline Taggart, Helen Woodhall, Sheila Boniface
Address: 122 Arlington Road, London NW1 7HP
Telephone: 020 7692 7215
Fax: 020 7692 7260
Email: kcathie@aol.com
Payment Details: Royalties paid twice yearly
Unsolicited Manuscripts: Yes

Catholic Institute For International Relations

A medium-sized development agency with a small publishing operation. Topics covered include human rights, international economic framework, civil society, peace processes, capacity-building of non-governmental organisations, environment, trade, food security, liberation theology. Areas: Latin America and Caribbean, Southern Africa, Middle East, South East Asia.

Editor(s): Adam Bradbury (Production Editor)
Address: Unit 3, Canonbury Yard, 190a New North Road, London N1 7BJ
Telephone: 020 7354 0883
Fax: 020 7359 0017
Email: ciir@ciir.org
Website: www.ciir.org
Imprints: CIIR, ICD
Parent Company: CIIR
Payment Details: Small fees negotiated
Unsolicited Manuscripts: Yes

C
Cavendish Publishing Limited

Publisher with offices in London and Sydney specialising in law and medical books for law students, academics and practitioners.

Editor(s): Ms Jo Reddy
Address: The Glass House, Wharton Street, London WC1X 9PX
Telephone: 020 7278 8000
Fax: 020 7278 8080
Email: info@cavendishpublishing.com
Website: http://www.cavendishpublishing.com
Imprints: Cavendish Publishing
Parent Company: Cavendish Publishing (Jersey) Ltd
Payment Details: Royalties
Unsolicited Manuscripts: No

Centaur Press

Subjects in the field of humane education, animal rights and classic literature.

Editor(s): Jeannie Cohen, Elisabeth Petersdorff
Address: 51 Achilles Road, London NW6 1DZ
Telephone: 020 7431 4391
Fax: 020 7431 5129
Email: books@opengatepress.co.uk
Website: www.opengatepress.co.uk
Imprints: Centaur Press, Linden Press
Parent Company: Open Gate Press
Unsolicited Manuscripts: Synopses and ideas for books only

Centre For Economic Policy Research

A network of over 500 Research Fellows, based primarily in European universities. The Centre coordinates its Fellows' research activities and communicates their results to the public and private sectors. CEPR is an entrepreneur, developing research initiatives with the producers, consumers and sponsors of research. Established in 1983, CEPR is a European economics research organisation with uniquely wide-ranging scope and activities. CEPR is a registered educational charity, supported by various charitable trusts and banks, none of which gives prior review to the Centre's publications, nor necessarily endorses the views expressed.

Address: 90-98 Goswell Road, London EC1V 7RR
Telephone: 020 7878 2900
Fax: 020 7878 2999
Email: cepr@cepr.org
Website: www.cepr.org
Imprints: CEPR
Payment Details: Confidential
Unsolicited Manuscripts: No

Centre For Information On Language Teaching & Research (CILT)

The Centre for Information on Language Teaching & Research provides a complete range of services for language professionals in every stage and sector of education, including publications designed to support teachers.

Editor(s): Head of Publishing: Emma Rees
Address: 20 Bedfordbury, London WC2N 4LB
Telephone: 020 7379 5101
Fax: 020 7379 5082
Email: publications@cilt.org.uk
Website: http://www.cilt.org.uk

C

Chalcombe Publications

Technical publications for agriculture, specialising in animal science, grassland and forage crops and animal production systems. The books are for farmers, veterinarians, students, teachers and research workers.

Editor(s): Dr J.M. Wilkinson
Address: Painshall, Church Lane, Welton, Lincoln LN2 3LT
Telephone: 01673 863023
Fax: 01673 863108
Email: mike@chalcombe.co.uk
Website: www.chalcombe.co.uk
Unsolicited Manuscripts: No

Chambers Harrap Publishers Ltd

Chambers - Publishers of the Chambers Dictionary, Chambers offers a full range of English dictionaries and thesauruses, ELT dictionaries and study aids, English usage guides, subject dictionaries, crossword and official Scrabble publications.

Harrap - French, Spanish, German, Italian and Portuguese bilingual dictionaries and study aids, plus a range of specialist French dictionaries.
Address: 7 Hopetoun Crescent, Edinburgh EH7 4AY
Telephone: 0131 556 5929
Fax: 0131 556 5313
Email: Admin@chambersharrap.co.uk
Website: www.chambersharrap.com
Imprints: Chambers and Harrap
Parent Company: Vivendi Universal Education France, Paris
Unsolicited Manuscripts: No

Chapman Publishing

Chapman New Writing series aims to present up-and-coming writers, Scottish and international (short fiction, poetry and plays). We also publish a quarterly literary magazine that includes poetry, fiction and critical work from around the world, and reviews of new publications. Previously unpublished poetry, fiction (up to 3,000 words) and critical pieces accepted.

Editor(s): Joy Hendry
Address: 4 Broughton Place, Edinburgh EH1 3RX
Telephone: 0131 557 2207
Fax: 0131 556 9565
Email: editor@chapman-pub.co.uk
Website: www.chapman-pub.co.uk
Imprints: Chapman New Writers Series, Chapman Magazine
Payment Details: Copies only
Unsolicited Manuscripts: Yes if accompanied by SAE/IRC

The Chartered Institute Of Personnel And Development

The Chartered Institute of Personnel and Development is the leading publisher of books and reports for personnel and training professionals, students, and all those concerned with the effective management and development of people at work.

Editor(s): Commissioning Editors: Robert Foss, Anne Cordwent
Address: CIPD Publishing, CIPD House, Camp Road, London SW19 4UX
Telephone: Customer Services 0208 263 3387, Reception 0208 971 9000
Fax: Publishing Department 0208 263 3850, Reception 0208 263 3333
Email: publish@cipd.co.uk
Website: www.cipd.co.uk
Imprints: CIPD
Parent Company: CIPD
Payment Details: Royalty agreement by negotiation
Unsolicited Manuscripts: Outline with SAE please for initial consideration

C
Zelda Cheatle Press

Specialist photography publishers.

Address: 99 Mount Street, London W1Y 5HF
Telephone: 020 7408 4448
Fax: 020 7408 1444
Email: photo@zcgall.demon.co.uk
Unsolicited Manuscripts: No

Checkmark Publications

Publishes 'The Step By Step Guide To Planning Your Wedding' by Lynda Wright (£5.95). Supplied through Gardners Books, Bertram Books, T.H.E. or Checkmark Publications.

Address: 2 Hazell Park, Amersham, Bucks HP7 9AB
Telephone: 01494 431289
Fax: As phone
Email: sales@checkmark-books.co.uk
Website: www.checkmark-books.co.uk
Unsolicited Manuscripts: No

Cherrytree Books

Cherrytree Press offers a superb range of books for PSE and full curriculum support. The highly aclaimed children's information book series, Cherrytree Books, offers a wide range of information books supporting the curriculum areas of PSE, Business Studies, ITC, English, History, Geography, Maths, Mythology and Science.

Editor(s): Angela Sheehan
Address: 2a Portman Mansions, Chiltern Street, London W1U 6NR
Telephone: 020 7487 0920
Fax: 020 7487 0921
Email: sales@evansbrothers.co.uk
Parent Company: Evans Brothers
Unsolicited Manuscripts: No

Child's Play (International) Ltd

Independent publisher of children's educational books, games and audio-visual materials - specialising in whole-child development, learning through play, life skills and values. Founded in 1972, Child's Play is non-sectarian, non-political, non-sexist, multi-cultural and eco-friendly. We encourage children to think about the world they want to live in, and provide challenging information books alongside beautifully illustrated fiction for the 2-10 age group.

Editor(s): Sue Baker
Address: Ashworth Road, Bridgemead, Swindon SN5 7YD
Telephone: 01793 616286
Fax: 01793 512795
Email: allday@childs-play.com
Website: www.childs-play.com
Imprints: Mission
Payment Details: Negotiable
Unsolicited Manuscripts: Yes - but no novels

The Children's Society

The Children's Society is one of Britain's leading charities for children and young people. Through its work and its publications, the Society aims to be a positive force for change in the lives of children, young people and their families. By publishing materials for professionals, policy makers and families themselves, we provide people with the resources they need to make a difference to the lives of children and young people.

Address: Edward Rudolf House, Margery Street, London WC1X 0JL
Telephone: 020 7841 4500
Fax: 020 7837 0211
Email: publishing@childsoc.org.uk
Website: www.the-childrens-society.org.uk
Unsolicited Manuscripts: No

Chivers Press

Chivers Press offers a range of large print and audio books for both adults and children. Titles include the very best of contemporary fiction, best sellers and classics. For children our Galaxy Large Print offers modern children's fiction in clear, large type, for reluctant readers or those with poor eyesight. Our audio books are complete and unabridged and can be enjoyed by everyone.

Address: Windsor Bridge Road, Bath BA2 3AX
Telephone: 01225 335336
Fax: 01225 310771
Email: sales@chivers.co.uk

The Christadelphian Magazine & Publishing Association Ltd

Publishes magazines, pamphlets and books on Bible topics, and to promote the Christadelphian faith.

Editor(s): M J Ashton
Address: 404 Shaftmoor Lane, Hall Green, Birmingham B28 8SZ
Telephone: 0121 777 6324
Fax: 0121 778 5024
Email: editor@thechristadelphian.com
Website: www.thechristadelphian.com
Imprints: The Christadelphian, Faith Alive!

Christchurch Publishers Ltd

General book publishers. Publications include reference, fine art, architecture and fiction.

Editor(s): James Hughes, Leonard Holdsworth
Address: 10 Christchurch Terrace, London SW3 4AJ
Telephone: 0207 351 4995
Fax: Same as phone
Imprints: Albyn Press, Charles Skilton Ltd, Luxor Press, Tallis Press, Caversham Communications Ltd
Parent Company: Christchurch Publications Ltd
Payment Details: By negotiation
Unsolicited Manuscripts: Letter before sending anything

C

Christian Education

Two areas of work: Christian Education Publications produces Bible reading notes, house group materials, prayers books, children's stories, activity books, and resources for Christian Education professionals. Religious Education Services provides publications and professional support for all involved in religious education in schools.

Editor(s): Elizabeth Bruce
Address: 1020 Bristol Road, Selly Oak, Birmingham B29 6LB
Telephone: 0121 472 4242
Fax: 0121 472 7575
Email: ebruce@ncec.fsbusiness.co.uk
Website: www.christianeducation.org.uk
Imprints: Christian Education Publications, International Bible Reading Association, RE Today Publishing
Payment Details: Varies
Unsolicited Manuscripts: No

Christian Focus Publications

Christian books for all ages. We are an evangelical publisher that produces board books to children's bibles for younger people and biographies to theological books for adults. For an idea of our range write for our full catalogue.

Editor(s): Willie Mackenzie (Editorial Manager), Malcolm Maclean (Ministry), Anne Norrie (Adult), Catherine Mackenzie (Children)
Address: Geanies House, Fearn, Tain, Ross-Shire Scotland IV20 1TW
Telephone: 01862 871 011
Fax: 01862 871 699
Email: info@christianfocus.com
Website: http://www.christianfocus.com
Imprints: Christian Focus, Christian Heritage, Mentor
Parent Company: Balintore Holdings
Payment Details: Negotiable royalty %, fixed fee
Unsolicited Manuscripts: Yes

Christian Music Ministries

CMM serves and resources churches, schools, bookshops and individuals through teaching, workshops, 'music in worship' seminars, musicals, training courses, day and weekend conferences and mail-order catalogue. Deals principally with the publishing, recording and marketing of music composed by Roger Jones, the Director. This includes his 16 musicals, the latest being Snakes And Ladders, published in 1999. He is currently working on his next Musical on the life and death of Stephen which will begin the first of three tours around the UK in November 2002, March/April 2003, and November 2003. He has released various collections of worship songs, Ways To Praise and Precious and Honoured being the two latest. CMM also run various Family Music Weeks during the summer which includes an annual visit to Lee Abbey in Devon.

Editor(s): Company Director: Roger W Jones
Address: 325 Bromford Road, Hodge Hill, Birmingham B36 8ET
Telephone: 0121 783 3291
Fax: 0121 785 0500
Email: Office@cmm.org.uk
Website: http://www.cmm.org.uk

Christian Research

Christian Research is a Christian charity serving all denominations. We are publishers of specialist reference books for leaders of churches and Christian organisations, including directories, handbooks, statistical works and an atlas. Also publish results of own research projects relating to Christian activity and behaviour, UK and worldwide.

Editor(s): Peter Brierley, Heather Wraight
Address: Vision Building, 4 Footscray Road, Eltham, London SE9 2TZ
Telephone: 020 8294 1989
Fax: 020 8294 0014
Email: admin@christian-research.org.uk
Website: christian-research.org.uk & ukchristianhandbook.org.uk
Unsolicited Manuscripts: No

C

Chrysalis Books

Publishers of non-fiction illustrated colour reference books covering craft, cookery, history, military, art, gardening, transport, humour, natural history, music, film.

Childrens list is Zig Zag (non-fiction and fiction illustrated).
Editor(s): Charlotte Davies, Will Steeds, John Lee, Tina Persaud
Address: Blenheim Court, Brewery Road, London N7 9NT
Telephone: 020 7700 7799
Fax: 0207 697 3001
Email: cdavies@chrysalisbooks.co.uk
Imprints: Salamander, Batsford, Zig-Zag - Childrens, Brassey, Conway Maritime, Putnam Aeronautical, Robson
Parent Company: Chrysalis Plc
Payment Details: Various / Subject to negotiation
Unsolicited Manuscripts: No

Church Pastoral Aid Society

The Church Pastoral Aid Society is a Christian charity associated with the Church of England. Dedicated to equipping church leaders, youth workers and small-group leaders. CPAS publish approximately 20 publications a year. Housing a direct marketing operation, CPAS combines both publishing and promotion to provide moral, biblical and religious resources. Books can be purchased online, see website for details.

Editor(s): Rory Keegan
Address: Athena Drive, Tachbrook Park, Warwick CV34 6NG
Telephone: 01926 458 458
Fax: 01926 458 459
Email: rkeegan@cpas.org.uk
Website: www.cpas.org.uk
Unsolicited Manuscripts: To the Editor

Church Society

Church Society is a long standing organisation working primarily within the National Church. Its regular publications include (A Theological Journal) and CrossWays (a magazine). Only occassional other titles are produced.

Editor(s): Revd David Phillips, Prof Gerald Bray
Address: Dean Wace House, 16 Rosslyn Road, Watford, Hertfordshire WD18 0NY
Telephone: 01923 235111
Fax: 01923 800362
Email: admin@churchsociety.org
Website: www.churchsociety.org
Unsolicited Manuscripts: Yes

Churches Together in Britain & Ireland - CTBI Publications

Absolutely all areas that Christianity impinges upon. For example: ecumenism, faith and order, interfaith relations, women and men in church and society, human sexuality, ethics, communication, racism, economics, healing, mission and evangelism, international students in Britain and Ireland, international affairs.

Address: Inter-Church House, 35-41 Lower Marsh, London SE1 7SA
Telephone: 020 7523 2121
Fax: 020 7928 0010
Email: communications@ctbi.org.uk
Website: www.ctbi.org.uk
Imprints: CTBI
Parent Company: Churches Together in Britain and Ireland
Payment Details: By negotiation
Unsolicited Manuscripts: Very rarely - work is usually commissioned

C

Financial World Publishing c/o Chartered Institute Of Bankers

Publisher of study workbooks, reference materials and practitioner manuals for the financial services industry. Titles are published in a variety of formats including perfect bound A5, A4, looseleaf and electronic (CD and Computer based training). Over 120 titles currently in print covering topics such as accountancy, IT, banking, risk, lending and marketing.

Editor(s): Finola McLaughlin, Teresa Hobson
Address: IFS House, 4-9 Burgate Lane, Canterbury, Kent CT1 2XJ
Telephone: 01227 818609
Fax: 01227 479641
Email: pblake@IFSlearning.com
Website: www.cib.org.uk
Imprints: CIB Publishing, Financial World, Institute of Financial Services
Parent Company: Chartered Institute of Bankers
Payment Details: Advance/royalty for practitioner texts. Royalties 8-12%. Most student study materials are commissioned on a fee only basis
Unsolicited Manuscripts: Yes

Cicerone Press

Activity guides - walking, climbing, cycling etc. We are the leading publishers in this field with around 300 titles.

Editor(s): Jonathan Williams
Address: 2 Police Square, Milnthorpe, Cumbria LA7 7PY
Telephone: 01539 562069
Fax: 01539 563417
Email: info@cicerone.demon.co.uk
Website: www.cicerone.co.uk
Payment Details: Royalties
Unsolicited Manuscripts: Yes

Claridge Press

Books on politics, philisophy, history, culture and the arts (no fiction). Also publishes The Salisbury Review.

Editor(s): Roger Scruton
Address: 33 Canonbury Park South, London N1 2JW
Telephone: 01666 510272
Fax: 020 7354 0383
Email: salisbury-review@easynet.co.uk
Imprints: Claridge Press
Parent Company: Claridge Ltd
Payment Details: Royalties
Unsolicited Manuscripts: Yes

T&T Clark Ltd

Theology and religion - international, non-denominational, academic and professional - books and journals.

Editor(s): Geoffrey Green
Address: 59 George Street, Edinburgh EH2 2LQ
Telephone: 0131 225 4703
Fax: 0131 220 4260
Email: ggreen@tandtclark.co.uk
Website: www.tandtclark.co.uk
Imprints: T&T Clark
Parent Company: The Continuum International Publishing Group Ltd
Payment Details: Royalties or fees
Unsolicited Manuscripts: Yes

James Clarke & Co Ltd/The Lutterworth Press

James Clarke & Co publish scholarly and academic works of religion, history, biography and reference. The Lutterworth Press imprint includes general trade titles of religion, children's fiction and non-fiction, and adult non-fiction (including art history, biography, history, crafts and pastimes, popular science, natural history and environment, and other subjects). Patrick Hardy books are children's fiction and picture books. Acorn Editions include local interest (East Anglia) titles and sponsored books.

Editor(s): Adrian Brink
Address: PO Box 60, Cambridge CB1 2NT
Telephone: 01223 350865
Fax: 01223 366951
Email: publishing@lutterworth.com
Website: http://www.lutterworth.com
Imprints: James Clarke & Co, The Lutterworth Press, Patrick Hardy, Acorn Editions
Parent Company: James Clarke & Co Ltd
Payment Details: Royalty
Unsolicited Manuscripts: Yes

Class Publishing

Popular health, medicine and law.

Address: Barb House, Barb Mews, London W6 7PA
Telephone: 020 7371 2119
Fax: 020 7371 2878
Email: class.co.uk
Unsolicited Manuscripts: Almost always rejected

Clwyd Family History Society

Publishers of parish register transcripts and indexes, and other indexes of value to the family and local historian.

Address: Pen y Cae, Ffordd Hendy, Gwernymynydd, Sir y Fflint CH7 5JP
Telephone: 01352 755138
Email: dafydd@wyddgrug.freeserve.co.uk
Website: www.clwydfhs.org.uk

Coachwise Ltd

Leading UK publisher in Sports Coaching resources. Mail order service for sports books and related products. Range of business to business solutions from research to bespoke publishing. 1st 4 Sport is a brand of sports coach UK all profits are reinvested back into UK Sport.

Editor(s): Nicola Cooke
Address: Units 2/3 Chelsea Close, Off Amberley Road, Armley, Leeds LS12 4HW
Telephone: 0113 231 1310
Fax: 0113 231 9606
Email: enquiries@1st4sport.com
Website: www.1st4sport.com
Imprints: National Coaching Foundation, 1st 4 Sport Publications
Parent Company: sports coach UK
Unsolicited Manuscripts: No

C

Vernon Coleman

Self publisher (with sales of over 400,000 books in the UK and translations in 22 languages). Published over 90 books including 'How To Publish Your Own Book' & 'How To Make Money While Watching TV'. No outside authors published.

Editor(s): Sue Ward
Address: Publishing House, Trinity Place, Barnstaple, Devon, EX32 9HJ
Telephone: 01271 328892
Fax: 01271 328768
Email: sue@vernoncoleman.com
Website: www.vernoncoleman.com
Imprints: Chilton Designs, European Medical Journal, Blue Books
Unsolicited Manuscripts: No

Peter Collin Publishing Ltd

We publish a wide range of dictionaries for students and professionals, in English, and in many other languages. We also publish ELT and travel material.

Editor(s): P H Collin and S Collin
Address: 32-34 Great Peter Street, London, SW1P 2DB
Telephone: 020 7222 1155
Fax: 020 7222 1551
Email: info@petercollin.com
Website: www.petercollin.com
Payment Details: Fee for smaller glossaries, royalty for larger works
Unsolicited Manuscripts: No, but draft proposals acceptable

Collins & Brown

Collins & Brown are publishers of non-fiction titles in the following areas: photography, lifestyle, gardening, crafts, health, mind, body and spirit, practical needlecraft, history and art and design. Paper Tiger (an imprint of Collins & Brown) is the leading publisher of fantasy art titles.

Address: Collins & Brown, London House, Great Eastern Wharf, Parkgate Road, London SW11 4NQ
Telephone: 0207 697 3000
Fax: 0207 697 3001
Email: info@cb-publishing.co.uk
Website: www.cb-publishing.co.uk
Imprints: Collins & Brown, Paper Tiger
Parent Company: C & B Publishing Plc
Payment Details: To be agreed
Unsolicited Manuscripts: Yes

Colourpoint Books

Educational textbooks. Transport: railways, buses, shipping, air transport, trams, etc. History: Irish subjects especially, but all subjects considered. Religion and theology.

Editor(s): Sheila Johnston, Norman Johnston, Ronnie Hanna
Address: Unit D5, Ards Business Centre, Jubilee Road, Newtownards, Co Down BT23 4YH
Telephone: 028 9182 0505
Fax: 028 9182 1900
Email: info@colourpoint.co.uk
Website: http://www.colourpoint.co.uk
Payment Details: Agreed individually
Unsolicited Manuscripts: Yes

The Columba Press

Religious publisher specialising in books of spirituality, theology, scripture, ministry and liturgy, primarily from the Roman Catholic and mainstream Protestant traditions. We also publish books of a more general interest on history, biographies, counselling and the arts.

Editor(s): Seán O Boyle
Address: 55a Spruce Avenue, Stillorgan Industrial Park, Blackrock, Co Dublin, Ireland
Telephone: 00353 129 42556
Fax: 00353 129 42564
Email: info@columba.ie
Website: http://www.columba.ie
Imprints: The Columba Press, Gartan
Parent Company: The Columba Press
Unsolicited Manuscripts: Send outline and sample chapter

Community Of Poets Press

An independent press with an increasing focus on printing and publishing poetry/text with original artwork and printmaking. Hand-sewn collections and collaborations with artists and printmakers are produced under the Pamphlet Poets and Poems by Post imprint. Some individual and special collections are produced either as artists books or by Community of Poets Press.

Editor(s): Philip Bennetta, Susan Bennetta
Address: 44 Cromwell Road, Whitstable CT5 1NN
Telephone: 01227 281806
Fax: Same as phone
Email: bennetta@artco@virginnet.co.uk
Imprints: Pamphlet Poets, Poems by Post
Parent Company: Community of Poets Press
Payment Details: By discussion
Unsolicited Manuscripts: No. Prefer to see one or two poems plus a SAE is essential for return of work

Compendium Publishing

We are an independent publisher and packager of illustrated reference books. The subjects that we publish include transport, military history, modelling and crafts, children's books, art and architecture and history.

Editor(s): Simon Forty
Address: 1st Floor, 43 Frith Street, London W1D 7SE
Telephone: 020 7287 4570
Fax: 020 7494 0583
Email: Compendiumpub@aol.com
Website: www.Compendiumpublishing.com
Imprints: WAG Books
Payment Details: Fee or royaly to be negotiated
Unsolicited Manuscripts: No

Computer Step

Established in 1991, the leading British publisher of computer books. All popular subject areas are covered in concise and easy-to-understand format. The main imprint is In Easy Steps and there are more of these titles in Booktrack's Top 50 best-selling list of computer books in UK than from most other publishers. Computer Step also exports, reprints and translates its work internationally. It is represented by Penguin for distribution to the book trade in South Africa, New Zealand and Australia.

Editor(s): Harshad Kotecha
Address: Southfield Road, Southam, Warwickshire CV47 0FB
Telephone: 01926 817999
Fax: 01926 817005
Email: publisher@ineasysteps.com
Website: http://www.computerstep.com and http://ineasysteps.com
Imprints: In Easy Steps
Payment Details: Advance and royalties paid
Unsolicited Manuscripts: Yes

C
Constable & Robinson Ltd

Constable & Co founded in 1890 by Archibald Constable, grandson of Walter Scott's publisher. Robinson Publishing Ltd founded in 1983 by Nick Robinson. In December 1999 Constable and Robinson combined their individual shareholdings into a single company, Constable & Robinson Ltd.

Imprints: Constable (Hardbacks) Editorial Director: Carol O'Brien. Publishes biography, crime fiction, general and military history, travel and endurance, climbing, landscape photography and outdoor-pursuits guidebooks.
Robinson (Paperbacks) Senior Commissioning Editor: Krystyna Green. Publishes crime fiction, sf, Daily Telegraph health books, the Mammoth series, psychology, true crime, military history and Smarties children's books.
Editor(s): Constable Editorial Director: Carol O'Brien, Robinson Senior Commissioning Editor: Krystyna Green
Address: 3 The Lanchesters, 162 Fulham Palace Road, London W6 9ER
Telephone: 020 8741 3663
Fax: 020 8748 7562
Email: enquiries@constablerobinson.com
Website: www.constablerobinson.com
Unsolicited Manuscripts: Unsolicited sample chapters, synopses and ideas are welcome. No mss; no e-mail submissions. Enclose return postage

Corpus Publishing Limited

Specialising in sports science and complementary therapies. List was started with a range of massage specific titles, but this will be expanded upon over the coming months.

Distributed by Human Kinetics.
Editor(s): Jonathan Hutchings
Address: 9 Roman Way, Fishbourne, Chichester PO19 3QN
Telephone: 01243 539106
Email: jonhutchings@corpus.fsbusiness.co.uk
Imprints: Otter Publications
Payment Details: Flat fee by negotiation
Unsolicited Manuscripts: Yes

Cottage Publications

Publisher of illustrationed colour books on irish interest subjects including books featuring specific geographical areas, walking books, arts, crafts and music books.

Address: Cottage Publications, Laurel Cottage, 15 Ballyhay Road, Donaghadee, Co Down BT21 0NG
Telephone: 028 9188 8033
Fax: 028 9188 8063
Email: info@cottage-publications.com
Website: www.cottage-publications.com

Council For British Archaeology

The Council For British Archaeology (CBA) is an educational charity which works to improve awareness and enjoyment of archaeology for the benefit of all. The CBA publishes two main series: research reports, which aim to disseminate information and stimulate further research, and practical handbooks which are aimed at a wider audience. Recent practical handbooks include 'Churches & Chapels: Investigating Places Of Worship' and 'Recording and Analysing Graveyards'. In addition, the CBA publishes educational titles such as the 'Guide To Archaeology In Higher Education'.

Editor(s): Jane Thorniley-Walker (Publications Officer)
Address: Bowes Morrell House, 111 Walmgate, York YO1 9WA
Telephone: 01904 671417
Fax: 01904 671384
Email: books@dial.pipex.com
Website: www.britarch.ac.uk
Payment Details: No royalty fees paid
Unsolicited Manuscripts: Proposals for new publications accepted

C

Council of Academic and Professional Publishers

Trade association for academic/professional publishers.

Address: No 1 Kingsway, London, WC2B 6XD
Telephone: 020 7565 7474
Fax: 020 7836 4543
Email: mail@publishers.org.uk
Website: www.publishers.org.uk
Parent Company: The Publishers Association
Unsolicited Manuscripts: No

Countryside Books

Established in 1976, we publish books of local interest, almost always relating to whole English counties. Non-fiction only. Main subjects local history and outdoor activities, especially walking.

Editor(s): Nicholas Battle
Address: Highfield House, 2 Highfield Avenue, Newbury RG14 5DS
Telephone: 01635 43816
Fax: 01635 551004
Email: info@countrysidebooks.co.uk
Website: www.countrysidebooks.co.uk
Unsolicited Manuscripts: Yes, but send outline and sample chapter first

R & E Coward

Publish Richard Coward's mystery thrillers only.

Address: 16 Sturgess Avenue, London NW4 3TS
Telephone: 020 8202 9592
Fax: 020 8201 6303
Email: richardcoward@onetel.net.uk
Unsolicited Manuscripts: No

Crabtree Press

The Press was incorporated in 1946 but since delimited, and now under the sole proprietorship of Ernie Trory, who uses it to publish his own extensive writings, some of which are partly autobiographical. Apart from a biography of the poet Percy Bysshe Shelley, and another of Thomas Hughes, author of Tom Brown's School Days, Crabtree Press publishes only contemporary history (1913 to date) from a Marxist viewpoint.

Address: 4 Portland Avenue, Hove, East Sussex BN3 5NP
Website: http://members.netscapeonline.co.uk/ernietrory/
Unsolicited Manuscripts: No

Crafthouse

Publishers of interactive CD-ROMS on diet and health, cookbooks, art and craft, travel. Under Vigara: Interactive Contact magazine (worldwide). Also Crafthouse Advertiser, an internet directory for various small companies; contains 'new writers' section where authors can display samples of their work for publishers' attention. Launched in 1999; details on application.

Editor(s): W Nicholas
Address: 122a Cambridge Road, Southend on Sea, Essex SS1 1ER
Telephone: 01702 354621
Fax: 01702 347353
Email: crafthouse@clara.net
Website: www.crafthouse.uk.com
Imprints: Winslow, Vigara
Parent Company: Crafthouse
Unsolicited Manuscripts: Accepted with return postage

Creative Monochrome Ltd

Specialist books and magazines on the art and craft of photography.

Editor(s): Roger Maile
Address: Courtney House, 62 Jarvis Road, South Croydon, Surrey CR2 6HU
Telephone: 020 8686 3282
Fax: 020 8681 0662
Email: cm@cremono.com
Imprints: Creative Monochrome, Digital Photo Art, Photo Art International
Payment Details: Negotiable
Unsolicited Manuscripts: No - contact first

Crescent Moon

Crescent Moon aims to publish the best in contemporary writing in the fields of poetry, literature, painting, sculpture, media, cinema, feminism and philosophy. Also publishes a quarterly magazine, Passion, and a bi-annual anthology of new American poetry, Pagan America.

Editor(s): J Robinson
Address: PO Box 393, Maidstone, Kent ME14 5XU
Telephone: 01622 729593
Imprints: Crescent Moon, Joe's Press
Payment Details: To be negotiated
Unsolicited Manuscripts: Yes, with letter and SAE or IRCs

Cressrelles Publishing Company Ltd

Established in 1972 to publish general books, now concentrates on plays and theatre books.

Address: 10 Station Road Industrial Estate, Colwall WR13 6RN
Telephone: 01684 540154
Fax: Same as phone
Imprints: J Garnett Miller Ltd, Kenyon-Deane, Actinic Press
Parent Company: Cressrelles Publishing Co Ltd

Cresta Booksellers Direct

Publishers and booksellers of books and manuals concerning industrial and commercial cleaning chemicals, methods and techniques, also kitchen cleaning manuals and books on industrial housekeeping.

Editor(s): J K P Edwards, A M Edwards
Address: 14 Beechfield Road, Liverpool, L18 3EH
Telephone: 0151 722 7400
Email: majohn.cresta@tesco.net
Website: www.cresta-books.co.uk
Imprints: Cresta Publishing Company

Critical Vision

Publishers of challenging, cutting-edge non-fiction plus several books on popular culture and the history of comic books.

Polyester in Australia recently called Critical Vision "The UK's most interesting publisher".

Our back catalogue includes, amongst others, the titles: The X Factory: Inside The American Hardcore Film Industry; Psychotropedia: A Guide to Publications on the Periphery; Bizarrism: Strange Lives, Cults & Celebrated Lunacy; Nasty Tales, the Story of Underground Comics in Britain; See No Evil: Banned Films & Video Controversy; and Psychedelic Decadence, Sex Drugs & Low-Art in Sixties & Seventies Britain.

Scheduled for imminent release are I Was Elvis Presley's Bastard Love-Child, a collection of rock interviews, and a new biography of Charles Fort.

We are always on the look-out for thought-provoking and esoteric new work but will only consider non-fiction submissions and proposals.

Critical Vision is an imprint of Headpress.

Editor(s): David Kerekes
Address: Headpress, 40 Rossall Avenue, Radcliffe, Manchester M26 1JD
Fax: 0161 796 1935
Email: david.headpress@zen.co.uk
Website: http://www.headpress.com/
Imprints: Critical Vision
Parent Company: Headpress
Payment Details: By arrangement with author
Unsolicited Manuscripts: Yes

Croner.CCH Group Ltd

Croner. CCH Group Ltd is a leading UK publisher of tax and financial information. Whether you need online, CD-ROM, loose-leaf, seminars, insurance or software services, we can deliver the service you require in the desired format. For more information on Croner.CCH and our tax partners, FDS and IRPC, please visit our website at www.tax-centre.net.

Address: 145 London Road, Kingston Upon Thames, Surrey, KT2 6BR
Telephone: 0870 241 5719
Fax: 020 8247 4124
Email: info@croner.cch.co.uk
Website: www.croner.cch.co.uk
Parent Company: Wolters Kluwer
Payment Details: Negotiable
Unsolicited Manuscripts: Brief explanatory letter invited as first step

G L Crowther

Author/publisher of a series of railway, tramway and waterway atlases of the UK (99 vols). They show navigable rivers; canals, locks, wharves, warehouses, towpaths; mineral tramroads; railways, locations of over 11000 railway stations including obscure and short-lived ones, tunnels, viaducts, rail-served factories, collieries and docks; horse, steam, cable and electric street tramways, termini and depots, as well as thousands of dates of use.

Address: 224 South Meadow Lane, Preston PR1 8JP
Telephone: 01772 257126

C
Cruithne Press

Publishes academic subjects: history, archaeology, Scottish literary criticism. Will not publish any other areas of non-fiction, will not even consider any non-academic submissions of non-fiction (no 'secrets of the Holy Grail' histories). Future plans include expanding into literary fiction, academic criticism, and maybe fiction itself (novels), Scottish focus preferred, will not publish poetry, short stories or autobiographies.

Editor(s): Contacts: Ross Samson, Valerie Lyon
Address: 197 Great Western Road, Glasgow G4 9EB
Telephone: 0141 632 8681
Fax: 0141 689 6089
Email: cruithne.press@virgin.net
Unsolicited Manuscripts: No proposals are ever considered if the text is not complete; always send a letter with descriptiion of work in the first instance with first two pages of typescript; never send entire unsolicited typescripts

Crux Press

Crux Press publishes Christian books. Most of their books are written or produced in-house, but they also publish books by authors outside the organisation. They specialise in bible-based puzzle books which encourage the study of the bible.

Editor(s): Mr Alick Hartley BSc
Address: Gwelfryn, Llanidloes Road, Newtown, Powys SY16 4HX
Telephone: 01686 623484
Fax: 01686 623784
Email: crux@press.mid-wales.net
Website: www.press.mid-wales.net/index.html
Imprints: Crux Press
Parent Company: Impart Books
Unsolicited Manuscripts: After permission obtained

C

Crécy Publishing Ltd

Publisher of aviation and military books, with over 150 titles in the range. Majority of titles second world war biographies and autobiographies. Also distribute for a number of other publishers.

Address: 1a Ringway Trading Estate, Shadowmoss Road, Manchester M22 5LH
Telephone: 0161 499 0024
Fax: 0161 499 0298
Email: books@crecy.co.uk
Website: www.crecy.co.uk
Imprints: Crécy, Goodall
Unsolicited Manuscripts: Yes with SAE

James Currey Publishers

Specialist publishers of academic paperbacks on Africa and the Caribbean in the fields of History, Social Anthropology, Geography, Politics, Literary Criticism, Development Economics; also on World Anthropology.

Editor(s): Douglas H. Johnson
Address: 73 Botley Road, Oxford OX2 0BS
Telephone: 01865 244111
Fax: 01865 246454
Website: www.jamescurrey.co.uk
Payment Details: Royalties paid
Unsolicited Manuscripts: Send proposal first

Curzon Press

Academic and reference books on all aspects of Asian and Middle Eastern studies, Central Asia and The Caucasus, and on religious studies and linguistics worldwide.

Editor(s): Jonathan Price, Rachel Saunders, Peter Sowden
Address: 51a George Street, Richmond, Surrey TW9 1HJ
Telephone: 020 8948 4660
Fax: 020 8332 6735
Email: publish@curzonpress.co.uk
Website: www.curzonpress.co.uk
Imprints: Curzon, Japan Library, Caucasus World
Unsolicited Manuscripts: Book Proposals: Jonathan Price, Rachel Saunders, Peter Sowden

Dalesman Publishing Company

3 regional magazines - Dalesman, Cumbria And Lake District Magazine, Peak District Magazine. Also regional books on each of these areas about history and culture. Walking guides for all abilities, cycling and town guides, humour books and illustrated books.

Editor(s): Terry Fletcher
Address: Stable Courtyard, Broughton Hall, Skipton, North Yorkshire BD23 3AZ
Email: editorial@dalesman.co.uk
Payment Details: Negotiable
Unsolicited Manuscripts: Yes

The C W Daniel Company Ltd

Alternative medicine and the metaphysical.

Editor(s): Sebastian Hobnut
Address: 1 Church Path, Saffron Walden, Essex CB10 1JP
Telephone: 01799 526216, 01799 521909
Fax: 01799 513462
Email: cwdaniel@dial.pipex.com
Website: www.cwdaniel.com
Imprints: Health Science Press, Neville Spearman Publishers, LN Fowler & Co Ltd
Unsolicited Manuscripts: No

Darf Publishers

Darf Publishers specialises in good quality facsimile reprints of out-of-print and rare books written in the eighteenth and nineteenth centuries. Our list is predominantly taken up with books on the geography culture, history, literature and theology of the Middle East and North Africa. As well as this we also publish original titles which will appeal to a different readership entirely - notably on cricket and racing.

Editor(s): A Bentaleb, John Cowen
Address: 227 West End Lane, West Hampstead, London NW6 1QS
Telephone: 020 7431 7009
Fax: 020 7431 7655
Email: Darf@freeuk.com
Website: www.darfpublishers.co.uk
Payment Details: Annual Royalties
Unsolicited Manuscripts: No

D
David & Charles

Craft, art techniques, decorative art and interiors, fine art, woodwork, photography, equestrian.

Editor(s): Publishing Manager: Miranda Spicer
Address: Brunel House, Forde Close, Newton Abbot TQ12 4PU
Telephone: 01626 323200
Fax: 01626 364463
Email: mail@davidandcharles.co.uk
Website: www.davidandcharles,co,uk
Imprints: Pevensey Press
Parent Company: Few Publications, Inc., Ohio, USA
Payment Details: Royalties paid twice-yearly
Unsolicited Manuscripts: Yes, synopsis only, above categories only.

Christopher Davies Publishers Ltd

Non-fiction: history, biography, natural history, and sport of Welsh interest only.

Editor(s): Christopher Davies
Address: PO Box 403, Swansea SA1 4YF
Telephone: 01792 648825
Fax: Same as phone
Imprints: Christopher Davies, Triskele Books
Payment Details: Royalty payments twice-yearly in April and October
Unsolicited Manuscripts: No

D

John Dawes Publications

Self-publisher of books about swimming pools: design, trade information etc. Catalogue available. Also consultant adviser to the Author-Publisher Network and the Institute of Swimming Pool Engineers, concerned with self-publishing information and technical issues.

Editor(s): John Dawes, Pam Davis
Address: 12 Mercers, Hawkhurst, Kent TN18 4LH
Telephone: 01580 753346
Fax: Same as phone
Imprints: John Dawes Publications
Payment Details: Self-payment by result
Unsolicited Manuscripts: Supplies information about author-publishing and willing to discuss means of publishing mss discussing swimming pool technology/design, also material concerning Hawkhurst Gang of Smugglers, 1750.

Giles de la Mare Publishers Ltd

Art and architecture, biography, history, music, general non-fiction.

Editor(s): Editor and Director: Giles de la Mare
Address: PO Box 25351, London NW5 1ZT
Telephone: 020 7485 2533
Fax: 020 7485 2534
Email: gilesdelamare@dial.pipex.com
Payment Details: Royalty
Unsolicited Manuscripts: No

D
Andre Deutsch Ltd

Biography, cookery, children's, humour, history, film and TV, music, natural history, photography, sport, politics and current affairs, lifestyle, fitness.

Editor(s): Louise Dixon, Nicky Paris, Ingrid Connell
Address: 76 Dean Street, London W1V 5HA
Fax: 020 7316 4499
Imprints: Andre Deutsch, Chameleon, Manchester United Books, Granada Media, Andre Deutsch Classics, Madcap
Parent Company: VCI
Unsolicited Manuscripts: No

Diehard Publishers

Small, specialist publisher of quality poetry and drama of Scottish and International interest. Run from an Antiquarian bookshop. We also publish the quarterly broadsheet Poetry Scotland which should be the first point of contact for poets. Poetry books by Ian Blake, Elizabeth Burns, Angus Calder, Bashabi Fraser, Alan Jackson, Richard Livermore, Richard Price, Martha Modena Vertreace, Colin Will and others, plays by John Cargill Thompson and others, also a new hardback craft bound series. ISBN prefix 0946230.

Editor(s): Ian W King and Sally Evans
Address: 91-93 Main Street, Callander, Scotland FK17 8BQ and 3 Spittal Street, Edinburgh EH3 9DY
Imprints: Diehard Poetry and Diehard Drama
Unsolicited Manuscripts: Rarely accepted

D

Dillons Publishing

Publish only commissioned books. Next publications, commissioned books: 1. 'Hurt, Hurt, Bitter Tears' by William Larkin. ISBN 1-901851-12-5. 2. 'Satan's Ireland' by William Larkin. ISBN 1-901851-15-X.

Editor(s): Anthony Grant
Address: 641 Castle Lane West, Bournemouth BH8 9TS
Telephone: 01202 396230
Imprints: 1-901851
Payment Details: By arrangement per commission
Unsolicited Manuscripts: No

Discovery Walking Guides Ltd

Walking guides/maps to popular holiday destinations. Essential to study our style, subject matter, on our website before approaching us.

Editor(s): David A Brawn, Ros Brawn
Address: 10 Tennyson Close, Northampton NN5 7HJ
Telephone: Initial contact by letter
Website: www.walking.demon.co.uk
Imprints: Warm Island Walking Guides, Tour & Trail Maps, Walk! Guidebooks
Payment Details: Negotiable
Unsolicited Manuscripts: No

D
Diva Books

Fiction and non-fiction books by and for lesbian and bisexual women. Send synopsis and sample chapter initially.

Editor(s): Helen Sandler - Commissioning Editor, Kathleen Bryson - Erotica Editor
Address: 116-134 Bayham Street, London, NW1 0BA
Telephone: 0207 482 2576
Fax: 0207 284 0329
Email: edit@divamag.co.uk
Website: www.divamag.co.uk
Imprints: Diva Books
Parent Company: Millivres-Prowler Group
Payment Details: Details on application
Unsolicited Manuscripts: Yes

Donhead Publishing Ltd

Donhead publishes books on building and architectural conservation, heritage and museum studies; scientific and technical books concerning the use of traditional building materials, and the conservation of those materials, looking at both the research and theory, along with the practical aspects of conservation. Would prefer it if potential authors were to contact us before sending a manuscript, either by telephone or letter to outline their ideas in order for us to assess whether it would be suitable for our list.

Editor(s): Jill Pearce, D Newberry (Publishing Manager)
Address: Lower Coombe, Donhead St Mary, Shaftesbury SP7 9LY
Telephone: 01747 828422
Fax: 01747 828522
Email: jillpearce@donhead.com
Website: www.donhead.com
Imprints: Donhead
Unsolicited Manuscripts: Only if relevant to our list

D

Douglas & McIntyre & Greystone Books

Publisher of general non-fiction and highly illustrated natural history titles with especial reference to North American wildlife, plus Canadian history (including native American) and ice hockey.

Editor(s): Rob Saunders
Address: C/o Roundhouse Publishing Ltd, Millstone, Limers Lane, Northam, Devon, EX39 2RG
Telephone: 01237 474474
Fax: 01237 474774
Email: round.house@fsbdial.co.uk
Website: www.roundhouse.net
Payment Details: Royalties twice yearly
Unsolicited Manuscripts: No

The Dovecote Press Ltd

The Dovecote Press publishes books reflecting the history, culture and way of life of individual English counties. The range is wide, and includes natural history, architecture, guide books, walking books and photographed portraits of individual counties in full colour. We take a great deal of trouble over production in an attempt to make every book we publish as well designed and of as high a quality as possible.

Editor(s): David Burnett
Address: Stanbridge, Wimborne, Dorset BH21 4JD
Telephone: 01258 840549
Fax: 01258 840958
Email: dovecote@mcmail.com
Unsolicited Manuscripts: Please enclose SAE - No fiction

D
Downlander Publishing

Highly selective publishers of poetry of outstanding merit. This is a non-profit foundation interested only in poetry which contributes in real terms to literature and which has both philosophical and technical quality. Selection of submitted titles (letter and examples initially) is rigorous.

Editor(s): D F Bourne-Jones, MA (Oxon)
Address: 'Downlander' 88 Oxendean Gardens, Lower Willingdon, Eastbourne, East Sussex BN22 0RS
Telephone: 01323 500 437
Payment Details: Applicant must be prepared to meet basic production cost
Unsolicited Manuscripts: None, letter and up to 10 examples of work, plus SAE

Downside Abbey Books

A department of the famous Somerset Benedictine monastery Downside Abbey, it specialises in English Roman Catholic history and produces about two books a year in addition to the quarterly periodical of theology, philosophy and history The Downside Review. This latter also reviews books in its subject area.

Address: Downside Abbey, Stratton on the Fosse, Bath BA3 4RH
Telephone: 01761 235 109
Fax: 01761 235 124
Email: books@downside.co.uk
Imprints: Downside Abbey
Parent Company: Downside Enterprise Ltd
Payment Details: No royalties on 1st editions
Unsolicited Manuscripts: Only after consultation

Drake Educational Associates

Drake Educational Associates publishes an extensive list of Teacher Reference books and videos alongside its list of classroom resources for Primary and Secondary schools. We also distribute Teacher Reference titles for three overseas publishers Pembroke, Eleanor Curtain and Highsmith.

Address: St Fagans Road, Fairwater, Cardiff CF5 3AE
Telephone: 01222 560333
Fax: 01222 554909
Email: E-bost:drakegroup@btinternet.com
Imprints: Pembroke, Eleanor Curtain, Highsmith
Parent Company: The Drake Group
Payment Details: Pro-forma

Dramatic Lines

Dramatic Lines is a small independent company dedicated to the publication of dramatic material for use in schools, acting examinations and theatres. Publications include monologues, duologues, an introduction to Shakespeare through one-act plays, a resource book of drama music and dance lessons for teachers, Shakespeare rewrites, plays linked to history national curriculum, performance pieces for three and four players and teenage plays on drugs and eating disorders. Musical plays include Introducing Oscar and Three Cheers for Mrs Butler.

Editor(s): John Nicholas
Address: PO Box 201, Twickenham, London
Telephone: 020 8296 9502
Fax: 020 8296 9503
Email: mail@dramaticlinespublishers.co.uk
Website: www.dramaticlines.co.uk
Imprints: Dramatic Lines
Payment Details: Royalties twice a year
Unsolicited Manuscripts: Yes. All unsolicited manuscripts must be accompanied by SAE

D
Dref Wen

Welsh and English language, children's books and books for adult Welsh learners.

Address: 28 Church Road, Whitchurch, Cardiff CF14 2EA
Telephone: 029 2061 7860
Imprints: Dref Wen
Unsolicited Manuscripts: No

Dublar Scripts

Publishers of pantomimes. Scripts aimed at the amateur theatre. Founded 1994.

Address: 204 Mercer Way, Romsey, Hants SO51 7QJ
Telephone: 01794 501377
Fax: 01794 502538
Email: scripts@dublar.freeserve.co.uk
Website: www.dublar.co.uk
Imprints: Sleepy Hollow Pantomimes
Unsolicited Manuscripts: All unsolicited manuscripts must be accompanied by SAE for return

Duncan Petersen Publishing Ltd

Trade publisher of travel guides, including the Charming Small Hotel Guides and the On Foot walking guides. Also a packager of quality illustrated reference books on a wide range of non-fiction subjects for the international co-edition market.

Editor(s): Editorial Director: Andrew Duncan
Address: 31 Ceylon Road, London, W14 0PY
Telephone: 0207 371 2356
Fax: 0207 371 2507
Email: dp@appleonline.net
Website: www.charmingsmallhotels.com
Imprints: Duncan Petersen Publishing Ltd
Parent Company: independent
Payment Details: Differs project to project
Unsolicited Manuscripts: No, synopses only for non-fiction illustrated reference

Eagle Publishing

Specialises in Christian books, primarily on prayer and spirituality, but also including a number of gift books incorporating classic and modern art.

Editor(s): Lynne Barratt
Address: 6-7 Leapale Road, Guildford, Surrey GU1 4JX
Telephone: 01483 306309
Fax: 01483 579196
Email: eagle_ips@compuserve.com
Imprints: Eagle
Parent Company: Inter Publishing Services (IPS) Ltd
Payment Details: On application
Unsolicited Manuscripts: Yes

E

Earlsgate Press

Earlsgate is a publisher of business management books.

Address: The Plantation, Rowdyke Lane, Wyberton, Boston, Lincs PE21 7AQ
Telephone: 01205 350764
Fax: 01205 359459
Email: earlsgatepress@btinternet.com
Website: www.earlsgatepress.com
Parent Company: Robertson Cox Ltd
Unsolicited Manuscripts: Yes but only business management

Earthscan Publications Ltd

Non-fiction publishers of books on environmental and sustainable development issues for academics, professionals, business people, policy makers and general readers. Broad categories within the fields of environment and development include: business and industry; cities and the built environment; climate; ecology and conservation; economics; food and agriculture; forestry; health; international relations; law; politics and society; popular science; natural resource management; risk; tourism.

Editor(s): Commissioning Editor: Pascale Mettam
Address: 120 Pentonville Road, London N1 9JN
Telephone: 020 7278 0433
Fax: 020 7278 1142
Email: earthinfo@earthscan.co.uk
Website: www.earthscan.co.uk
Parent Company: Kogan Page Ltd
Unsolicited Manuscripts: Yes

Ebury Press

Division of Random House UK, specialising in adult non-fiction publishing over a broad range of subjects, from cookery, gardening and lifestyle to psychology, health and personal development, and including high-quality illustrated books, film and television tie-ins, sports and popular music. Sales force of 15 reps working across the UK, supported by 25 head office sales staff, a dedicated marketing and publicity team; sales offices in the USA, Canada, Australia, New Zealand and South Africa; and a rights department selling rights in all languages throughout the world.

Editor(s): Fiona MacIntyre, Julian Shuckburgh, Denise Bates, Jake Lingwood, Hannah MacDonald, Lisa Pendreigh (Ebury Press); Jacquline Burns (Vermilion); Judith Kendra (Rider Books)
Address: Random House, 20 Vauxhall Bridge Road, London SW1V 2SA
Telephone: 020 7840 8400
Fax: 020 7840 8406
Website: www.randomhouse.co.uk
Imprints: Ebury Press, Vermilion, Rider Books, Fodor's Travel Guides
Parent Company: Random House UK Ltd
Unsolicited Manuscripts: Yes with return postage

Eco-Logic Books

Promoting and publishing books that provide practical solutions to environmental problems eg Agenda 21 issues, Permaculture, Sustainability, Alternative Energy and Organic Gardening.

Address: 10-12 Picton Street, Bristol BS6 5QA
Telephone: 0117 942 0165
Fax: 0117 942 0164
Email: books@eco-logic.demon.co.uk
Imprints: Grover Books, Eco-Logic Books
Parent Company: Eco-Logic Books
Unsolicited Manuscripts: Yes with return postage

E

Eddison Sadd Editions

A packaging company creating illustrated non-fiction titles as international co-editions for publisher clients. Experience in producing kits. Particularly interested in all self-help titles - new age, health, craft, gardening, sex. Authors often need to write to fit a layout and be closely involved in design stages.

Editor(s): Ian Jackson
Address: St Chad's House, 148 King's Cross Road, London WC1X 9DH
Telephone: 020 7837 1968
Fax: 020 7837 2025
Email: reception@eddisonsadd.co.uk
Payment Details: Fees when appropriate, or royalties based on net receipts
Unsolicited Manuscripts: No - synopsis first

Edinburgh University Press

Academic textbooks aimed at undergraduates: humanities subjects including: Literature, Politics, Philosophy, American Studies, History, Media and Film, Cultural Studies, Linguistics, Literary Theory, Islamic Studies, Religious Studies, Natural History, African Studies, Geography, Ancient History, Archaeology.

Editor(s): Jackie Jones (Philosophy/Literature, Culture), Nicola Carr (Islamic, Politics, American Studies), Sarah Edwards (Linguistics)
Address: 22 George Square, Edinburgh, EH8 9LF
Fax: 0131 662 0053
Website: www.eup.ed.ac.uk
Imprints: Polygon, Polygon at Edinburgh
Parent Company: Edinburgh University Press
Unsolicited Manuscripts: Yes

E

Educational Publishers Council

Trade association for school publishers.

Address: No 1 Kingsway, London WC2B 6XD
Telephone: 020 7565 7474
Fax: 020 7836 4543
Email: mail@publishers.org.uk
Website: www.publishers.org.uk
Parent Company: The Publishers Association
Unsolicited Manuscripts: No

Egmont Children's Books

Egmont Children's Books is the leading publisher of award-winning fiction and picture book titles, non-fiction and educational titles and a powerful range of children's classic and contemporary licenses including Thomas the Tank Engine and Winnie-the-Pooh.

Editor(s): Various
Address: 239 Kensington High Street, London W8 6SA
Telephone: 020 7761 3500
Fax: 020 7761 3510
Email: firstname.surnam@ecb.egmont.com
Website: In development
Imprints: Mammouth, Methuen, Egmont World, Heinemann, Dean Joint Ventrue
Parent Company: The Egmont Group
Unsolicited Manuscripts: No

E
Egmont World Ltd

Specialises in children's books for home and international markets: activity, sticker, baby, early learning, novelty, character books and annuals. Series - Mr Men; I Can Learn; Learning Rewards.

Editor(s): Nina Filipek, Stephanie Sloan, Rachel Murawa
Address: Deanway Technology Centre, Wilmslow Road, Handforth, Cheshire SK9 3FB
Parent Company: Egmont Group, Denmark
Unsolicited Manuscripts: Very rarely used. No responsibility can be taken for the return of unsolicited submissions

Edward Elgar Publishing

Edward Elgar Publishing was founded in 1986 by Edward Elgar. We are a privately owned scholarly publisher with a focus on economics, finance and public policy. We have an ambitious, high quality list of monographs, reference works and advanced textbooks by important scholars working in North America, Europe, Asia and Australia. We continue to commission actively, with over 1,200 books in print and over 220 new titles a year. We now have 3 offices and over 30 members of staff. We are committed to providing a personal and efficient service to our authors and customers throughout the World.

Editor(s): Edward Elgar
Address: Glensanda House, Montpellier Parade, Cheltenham GL50 1UA
Telephone: 01242 226934
Fax: 01242 262111
Email: info@e-elgar.co.uk
Website: www.e-elgar.co.uk
Imprints: EE
Parent Company: Edward Elgar Publishing Inc
Unsolicited Manuscripts: Yes

Elliot Right Way Books

We specialise in practical self-help instructional books covering a wide range of subjects, including: cookery, wine and beer making, weddings, speeches, letters, family finance, job search, business, health, quizzes, games and pastimes, pets, equestrian, motoring, fishing, sport and hobbies. Non-fiction only. Low prices - big sales.

Editor(s): Clive Elliot, Malcolm Elliot
Address: Kingswood Buildings, Brighton Road, Lower Kingswood, Tadworth, Surrey KT20 6TD
Telephone: 01737 832202
Fax: 01737 830311
Email: info@right-way.co.uk
Website: www.right-way.co.uk
Imprints: Right Way, Clarion (bargain books)
Payment Details: Choice of royalty and advance or outright copyright payment
Unsolicited Manuscripts: Yes

Aidan Ellis Publishing

History, biography/autobiography, gardening, cookery, maritime; some novels.

Editor(s): Aidan Ellis, Lucinda Ellis
Address: Whinfield, Herbert Road, Salcombe, Devon TQ8 8HN
Telephone: 01548 842755
Fax: 01548 844356
Email: aidan@aepub.demon.co.uk
Website: www.demon.co.uk/aepub
Imprints: Aidan Ellis
Payment Details: Royalties
Unsolicited Manuscripts: Yes if non-fiction - synopsis and sample chapters and return postage. No fiction please

ELM Publications/Training

Independent publisher of business and law textbooks and teaching resources. Also of training materials for business management skills for first level supervisory up to middle management level in negotiating, group and team work and dynamics, motivation, personal and interpersonal skills.

Editor(s): Sheila Ritchie
Address: Seaton House, Kings Ripon, Huntingdon PE28 2NJ
Telephone: 01487 773254
Email: elm@elm-training.co.uk
Website: www.elm-training.co.uk
Payment Details: Annual in arrears, usually 10-25% depending on medium/format, eg printed materials usually 10%
Unsolicited Manuscripts: Do not send - outline preferred in first instance

Elmwood Press

Elmwood Press publish material for use in schools from KS2 to KS3 and KS4. So far mainly Mathematics, Science and English.

Editor(s): Various
Address: 80 Attimore Road, Welwyn Garden City, Herts AL8 6LP
Telephone: 01707 333232
Fax: 01707 333885
Website: www.elmwoodpress.co.uk
Payment Details: By arrangement
Unsolicited Manuscripts: Welcome from teachers

E

Emissary Publishing

Founded 1992. Publishes mainly humorous paperback books; no poetry or children's. Run's a biennial Humorous Novel Competition in memory of the late Peter Pook and publishes the winning novel. Next competition 1903 (SAE for details). No unsolicited mss or synopses.

Editor(s): Val Miller - Editorial Director
Address: PO Box 33, Bicester, OX26 4ZZ
Telephone: 01869 322552 or 01869 323447
Fax: 01869 324096
Parent Company: Manuscript Research
Payment Details: Six monthly
Unsolicited Manuscripts: No

Training Publications (Engineering) Ltd

Main areas: basic engineering manufacture, including NVQ-related material, science and technology. Subsidiary areas: small but expanding archaeological and ancient history list, also biology and natural history.

Editor(s): Publishing Manager: Mrs Lesley Page
Address: 3 Finway Court, Whippendell Road, Watford WD18 7EN
Telephone: 01923 243730
Fax: 01923 213144
Email: tpl@emta.org.uk
Website: ww.training-publications.com
Imprints: Entra, EMTA, EIT, EITB
Parent Company: Engineering and Marine Training Authority
Payment Details: Negotiable
Unsolicited Manuscripts: Yes

E

The Eothen Press

An academic press devoted to publishing scholarly, but generally accessible, books on Turkey and Cyprus, particularly in the fields of modern history and politics, foreign policy, economics and economic history, social anthropology and sociology.

Address: 10 Manor Road, Hemingford Grey, Huntingdon PE28 9BX
Telephone: 01480 466106
Fax: Same as phone
Email: theeothenpress@btinternet.com
Website: www.btinternet.com/~theeothenpress
Imprints: The Eothen Press
Unsolicited Manuscripts: No

EPA Press

Publishers of guides to electrical and electronic regulations.

Address: Bulse Grange, Wendens Ambo, Saffron Walden CB11 4JT
Telephone: 01799 541207
Fax: 01799 541166

Epublish Scotland

Publishers of educational resources with an emphasis on maths/IT. These are intended to be of use to teachers and lecturers in schools and colleges. All are produced in electronic format, but some are also available in printed format.

Editor(s): John Brewer
Address: 236 Magdala Terrace, Galashiels, TD1 2HT
Telephone: 01896 752109
Email: info@epublish-scotland.com
Website: www.epublish-scotland.com
Unsolicited Manuscripts: No, contact by email in first instance

Epworth Press

Academic and theological works.

Editor(s): Gerald M Burt
Address: 20 Ivatt Way, Peterborough, Cambs PE3 7PG
Imprints: Epworth Press
Parent Company: Methodist Publishing House
Payment Details: Subject to negotiation
Unsolicited Manuscripts: Yes

The Erskine Press

Founded in 1986, the Erskine Press publishes, twice a year, books on the 'Heroic Age' of Antarctic exploration, covering facsimiles of diaries long out of print, new diaries and previously unpublished works, as well as first English translations of European expeditions of the late 19th and early 20th centuries. In recent years it has expanded its titles to cover general interest autobiographies and medical-related 'Patient's Guides' (Hip and Knee Replacement, Chronic Fatigue Syndrome). Its founding company Archival Facsimiles Limited produces scholarly reprints and high quality limited edition publications for academic/business organisations, ranging from leather-bound folios of period print reproductions to small illustrated books. It undertakes private publications as well for individuals and organisations.

Editor(s): Crispin de Boos
Address: The Old Bakery, Banham, Norwich, Norfolk NR16 2HW
Telephone: 01953 887277
Fax: 01953 888361
Email: erskpres@aol.com
Website: www.erskine-press.com
Imprints: Archival Facsimiles Ltd
Payment Details: Royalties paid 6 monthly
Unsolicited Manuscripts: No

E
Euromoney Books

A division of Euromoney, Euromoney Books is the world's leading publisher of specialist financial books. Publishing over 100 titles, including textbooks, country guides and self-study workbooks, the company provides authoritative and up-to-date information on financial products, practices and markets worldwide. Visit the website bookshop for more information about the full range of books that Euromoney publishes or contact:

Editor(s): Managing Editor: Stuart Allen
Address: Nestor House, Playhouse Yard, London EC4V 5EX
Telephone: 020 7779 8955
Fax: 020 7779 8541
Email: books@euromoneyplc.com
Website: www.euromoneybooks.com
Imprints: Euromoney Books
Parent Company: Associated Newspapers
Unsolicited Manuscripts: Yes, to Elizabeth Gray, Commissioning Editor

Europa Publications

Publisher of international reference books on political, economic, geographical, academic and biographical subjects. Leading publications include The Europa World Year Book, The World of Learning, The International Who's Who and the Regional Surveys of the World Series. Most titles are revised annually.

Editor(s): Paul Kelly (Editorial Director)
Address: 11 New Fetter Lane, London EC4P 4EE
Telephone: 020 7822 4300
Fax: 020 7822 4319
Email: paul.kelly@tandf.co.uk
Website: www.europapublications.co.uk
Parent Company: Taylor & Francis Group Plc
Payment Details: Agreed fee or royalty
Unsolicited Manuscripts: Yes

Evangelical Press

Publishers of evangelical Christian literature and Bible study material.

Address: Grange Close, Faverdale North Industrial Estate, Darlington DL3 0PH
Telephone: 01325 380232
Fax: 01325 466153
Email: sales@evangelical-press.org
Website: www.evangelical-press.org
Imprints: Grace Publications Trust, Carey Press
Payment Details: Royalty paid on publication
Unsolicited Manuscripts: Prefer outlines and contents list on first contact

Evans Brothers Ltd

Children's publishers specialising in educational non-fiction texts for school age children. We also publish in overseas markets, especially in Africa.

Editor(s): Su Swallow
Address: 2a Portman Mansions, Chiltern Street, London, W1U 6NR
Telephone: 020 7487 0920
Fax: 020 7487 0921
Email: sales@evansbrothers.co.uk
Website: www.evansbooks.co.uk
Imprints: Zero to Ten, Cherrytree Books.
Unsolicited Manuscripts: No

Ex Libris Press

Illustrated paperbacks on West Country, mainly Wiltshire and Somerset; also books on various country topics and books on the Channel Islands. Also book production service.

Editor(s): Roger Jones
Address: 1 The Shambles, Bradford-on-Avon BA15 1JS
Telephone: 01225 863595
Fax: Same as phone
Email: rogerjones@ex-librisbooks.co.uk
Website: www.ex-librisbooks.co.uk
Imprints: Ex Libris Press, Seaflower Books
Payment Details: 10% royalty twice-yearly
Unsolicited Manuscripts: Prefer initial letter with outline

Executive Grapevine International Ltd

A specialist information provider, Executive Grapevine publishes an annual series of directories and a monthly newsletter - The Head-hunter.

The directories provide in-depth information about UK and international executive recruitment consultants, training and development consultants and interim management providers. Each directory contains detailed information on the leading suppliers in their respective fields.

EG also publishes a complementary range of directories which detail the leading executives in the UK's top companies. These titles are organised by functions areas: Chairmen, Chief Executives and Managing Directors; Finance Executives; HR Executives, Sales and Marketing Executives and Information Technology Executives. These directories are used by executive recruiters and researchers worldwide.

The Head-hunter, is circulated to over 7,000 executive recruiters every month throughout Europe and parts of the USA. The Head-hunter keeps corporate and professional recruiters informed on the latest developments in the human capital marketplace.

Editor(s): Helen Barrett - Editor-in-Chief, Victoria Bates - Editorial Director, Global, Emma Abbott - Assistant Editor
Address: 2nd Floor, New Barnes Mill, Cottonmill Lane, St Albans AL1 2HA
Telephone: 01727 844335
Fax: 01727 844779
Email: enquiries@executive-grapevine.co.uk
Website: www.askgrapevine.com
Unsolicited Manuscripts: No

E

Eyelevel Books

Publishers of biographical and historical titles, plus some children's material. Specialises in niche and unusual titles.

Editor(s): Jon Moore
Address: The Flat, Oldbury Grange, Lower Broadheath, Worcester WR2 6RQ
Telephone: 01905 427825
Email: books@eyelevelbooks.co.uk
Website: www.eyelevelbooks.co.uk
Imprints: Eyelevel Books
Payment Details: By negotiation
Unsolicited Manuscripts: To Editor, non-returnable

Fabian Society

Britain's senior think-tank. Affiliated to Labour Party, but editorially independent. Publishes pamphlets and quarterly magazine. Aims to help shape the agenda for the medium and long term of the Labour Government. Also holds seminars and conferences. The Fabian Society has 6000 members and 60 local societies, as well as corporate, trade union and non-governmental organisation subscribers.

Editor(s): Adrian Harvey
Address: 11 Dartmouth Street, London SW1H 9BN
Telephone: 020 7227 4900
Fax: 020 7976 7153
Email: info@fabian-society.org.uk
Website: www.fabian-society.org.uk
Imprints: Fabian Society
Unsolicited Manuscripts: Please send synopsis

ℱ

Fairview Press

Fairview Press publishes books that educate families and individuals about their physical, emotional, and spiritual health and motivate them to seek positive changes in themselves and their communities.

Editor(s): Steve Deger
Address: C/o Roundhouse Publishing Ltd, Millstone, Limers Lane, Northam, Devon, EX39 2RG
Telephone: 01237 474474
Fax: 01237 474774
Email: round.house@fsbdial.co.uk
Website: www.roundhouse.net
Payment Details: Royalties twice yearly
Unsolicited Manuscripts: No

Famedram Publishers Ltd

Publishers of Scotland's liveliest leisure guides.

Address: PO Box 3, Ellon, Aberdeenshire AB41 9EA
Telephone: 01651 842429
Fax: 01651 842180
Email: eleanor@northernbooks.co.uk
Website: www.northernbooks.co.uk
Imprints: Northern Books

F
Farming Press

Books relating to rural life; farming and veterinary; tractor and transport history and technology; children's books related to farming.

Editor(s): Liz Ferretti, Hal Norman
Address: CMP Information Ltd, Sovereign House, Sovereign Way, Tonbridge TN9 1RW
Telephone: 01732 377539
Email: farmingpress@cmp.information.com
Website: www.farmingpress.com
Parent Company: United Business Media
Unsolicited Manuscripts: Synopses only. SAE for return

Feather Books

Publishes secular and religious books and music. Adult fiction includes the Blake Hartley mystery novels. Children's fiction includes the Quill Hedgehog novels. Also humorous verse and CDs/cassettes. Religious publications include Feather Books Poetry Series. Drama list includes 'Garlic Lane' (Winner of the Burton Award 1999) and 'Easy Street'. Publishes a leading Anglo-American Christian poetry/prayers quarterly, The Poetry Church, 40 pages in length, £7 pa.

Editor(s): John Waddington-Feather, Tony Reavill, David Grundy, Paul Evans, Anna Waddington-Feather, Jo Fulwood
Address: PO Box 438, Shrewsbury, SY3 0WN
Telephone: 01743 872177
Fax: Same as phone
Email: john@waddysweb.freeuk.com
Website: www.waddysweb.com, poetry-church.com
Parent Company: Feather Books
Payment Details: Nil for poetry, but free copies
Unsolicited Manuscripts: With SAE, otherwise non-returnable

Fernhurst Books

Watersports publisher specialising in 'how-to' books written by the leading expert in each field and where relevant endorsed by the National Authority. Books enable readers to get the very most out of their chosen sport. Covering all aspects of dinghies, catamarans, yachts and motorboats, whether racing or cruising; also seamanship, navigation, craft maintenance and equipment, plus surfing, waterskiing, kayaking.

Editor(s): Tim Davison
Address: Duke's Path, High Street, Arundel, West Sussex BN18 9AJ
Telephone: 01903 882277
Fax: 01903 882715
Email: sales@fernhurstbooks.co.uk
Website: www.fernhurstbooks.co.uk
Unsolicited Manuscripts: No, please phone and enquire

FHG Publications Ltd

FHG Publications based in Paisley, publish 12 annual holiday guides covering all forms of accomodation throughout the UK. With over 50 years' experience in providing up-to-date information for thousands of holiday destinations to suit every taste and pocket, you're sure to find the perfect holiday choice from the books in our range.

Editor(s): Anne Cuthbertson
Address: Abbey Mill Business Centre, Seedhill, Paisley PA1 1TJ
Telephone: 0141 887 0428
Fax: 0141 889 7204
Email: fhg@ipcmedia.com
Website: www.holidayguides.com
Parent Company: IPC Media
Unsolicited Manuscripts: No

ℱ
First And Best In Education Ltd

First and Best specialises in educational books for teachers. These can be categorised in two ways: subject specific books for teaching in the classroom; and school management books. All books come in photocopiable format and many are available on disk. First and Best will look at unsolicited proposals - non fiction only. The company is also involved in e-publishing.

Editor(s): Anne Cockburn
Address: Earlstrees Court, Earlstrees Road, Corby, Northants NN17 4HH
Telephone: 01536 399000
Fax: 01536 399012
Email: firstandbest@themail.co.uk
Website: www.firstandbest.co.uk
Payment Details: 7.5%
Unsolicited Manuscripts: Send SAE for details of requirements and current projects. Please do not telephone

First Class Books

Specialises in study guides to help people working to obtain NVQ in Care awards at level 2 and level 3.

Address: PO Box 1, Portishead, Bristol BS20 9BR
Telephone: 01823 323126
Fax: 01823 321876
Email: ebw@dircon.co.uk
Unsolicited Manuscripts: No

Fitzroy Dearborn Publishers

Our reference books are designed to meet the needs of university, professional, secondary school, and public libraries. Our editorial staff, contributors, and boards of advisers are all committed to providing detailed and comprehensive analysis of subjects in the arts, humanities, business, and the sciences. Fitzroy Dearborn reference books are international in scope and appropriate for the general reader as well as the serious researcher.

Editor(s): Daniel Kirkpatrick, Lesley Henderson, Roda Morrison, Anne-Lucie Norton, Mark Hawkins-Dady, Gillian Lindsay, Jonathan Dore
Address: 310 Regent Street, London W1B 3AX
Telephone: 020 7636 6627
Fax: 020 7636 6982
Email: post@fitzroydearborn.co.uk
Website: www.fitzroydearborn.com
Unsolicited Manuscripts: No thank you

Flambard Press

Flambard, founded in 1991, is particularly sympathetic to new or neglected writers and is keen to nourish developing talent. Based in the North and supported by Northern Arts, Flambard sees itself as having a role to play in the literary life of the region, but is open to all-comers and is not a regional publishing house. Flambard began as a poetry press and still concentrates on poetry, but now includes fiction in its list. It is developing a crime fiction series.

Editor(s): Margaret Lewis, Peter Lewis
Address: Stable Cottage, East Fourstones, Hexham NE47 5DX
Telephone: 01434 674360
Fax: 01434 674178
Website: www.flambardpress.co.uk
Imprints: Flambard
Payment Details: Royalty for fiction. Usually fixed fee for poetry.
Unsolicited Manuscripts: We accept these, but much prefer a preliminary letter. Informative letter about writer needed with manuscript.

F

Flicks Books

Specialist publishers of books and journals on film and cinema, and related media such as television. Our list covers fiction and non-fiction film, archival collections, histories of filmmaking in individual countries, monographs on important directors and films, reference works and directories, interviews with filmmakers, film scripts, and the reissue of out-of-print documents.

Editor(s): Matthew Stevens
Address: 29 Bradford Road, Trowbridge, Wiltshire BA14 9AN
Telephone: 01225 767728
Fax: 01225 760418
Email: flicks.books@dial.pipex.com
Payment Details: Royalty or fee system
Unsolicited Manuscripts: Yes

Floris Books

Adult non-fiction, new thinking in science, philosophy, religion, ecology, Celtic studies and literature. Children's and parenting. Fiction, including Flyways series (8-14), picture books, craft books, anthologies. Education and social issues.

Editor(s): Christopher Moore, Gale Winskill
Address: 15 Harrison Gardens, Edinburgh EH11 1SH
Telephone: 0131 337 2372
Fax: 0131 346 7516
Email: floris@floris.demon.co.uk
Imprints: Floris Classics (Celtic), Flyways (Children's fiction)
Payment Details: Annual
Unsolicited Manuscripts: Yes, Proposal / Sample only

Folens Publishers

Folens is Britain's largest publisher of teacher ideas materials and a significant publisher of curriculum resources. The Dunstable site provides product creation, sales and marketing, financial and distribution services and employs over 100 staff. Growth has been rapid and sustained. We publish in excess of 1000 of our own titles and produce over 150 new titles per year for ages 4-16. Folens publish over 80 Big Books, 50 Belair books, 350 reading books, poetry, major resources for every curriculum area plus a wide range of teacher idea books.

Editor(s): Publishing Director - Steve Harrison
Address: Albert House, Apex Business Centre, Boscombe Road, Dunstable, Beds LU5 4RL
Telephone: 01582 472005
Fax: 01582 475524
Email: folens@folens.com
Website: http://www.folens.com
Imprints: Folens Publications, Belair Publications
Parent Company: Folens Publishers, Ireland
Unsolicited Manuscripts: To Steve Harrison, Publishing Director

Folly Publications

38 paperback titles published since 1988 about British castles up to the 1660s and parish churches up to 1800. All are lavishly illustrated with plans and photos by author-publisher Mike Salter and old prints and postcards. Format ranges from 40 pages 40 page saddlestitch volumes to a 224 page volume perfect bound with sewn sections. Comprehensive gazetteer coverage of all castles and churches in Scotland (5 castle vols, 1 churches), Wales (4 castles vols, 4 churches vols), Isle of Man, and counties of Cumbria, Northumberland, Shropshire, Staffordshire, Warwickshire, Worcestershire, Herefordshire, Devon, Cornwall, Sussex. Churches books only for Cheshire, Derbyshire and Forest of Dean. Irish castle book is not comprehensive of all sites there. Volumes in preparation for release 2000-1: Surrey churches, Kent castles, East Anglia castles. Four volumes for Shropshire and Gwent & Glamorgan currently out of print awaiting preparation of new editions.

Address: Folly Cottage, 151 West Malvern Road, Malvern, Worcs WR14 4AY
Unsolicited Manuscripts: No

F
Food Trade Press Ltd

Books on food technology, science and processing, general food industry books, food hygiene, food engineering and historical books on food, plus directories.

Editor(s): Adrian Binsted
Address: Station House, Hortons Way, Westerham, Kent TN16 1BZ
Telephone: 01959 563944
Fax: 01959 561285
Email: foodtradereview@aol.com
Imprints: Food Trade Press, Food Trade Review
Payment Details: 10% royalty on retail price of books
Unsolicited Manuscripts: Yes

Footprint Handbooks

Footprint Handbooks are the ultimate guidebooks for all independently-minded travellers, providing expert knowledge, and explaining culture, places and people in a balanced, lively, and clear way. The handbooks cover Latin America, the Caribbean, Africa, India, Southeast Asia, the Middle East and Europe.

Address: 6 Riverside Court, Lower Bristol Road, Bath BA2 3DZ
Telephone: 01225 469141
Fax: 01225 469461
Email: discover@footprintbooks.com
Website: www.footprintbooks.com
Imprints: Footprint Handbooks

The Forth Naturalist And Historian (FNH)

An informal enterprise of the University of Stirling. Set up 1975 to provide focus for activities and publications of environmental, heritage, historical interest for the area of mid Scotland. The annual FNH journal publishes papers, reviews - many authoritative and significant including annual bird and weather reports. A major work is the survey book Central Scotland - land, wildlife, people - others are on Loch Lomond, Mines of the Ochils, The Ochils Hills, Woollen Mills of the Hillfoots. An annual symposium Man and the Landscape had its jubilee (25 years) in November 1999.

Editor(s): Hon. Sec. L Corbett and Neville Dix
Address: University of Stirling, Stirling FK9 4LA and 30 Dunmar Drive, Alloa FK10 2EH
Telephone: 01259 215091
Fax: 01786 494994
Email: Lindsay.Corbett@stir.ac.uk
Website: http://www.stir.ac.uk/departments/naturalsciences/Forth_naturalist/index.htm
Imprints: FNH is a member of the Scottish Publishers Association
Payment Details: No payments have been made to contributors
Unsolicited Manuscripts: Welcomed, and all refereed

W Foulsham & Co Ltd

All non-fiction subject areas, especially new age, cookery and lifestyle.

Editor(s): Wendy Hobson, Jane Hotson
Address: The Publishing House, Bennetts Close, Cippenham, Slough, Berkshire SL1 5AP
Telephone: 01753 526769
Fax: 01753 535003
Imprints: Foulsham, Foulsham Educational, Quantum
Unsolicited Manuscripts: Yes

Four Courts Press

Founded in 1972. Publishes mainly scholarly books in the humanities. About 65 titles a year which include history, Celtic and medieval studies, law, literature, art and theology. The chairman and managing director is Michael Adams, Martin Healy is a fellow director and production manager and there are five full - time members of staff in total. Synopses and ideas for new books are always welcome.

Editor(s): Michael Adams, Martin Fanning
Address: Four Courts Press, Fumbally Lane, Dublin 8, Ireland
Telephone: 00353 1 453 4668
Fax: 00353 1 453 4672
Email: info@four-courts-press.ie
Website: http://www.four-courts-press.ie
Imprints: Four Courts Press, Open Air
Payment Details: Royalties once a year
Unsolicited Manuscripts: Generally no

Four Seasons Publishing Limited

Publishers of illustrated record books (eg Grandparents Books, Baby Books, Address Books) and, increasingly, illustrated anthology books for the International gift trade and book trade. Emphasis is on titles which enlarge people's enjoyment of life and their relationships.

Editor(s): C. Shepheard-Walwyn (Managing Director)
Address: Four Seasons Publishing Limited, 16 Orchard Rise, Kingston Upon Thames, Surrey KT2 7EY
Telephone: 020 8942 4445
Fax: 020 8942 4446
Email: info@fourseasons.net
Payment Details: By negotiation
Unsolicited Manuscripts: Outlines of concepts only please

Fourth Estate Ltd

General trade publisher. Publisher of the Year 1997. Literary fiction. Commercial fiction. General non-fiction: biography, autobiography, history, travel, popular science, popular culture. Humour. Illustrated non-fiction: cookery.

Editor(s): Louise Haines, Andy Miller, Nicholas Pearson, Christopher Potter, Clive Priddle, Leo Hollis, Courtney Hodell, Catherine Blyth
Address: 77-85 Fulham Palace Road, London, W6 8JB
Telephone: 0208 741 4414
Fax: 0208 307 4466
Email: general@4thestate.co.uk
Website: www.4thestate.uk
Imprints: 4th Estate
Parent Company: Harpercollins Publishers
Unsolicited Manuscripts: No

Free Association Books Ltd

Psychotherapy, psychiatry, psychoanalysis, counselling, social welfare, addiction studies, organisational studies, child and adolescent studies, women's studies, cultural and social studies, philosophy, health and complementary medicine.

Editor(s): Publisher: Trevor Brown; Editors: David Stonestreet, Christian Braun, Kieran Corless
Address: 57 Warren Street, London W1P 5PA
Telephone: 020 7388 3182
Fax: 020 7388 3187
Email: fab@fa-b.com
Website: www.fa-b.com
Payment Details: Standard academic terms
Unsolicited Manuscripts: Yes

Samuel French Ltd

Scripts of stage plays only, intended for performance by amateur and professional theatre companies and therefore accompanied by stage directions, lighting, sound effects, plots etc. Seldom text books and no screenplays or scripts for other media.

Address: 52 Fitzroy Street, Fitzrovia, London W1T 5JR
Telephone: 020 7387 9373
Fax: 020 7387 2161
Email: theatre@samuelfrench-london.co.uk
Website: www.samuelfrench-london.co.uk
Imprints: French's Acting Editions
Parent Company: Samuel French Inc, New York
Unsolicited Manuscripts: Yes

The Frogmore Press

Publishes the bi-annual literary magazine The Frogmore Papers (founded 1983) as well as occasional anthologies and collections by individual poets, most recently A Plutonian Monologue by Adrian Aldiss. The Frogmore Poetry Prize will be awarded for the 15th consecutive year in 2001. Previous winners include Tobias Hill, John Latham, Caroline Price and Mario Petrucci.

Editor(s): Jeremy Page
Address: 42 Morehall Avenue, Folkestone, Kent CT19 4EF
Imprints: Crabflower Pamphlets (1989-1997)
Unsolicited Manuscripts: No

David Fulton Publishers Ltd

David Fulton Publishers, established in 1987, has over 400 titles in print, covering the full range of education and teaching from 3 to 19 years. The Fulton list has a distinctive focus on textbooks for student teachers and practical, professional books for teachers, coordinators and managers in mainstream and special schools. We are always interested in ideas for new books. Prospective authors should contact Nina Stibbe at our London address.

Editor(s): Nina Stibbe (Early years), Jude Bowen (Special Education), Margaret Haigh (Mainstream)
Address: 26-27 Boswell Street, London WC1N 3JZ
Telephone: 020 7405 5606
Fax: 020 7831 4840
Email: mail@fultonpublishers.co.uk
Website: www.fultonpublishers.co.uk
Payment Details: Royalty (no advances) paid twice a year
Unsolicited Manuscripts: No

Funfax Ltd

Children's books and organizers - from pre-school to early teens, non fiction activity and novelty.

Editor(s): Sue Grabham (Publishing Manager)
Address: 13 King Street, London WC2E 8HN
Imprints: Funfax, Microfax, Quiz Quest, The Lettermen, Mad Jack, Funpax, DK Stickers.
Parent Company: Dorling Kindersley Ltd
Payment Details: Flat fee no royalties
Unsolicited Manuscripts: No

Garnet Publishing Ltd

Since its foundation Granet Publishing has expanded its list to include a wide range of subjects from translated fiction to high quality illustrated books. Art, architecture, travel and photography feature strongly in our list as does religious studies.

1999 saw the launch of our new imprint South Street Press. Its first series 'Behind the Headlines' provides small factual books on topical subjects. Our educational division continues to expand its TEFL activities, while Ithaca Press, our academic imprint, specialises in political, historical and social studies on the Middle East and other regions.

Editor(s): Emma Hawker (Editorial Manager)
Address: 8 Southern Court, South Street, Reading, Berkshire RG1 4QS
Telephone: 0118 959 7847
Fax: 0118 959 7356
Email: enquiries@garnet-ithaca.demon.co.uk
Website: www.garnet-ithaca.co.uk
Imprints: Ithaca Press, South Street Press
Parent Company: Garnet Publishing
Unsolicited Manuscripts: Yes

Gateway Books
(Now An Imprint Of Gill & Macmillan)

Alternative health, alternative science, cosmic questions, healing, self-help and psychology. Gateway publishes books which try to represent different ways of understanding the unfolding new spiritual and social changes of the new millennium.

Editor(s): Submissions Editor: Alick Bartholomew
Address: The Hollies, Wellow, Bath BA2 8QJ
Parent Company: Gill & Macmillan Publishers
Unsolicited Manuscripts: No - synopsis only

Geddes & Grosset

Publishers of reference and children's books directed at the mass market.

Editor(s): Mike Miller, Ron Grosset
Address: David Dale House, New Lanark, Scotland ML11 9DJ
Telephone: 01555 665000
Fax: 01555 665694
Email: info@gandg.sol.co.uk
Imprints: Geddes & Grosset, Beanobooks
Parent Company: DC Thomson & Co Ltd
Payment Details: Various
Unsolicited Manuscripts: No

Society Of Genealogists

Educational charity. Publishes books related to genealogy and family history. Prospective authors should first contact the Society with a proposal.

Address: 14 Charterhouse Buildings, Goswell Road, London EC1M 7BA
Telephone: 020 7251 8799
Fax: 020 7250 1800
Email: sales@sog.org.uk
Website: www.sog.org.uk
Payment Details: Half-yearly royalties by cheque
Unsolicited Manuscripts: No

The Geographical Association

The Geographical Association is the national subject teaching association for all geographers. It has around 11,000 members and 60 branches in England, Wales and Northern Ireland. The GA offers curriculum support for teachers at all levels, publishing three journals: Geography (quarterly: Honorary Editor Dr Hazel Barrett), Teaching Geography (quarterly: Honorary Editor Ms Elisabeth Barratt Hacking) and Primary Geographer (termly: Honorary Editor Dr Margaret Mackintosh). The GA also publishes resources to support the teaching and learning of geography, from reception to post-16, and a growing range of titles on geographical subjects for the general public. The Geographical Association is a registered charity.

Editor(s): Publications Officer: Dr David Lambert; Production Editor: Fran Royle
Address: The Geographical Association, 160 Solly Street, Sheffield S1 4BF
Telephone: 0114 296 0088
Fax: 0114 296 7176
Email: ga@geography.org.uk
Website: http://www.geography.org.uk
Imprints: The Geographical Association
Parent Company: The Geographical Association
Payment Details: Royalty on resources for sale; no payment for journal articles
Unsolicited Manuscripts: Yes, but prefer synopsis first

The Geological Society Publishing House

The Geological Society Publishing House is part of the Geological Society of London. The Publishing House is responsible for the production of 7 journals and approximately 25 books per year. Publications include the highly acclaimed 'Geological Society Special Publications Series', 'Engineering Geology Special Publications', 'Memoirs' and Special Reports.

Editor(s): Mike Collins - Publications Manager
Address: Unit 7, Brassmill Enterprise Centre, Brassmill Lane, Bath BA1 3JN
Telephone: 01225 445046
Fax: 01225 442836
Email: mike.collins@geolsoc.org.uk
Website: bookshop.geolsoc.org.uk
Imprints: The Geological Society Publishing House
Parent Company: The Geological Society

George Mann Books

We aim to publish worthwhile books of adventure and experience - real-life, first-hand, personal accounts. No fiction. No poetry. Sometimes joint-venture publishing arrangements.

First approach should be by letter, with a full synopsis which must relate to a completed manuscript. We do not commission books. Finished length in 000s of words should always be given and a stamped, self-addressed envelope enclosed for our reply. All unsolicited manuscripts are NEVER read and, like synopses - unless accompanied by return postage - are promptly binned.

Editor(s): George Mann, John Arne
Address: PO Box 22, Maidstone, Kent, ME14 1AH
Telephone: 01622 759591
Fax: 01622 209193
Imprints: George Mann, George Mann Books, Arnefold
Payment Details: By arrangement, half yearly
Unsolicited Manuscripts: No

Robert Gibson & Sons Ltd

Educational publishers of primary and secondary school books.

Address: 17 Fitzroy Place, Glasgow G3 7SF
Telephone: 0141 248 5674
Fax: 0141 221 8219
Email: robert.gibsonsons@btinternet

Ginn & Co

Publishes materials for the teaching of a variety of subjects in primary schools. Provides a comprehensive range of resources offering solutions for the Numeracy and Literacy Strategies and other curriculum areas, for teachers and schools throughout the UK and beyond. Aims to provide high quality materials and service to primary schools through a wide variety of resources to meet teachers' changing needs.

Editor(s): Publishers: Catherine Baker (literacy), Ruth Burdett (science, mathematics and foundation)
Address: Linacre House, Jordan Hill, Oxford OX2 8DP
Telephone: 01865 888000
Fax: 01865 314222
Email: services@ginn.co.uk
Website: www.ginn.co.uk
Parent Company: Reed Elsevier

Gomer Press

Literature and non-fiction with a welsh background or relevance in english and welsh. Children's books. Founded in 1892.

Editor(s): Mairwen Prys Jones, Gordon Jones, Bethan Mais, Francesca Rhyddorch
Address: Gomer Press, Llandysul, Ceredigion SA44 4QL
Telephone: 01559 362371
Fax: 01559 363758
Email: gwasg@gomer.co.uk
Website: www.gomer.co.uk
Imprints: Pont
Payment Details: Royalties paid twice yearly
Unsolicited Manuscripts: No unsolicited mss, preliminary letter essential

Gospel Standard Trust Publications

The Trust publishes books that commend the free and sovereign grace of God. Writers are usually invited to write on given subjects. Titles cover the interest of the very young child through to the serious theologian.

Editor(s): B A Ramsbottom
Address: 12b Roundwood Lane, Harpenden, Herts AL5 3DD
Telephone: 01582 765448
Fax: 01582 469148
Email: gospelstandardpublications@btinternet.co
Imprints: Gospel Standard Trust Publications
Payment Details: By agreement
Unsolicited Manuscripts: No

Graham & Whiteside Ltd

Graham & Whiteside is one of the leading publishers of high-quality printed and electronic data on major companies throughout the world. The Major Companies Series of Directories are long established, the oldest having been published annually for the past 22 years. Our databases of 80,000 companies are updated rigorously by teams of editors and researchers, who contact every company directly to obtain information. This accurate and comprehensive series has become established as an essential business reference tool for many of the leading national and international coroporations and institutional and business libraries.

Editor(s): Please refer to individual titles
Address: Tuition House, 5-6 Francis Grove, London SW19 4DT
Telephone: 020 8947 1011
Fax: 020 8947 1163
Email: sales@graham-whiteside.com
Website: www.graham-whiteside.com
Parent Company: The Thomson Corporation
Unsolicited Manuscripts: No

W F Graham (Northampton) Ltd

Publishers of the most extensive range of quality low priced mass market children's activity books representing excellent value for money within this competitive sector. The substantial and varied list includes colouring, puzzle, dot, magic painting, wordsearch, cut out, story books, activity and play packs. Several series of outstanding nature, animal and countryside to colour books popular with children and adults. New titles and finishes continually introduced. WF Graham have an established reputation as publishers of specialist and customer branded books. Experienced in foreign language overlays. Importers of fibre tip pens.

Address: 2 Pondwood Close, Moulton Park, Northampton NN3 6RT
Telephone: 01604 645537
Fax: 01604 648414

Graham-Cameron Publishing & Illustration

We act as packagers for other publishers usually on their initiatives. We also provide full editorial and production services for self-publishers. For this reason, please don't send us mss. We are also agents for 37 illustrators of educational and children's books.

Editor(s): Helen Graham-Cameron, Mike Graham-Cameron
Address: The Studio, 23 Holt Road, Sheringham, Norfolk NR26 8NB
Telephone: 01263 821 333
Fax: 01263 821 334
Imprints: Graham-Cameron Illustration, Graham-Cameron Publishing
Unsolicited Manuscripts: No

Grandreams Ltd

Children's book publishers. Novelty books, story books, pop-ups, annuals, colouring and activity, poster books and calendars. Minimum order £500 net in UK.

Address: 435-437 Edgware Road, London W2 1TH
Telephone: 020 7724 5333
Fax: 020 7724 5777
Email: salesgdl@aol.com
Website: www.grandreams.com
Imprints: Goodnight Sleeptight
Unsolicited Manuscripts: No

Grant Books

Specialists in golf books; publishers of limited edition golf books and golf club histories.

Address: The Coach House, New Road, Cutnall Green, Droitwich WR5 0PQ
Telephone: 01299 851 588
Fax: 01299 851 446
Email: golf@grantbooks.co.uk
Website: www.golfbooks-memorabilia.com
Unsolicited Manuscripts: On golf subjects (but not fiction or instructional) especially golf course architecture, biography, history and reference

Granta Books

Small independent publisher of fiction and non-fiction, including biography, travel writing and current affairs.

Editor(s): Neil Belton
Address: 2/3 Hanover Yard, Noel Road, London N1 8BE
Telephone: 020 7704 9776
Fax: 020 7354 3469
Website: www.granta.com
Unsolicited Manuscripts: Yes - looked at

Green Books

Environment, eco-spirituality, politics and cultural issues. No fiction or children's books. Publish around ten new books per year.

Editor(s): John Elford
Address: Foxhole, Dartington, Totnes, Devon TQ9 6EB
Email: greenbooks@gn.apc.org
Website: www.greenbooks.co.uk
Imprints: Green Books, Resurgence Books, Green Earth Books
Payment Details: Twice-yearly royalties
Unsolicited Manuscripts: No, brief synopsis intitially please

W Green - The Scottish Law Publisher

W Green, the Scottish law publishing company of Sweet and Maxwell, publishes an unrivalled collection of books, periodicals and encyclopaedias on Scots law, as well as digital products.

Address: 21 Alva Street, Edinburgh EH2 4PS
Telephone: 0131 225 4879
Fax: 0131 225 2104
Website: www.wgreen.co.uk
Parent Company: Thomson Corporation

Greenhill Books

Specialist publishers of books on military history, from ancient times to current.

Editor(s): Lionel Leventhal, Jonathan North
Address: Park House, 1 Russell Gardens, London NW11 9NN
Telephone: 020 8458 6314
Fax: 020 8905 5245
Email: LionelLeventhal@compuserve.com
Website: www.greenhillbooks.com
Imprints: Greenhill Books
Parent Company: Lionel Leventhal Ltd
Payment Details: Royalties
Unsolicited Manuscripts: Preliminary letter with information about project in advance of submission

Gresham Books Ltd

Specialised publisher offering hymnbooks, service books and prayer books in limited editions for schools and churches. Gresham Books also publish school histories, anniversary books and personalised music folders.

Editor(s): Paul Lewis
Address: 46 Victoria Road, Summertown, Oxford OX2 7QD
Telephone: 01865 513582
Fax: 01865 512718
Email: greshambks@btinternet.com
Website: www.gresham-books.co.uk
Imprints: Gresham Books
Payment Details: Negotiable
Unsolicited Manuscripts: No

Grevatt & Grevatt

Small print runs in the following areas: descriptive linguistics; poetry; religious studies, especially Hinduism. Privately funded, so generally no royalties unless more than 500 copies are sold. Authors receive 2-10 complimentary copies.

Editor(s): S Y Killingley
Address: 9 Rectory Drive, Newcastle Upon Tyne NE3 1XT
Imprints: Grevatt & Grevatt, S Y Killingley
Unsolicited Manuscripts: No. All enquiries must include SAE

Grub Street

Cookery, wine, health, aviation, military history.

Editor(s): John Davies, Anne Dolamore
Address: The Basement, 10 Chivalry Road, London SW11 1HT
Telephone: 020 7924 3966/020 7738 1008
Fax: 020 7738 1009
Email: post@grubstreet.co.uk
Payment Details: Standard contracts
Unsolicited Manuscripts: Yes, but must include return postage

Gryphon House & Robins Lane Press

Publisher of a comprehensive range of pre-school and early-childhood resources for both parents and teachers, to promote active learning, philosophical enquiry, and general development.

Editor(s): Justin Rood
Address: C/o Roundhouse Publishing Ltd, Millstone, Limers Lane, Northam, Devon, EX39 2RG
Telephone: 01237 474474
Fax: 01237 474774
Email: round.house@fsbdial.co.uk
Website: www.roundhouse.net
Payment Details: Royalties twice yearly
Unsolicited Manuscripts: No

Guild of Master Craftsman Publications Ltd

Publishers that specialise in publishing 'how to' books for subjects including miniatures, photography, gardening, crafts, woodworking and self-build.

Editor(s): Stephen Haynes, Linda Dunlop, David Arscott, Kylie Johnston
Address: 86 High Street, Lewes, East Sussex, BN7 1XN
Telephone: 01273 402830
Fax: 01273 487692
Email: Aprilm@thegmcgroup.com
Parent Company: Guild of Master Craftsman
Payment Details: Royalties or outright payment
Unsolicited Manuscripts: Yes

Gwasg Carreg Gwalch

Welsh publishers, specialising in all kinds of publications in the Welsh language and also all kinds of Welsh interest titles in English.

Editor(s): Myrddin ap Dafydd, Heledd Jones
Address: 12 Iard Yr Orsaf, Llanrwst, Conwy, Wales, LL26 0EH
Telephone: 01492 642031
Fax: 01492 641502
Email: books@carreg-gwalch.co.uk
Website: www.carreg-gwalch.co.uk
Payment Details: 10% Royalties
Unsolicited Manuscripts: Yes (please supply a reply envelope)

Gwasg Gwenffrwd

Academic; reference; bibliographies; Africa; Latin America; Pacific Islands; Czechoslovakia; poetry; labour history; local history: Wales and Welsh; linguistics; anthropology; history and mission history.

Editor(s): H G A Hughes
Address: Hendre Bach, Cerrigydrudion, Corwen, LL21 9TB
Telephone: 01490 420560
Email: astic@britishlibrary.net
Imprints: Astic, Bronant, Gwenffrwd, Translations Wales, Hanes Gweithwyr Cymru, Hyddgen, South Seas Studies
Payment Details: By agreement
Unsolicited Manuscripts: No, all work commissioned

Peter Halban Publishers

Publishers of general non-fiction, including biography, politics, history, with concentration on Jewish subjects and Middle East. NB all trade orders to Littlehampton Book Services, Centre Warehouse, Columbia Building, Faraday Close, Durrington, Worthing BN13 3HD.

Editor(s): Martine Halban, Peter Halban
Address: 22 Golden Square, London W1F 9JW
Telephone: 020 7437 9300
Fax: 020 7437 9512
Email: books@halbanpublishers.com
Website: www.halbanpublishers.com
Unsolicited Manuscripts: Synopsis and letter essential

Robert Hale Ltd

Independent general publishers established in 1936. Diverse fiction and non-fiction lists with most subject areas covered. Specialist imprints are JA Allen: equestrian and NAG Press: horological.

Editor(s): John Hale
Address: Clerkenwell House, 45/47 Clerkenwell Green, London EC1R 0HT
Telephone: 020 7251 2661
Fax: 020 7490 4958
Email: enquire@halebooks.com
Website: www.halebooks.com
Imprints: NAG Press, JA Allen
Payment Details: Royalties paid twice a year
Unsolicited Manuscripts: Yes, but no submissions by email will be considered.

Halsgrove Publishing

Non-fiction - Southern England Specialist, but general history, natural history, art and military history lists in addition. Regional magazines (quarterly, Countryside).

Editor(s): Steven Pugsley, Simon Butler
Address: Halsgrove House, Lower Moor Way, Tiverton, Devon EX16 6SS
Telephone: 01884 243242
Fax: 01884 243325
Website: www.halsgrove.com
Imprints: Halsgrove, Devon Books, Dorset Books, Exmoor Books, Exmoor Press, Somerset Books, etc
Parent Company: DAA Halsgrove Ltd
Unsolicited Manuscripts: No

Hambledon And London

Hambledon and London specialises in History. We publish original scholarly books which can be read and enjoyed by both the historian and the general reader.

Our books are published promptly and priced affordably. We promote them vigorously to high street bookshops. Our list is designed to embody the best in research and historical writing.

Hambledon and London is the joint enterprise of Martin Sheppard, founder of the Hambledon Press, and Tony Morris, History Editor at Oxford University Press from 1989 to 1997.

Titles include: Geoffrey Best - Churchill: A Study in Greatness; Thomas Dormandy - The White Death: A History of Tuberculosis; David Hey - Family Names and Family History; Stephen Wilson - The Magical Universe: Everyday Ritual and Magic in Pre-Modern Europe; Irene Collins - Jane Austen and the Clergy.

We welcome proposals on all historical topics. A brief synopsis in the first instance will guarantee a rapid response.

Editor(s): Tony Morris (Commissioning Director), Martin Sheppard (Editorial Director)
Address: 102 Gloucester Avenue, London NW1 8HX
Telephone: 020 7586 0817
Fax: 020 7586 9970
Email: office@hambledon.co.uk
Website: www.hambledon.co.uk
Payment Details: Royalties paid twice yearly
Unsolicited Manuscripts: Yes, write first describing book

Hamlyn Octopus

Cookery, health and sex, interiors and crafts, gardening, sport, pet care, natural history.

Address: 2-4 Heron Quays, London E14 4JP
Telephone: 020 7531 8400
Fax: 020 7531 8650
Website: http://www.hamlyn.co.uk
Imprints: Hamlyn Octopus
Parent Company: Division of Octopus Publishing Group Ltd

Hanbury Plays

Publishers of plays, sketches, monologues, books about theatre and plays for all-women casts.

Editor(s): Brian J Burton
Address: Keeper's Lodge, Broughton Green, Droitwich WR9 7EE
Telephone: 01905 23132
Fax: Same as phone
Imprints: Hanbury Plays
Payment Details: Negotiable, but no charge to authors for publications accepted
Unsolicited Manuscripts: No - synopsis first

Happy Cat Books Ltd

Children's books for under 5's: board books, sticker books, picture books with simple texts.

Editor(s): Martin C West
Address: Fieldfares, Mill Lane, Bradfield, Essex CO11 2UT
Telephone: 01255 870902
Fax: Same as phone
Email: mcwest@happycat.co.uk
Payment Details: Fee basis
Unsolicited Manuscripts: No

Harden's Limited

Publishers of quality consumer guides to London and the UK, both in hard copy and on the internet, with a particular emphasis on restaurant guides. Leading publishers of quality corporate gifts.

Editor(s): Richard Harden, Peter Harden
Address: 14 Buckingham Street, London WC2N 6DF
Telephone: 020 7839 4763
Fax: 020 7839 7561
Email: mail@hardens.com
Website: www.hardens.com

Harlequin Mills & Boon Ltd

Romance novels in varying lengths. Tipsheets available with SAE, or on website.

Editor(s): Editorial Director: K Stoecker
Address: Eton House, 18-24 Paradise Road, Richmond, Surrey TW9 1SR
Telephone: 020 8288 2800
Fax: 020 8288 2899
Website: www.millsandboon.co.uk
Imprints: Mills & Boon, Silhouette, Mira
Parent Company: Harlequin Enterprises Ltd
Payment Details: Advance against royalties
Unsolicited Manuscripts: Prefer query first

ℋ
Harley Books

Natural history publishers, specializing in Entomology and Botany with a worldwide market. Books are published to the highest editorial and production standards. Special attention is paid to the quality of illustration, references and indexing, and many titles are regarded as the definitive works in their fields.

Editor(s): Basil Harley, Annette Harley, and specialist editorial panel for 'The Moths & Butterflies of G.B. & I.' series.
Address: Martins, Great Horkesley, Colchester, Essex, CO6 4AH
Telephone: 01206 271216
Fax: 01206 271182
Email: harley@keme.co.uk
Parent Company: B.H. & A. Harley Ltd
Unsolicited Manuscripts: Yes

Harvey Map Services Ltd

Publishers of specialist maps for walking, climbing and cycling. Popular areas throughout Great Britain covered, in easy to read waterproof maps which show extra detail necessary for sure navigation. Harvey also publish an assortment of books relating to orienteering. Teacher's and coach's manuals covering the basics to more specialised skills. Full catalogue of publications and equipment available.

Address: 12-22 Main Street, Doune, Perthshire FK16 6BJ
Telephone: 01786 841202
Fax: 01786 841098
Email: sales@harveymaps.co.uk
Website: www.harveymaps.co.uk
Unsolicited Manuscripts: No

The Harvill Press

Independent publisher, chiefly of literature in translation. Also publishes illustrated books in the fields of ethnography, travel, natural history, gardening and sailing.

Editor(s): Guido Waldman, Ian Pindar, Margaret Stead, Victoria Millar, Editorial Consultants: Euan Cameron, Andrea Belloli
Address: 2 Aztec Row, Berners Road, London N1 0PW
Telephone: 020 7704 8766
Fax: 020 7704 8805
Email: m.stead@harvill-press.com
Website: www.harvill-press.com
Imprints: Panther
Payment Details: Royalties paid twice yearly
Unsolicited Manuscripts: Yes, but outline and specimen chapter first

Hawthorns Publications Ltd

Children's illustrated story books; children's and adult fiction; school aid books; biography; history.

Address: Pond View House, 6A High Street, Otford, Sevenoaks, Kent TN14 5PQ
Telephone: 01959 522368
Fax: 01959 522368
Imprints: Pond View Books
Payment Details: Royalties paid twice-yearly
Unsolicited Manuscripts: Not at present

Hayes Press

Christian publisher of hymn books, doctrinal and evangelical books, gospel tracts and calendars.

Address: Essex Road, Leicester LE4 9EE
Telephone: 01162 740 204
Fax: 01162 740 200
Email: info@hayespress.org
Website: www.hayespress.org
Unsolicited Manuscripts: No

Haynes Publishing

Publishers of car and motorcycle service and repair manuals, car handbooks, servicing guides, books on cars, motorcycles, motorsport and related biographies, caravanning, cycling and home DIY.

Editor(s): Matthew Minter (Editorial Director - manuals), Mark Hughes (Editorial Director - books), Flora Myer - (Senior Editor - books)
Address: Sparkford, Near Yeovil, Somerset BA22 7JJ
Telephone: 01963 440635
Fax: 01963 440001
Email: sales@haynes-manuals.co.uk
Website: www.haynes.com
Imprints: Patrick Stephens Limited, G T Foulis & Co., Oxford Illustrated Press, Sutton Publishing.
Payment Details: Royalty or fee-paid contract with bi-annual settlement
Unsolicited Manuscripts: Yes

Hazar Publishing Ltd

Hazar is an independent publisher of high-quality children's picture books and illustrated adult books on architecture and design.

Editor(s): Marie Clayton
Address: 147 Chiswick High Road, London W4 2DT
Telephone: 020 8742 8578
Fax: 020 8994 1407
Email: hazar@compuserve.com
Imprints: Hazar
Payment Details: Twice yearly, Jan and July
Unsolicited Manuscripts: No

Hazleton Publishing

Widely recognised as the world's leading motorsport publisher. Our range of motor sport annuals dates back to 1951 with the birth of Autocourse, dedicated to reviewing the Formula 1 season. Similarly, Motocourse reviews the two-wheeled world championships, and last year marked the celebration of their 50th and 25th anniversary, respectively. Rallycourse, now in its 20th year, covers the World Rally Championship. In addition we publish the official CART Annual and The Official Wimbledon and Open Golf Annuals, as well as a range of technical and historical series on motor sports.

Editor(s): Robert Yarham
Address: 3 Richmond Hill, Richmond, Surrey TW10 6RE
Telephone: 020 8948 5151
Fax: 020 8948 4111
Email: info@hazletonpublishing.co.uk
Website: www.hazletonpublishing.com
Imprints: Autocourse, Motocourse, Rallycourse
Unsolicited Manuscripts: No

Headline Book Publishing Ltd

Fiction: general, saga, historical, romance, literary, thriller, crime, horror. Non-fiction: sport and sports yearbooks, humour, cookery, reference, biography, autobiography, popular culture, gardening, history, science, TV tie-ins.

Editor(s): Publishing Directors: Jane Morpeth (Fiction); Heather Holden-Brown (Non-fiction)
Address: 338 Euston Road, London NW1 3BH
Telephone: 020 7873 6000
Fax: 020 7873 6124
Email: headline.books@headline.co.uk
Website: www.headline.co.uk
Imprints: Headline, Headline Feature, Review
Parent Company: Hodder Headline Limited
Payment Details: Negotiable
Unsolicited Manuscripts: Synopsis and 5 chapters only; return postage

Health Promotion England

Health Promotion England develops and delivers public education programmes and health promotion programmes for England in the areas of drugs and alcohol misuse, immunisation, sexual health, older people, and children and families. It publishes a range of resources including leaflets, books, videos and new media.

Editor(s): Liz Niman, Gillian Sturgess
Address: 50 Eastbourne Terrace, London W2 3QR
Telephone: 020 7413 2627
Fax: 020 7413 2049
Email: chris.owen@hda-online.org.uk
Website: www.hpe.org.uk
Unsolicited Manuscripts: No

Heart Of Albion Press

Books, booklets and computer-readable publications on local history (especially Leicestershire), folklore, mythology and archaeology.

Editor(s): R N Trubshaw
Address: 2 Cross Hill Close, Wymeswold, Loughborough LE12 6UJ
Telephone: 01509 880725
Email: albion@indigogroup.co.uk
Website: www.indigogroup.co.uk/albion/
Imprints: Heart of Albion Press
Payment Details: Contact Editor
Unsolicited Manuscripts: Future publications will be CD-ROM only so conventional mss not of interest

Heinemann Educational

Atlases and maps; educational and textbooks; electronic (Educational); African writers series; Caribbean writers series; school library books.

Address: Halley Court, Jordan Hill, Oxford OX3 8EJ
Telephone: 01865 311 366
Fax: 01865 310 043
Email: uk.schools@repp.co.uk
Website: www.heinemann.co.uk
Imprints: Rigby, Ginn
Parent Company: Reed Educational and Professional Publishing
Unsolicited Manuscripts: Yes

H

Helicon Publishing (Publishers of Hutchinson encyclopedias & dictionaries)

Publishers of the Hutchinson encyclopedias and dictionaries, Helicon was formed in 1992 through a management buyout of the Hutchinson titles from the reference division of Random House. The first British company to publish a multimedia encyclopedia, and the first to put that encyclopedia online, Helicon continues to publish in book, CD-ROM and online form.

Editor(s): Hilary McGlynn - Editorial Director
Address: 3rd Floor, Clarendon House, Shoe Lane, Oxford, OX1 2DP
Telephone: 01865 204204
Fax: 01865 204205
Email: admin@helicon.co.uk
Website: www.helicon.co.uk
Parent Company: WHSmith

Hendon Publishing Co

Publisher of local history books. A4 landscape 44 pages, mainly photographs, with some text.

Address: Hendon Mill, Nelson, Lancashire BB9 8AD
Telephone: 01282 613129
Fax: 01282 870215
Parent Company: Hendon Trading Co Ltd
Payment Details: Negotiable
Unsolicited Manuscripts: Send sample of work with SAE

Henry Stewart Publications

International publisher of business journals. Range includes journals of the following: brand management; database marketing; consumer behaviour; communication management; targeting measurement and analysis for marketing; non-profit and voluntary sector marketing; change management; medical marketing; corporate reputation review; financial services marketing; corporate real estate; financial crime; financial regulation and compliance; international banking regulation, money laundering control; asset management; pensions management, small businesses and enterprise development; interactive marketing; vacation marketing, tourism and hospitality research, medical marketing, commercial biotechnology, bioinformatics educational advancement and aerospace management.

Editor(s): International editorial boards
Address: Russell House, 28-30 Little Russell Street, London WC1A 2HN
Telephone: 020 7404 3040
Fax: 020 7404 2081
Email: jon@hspublications.co.uk
Website: www.henrystewart.co.uk

The Herb Society

Exists for amateurs and professionals alike with a keen interest in any aspect of herbs. We produce a quarterly magazine Herbs, which covers topics such as culinary, medicinal, aromatic, history, future and cultivation of herbs.

Editor(s): The Editorial Board
Address: Deddington Hill Farm, Warmington, Banbury OX17 1XB
Telephone: 01295 692000
Fax: 01295 692004
Email: herbsociety.co.uk
Website: www.herbsociety.co.uk
Parent Company: The Herb Society
Unsolicited Manuscripts: Yes

Highfield Publications

Highfield Publications is the leading independent supplier of food safety training materials to all sectors of the food industry. Highfield Publications has been publishing food safety books since 1982. Many of its publications have been translated and are distributed all over the world.

The company, which is a family run business, sincerely believes in providing quality, value and service and strives to ensure customer satisfaction.

Editor(s): Mr Richard A Sprenger
Address: Vue Pointe, Spinney Hill, Sprotbrough, Doncaster DN5 7LY
Telephone: 01302 391999
Fax: 01302 783303
Email: jayne@highfieldpublications.com
Website: www.highfield.co.uk

Highgate Publications (Beverley) Ltd

Interested primarily in books on East Yorkshire. The policy is to publish manuscripts of good academic quality predented in a readable style. No autobiographies, poetry or fiction.

Editor(s): John Markham
Address: 4 Newbegin, Beverley, East Yorkshire HU17 8EG
Telephone: 01482 866826
Fax: 01482 225257
Imprints: Highgate of Beverley
Payment Details: 10% of trade price, paid quarterly
Unsolicited Manuscripts: No

Hilmarton Manor Press

Publishers, distributors and mail order booksellers of art and antique reference books.

Editor(s): Charles Baile de Laperierre
Address: Calne, Wiltshire, SN11 8SB
Telephone: 01249 760208
Fax: 01249 760379
Email: mailorder@hilmartonpress.co.uk
Imprints: Hilmarton Manor Press
Unsolicited Manuscripts: No

Hippopotamus Press

Founded in 1974 and specialises in first collections of new verse by those that have had the usual magazine appearances and are ready for book publication. We also publish occasional larger books of selected poems by those that we feel are unfairly neglected. Recently we have added a few titles of criticism and literary essays. Our current list consists of 70% first collections, 15% of second and third books from these authors, 10% selected poems, the remaining 5% is prose. We only publish a narrow range of contemporary verse, so it is important to read some of our authors before submitting a collection.

Editor(s): Roland John, Anna Martin
Address: 22 Whitewell Road, Frome, Somerset BA11 4EL
Fax: 01373 466653
Imprints: Outposts Poetry Quarterly Magazine
Parent Company: Hippopotamus Press
Payment Details: 7½% royalty
Unsolicited Manuscripts: Yes

Hodder & Stoughton

Commercial and literary fiction, biography, autobiography, history, self-help, humour, travel and general interest non-fiction, audio.

Editor(s): Sue Fletcher, Roland Philipps, Carole Welch, Carolyn Mays, Carolyn Caughey, Rupert Lancaster
Address: 338 Euston Road, London NW1 3BH
Telephone: 020 7873 6000
Fax: 020 7873 6024
Website: www.hodder.co.uk
Imprints: Hodder & Stoughton, Sceptre, Coronet, Nel, Flame, LIR
Parent Company: W H Smith
Unsolicited Manuscripts: No

Hodder & Stoughton Educational

We publish books for schools, colleges of further education, universities and general interest. Subject areas include: science, mathematics, information technology, tests and assessment, psychology, business studies, child care, teacher education, geography, beauty therapy, history, religious education, PSE and English.

Editor(s): Various
Address: 338 Euston Road, London NW1 3BH
Telephone: 020 7873 6000
Fax: 020 7873 6299
Website: www.educational.hodder.co.uk
Imprints: Teach Yourself
Parent Company: Hodder Headline
Unsolicited Manuscripts: No

Hodder Children's Books

All Hodder's books are designed to hook children into the reading habit and hold them there. Several formats: Picture Books - Picture story books illustrated in full colour, approx 1,000 words, aimed at 2-5 year olds. Young Fiction range for 6 to 9 year olds. Novels - 20-50,000 words, for children of 8 and upwards, on any theme; a strong original story and good characters, as well as particular relevance to children, are most important. Information Books - For ages 6-8, 7-11, teen - looking for original, accessible, child-centred approaches. We also offer an extensive list of classics by authors like Enid Blyton, Joan Aiken, Helen Cresswell as well as 'modern' classics such as David Almond's 'Skellig'.

Editor(s): Publishing Director: Margaret Conroy
Address: 338 Euston Road, London NW1 3BH
Telephone: 0207 873 6000
Fax: 0207 873 6024
Imprints: Young Fiction, Bite, Signature, Hodder Home Learning, Silver, Hodder Toddler, Hodder Wayland
Parent Company: W H Smith Group
Payment Details: Subject to contract
Unsolicited Manuscripts: Yes, but no poetry, rhyming texts, counting books or ABC's

Honeyglen Publishing Ltd

Small publisher specialising in history, biographies, belles-lettres and selected fiction.

Editor(s): Nadia Poderegin, Jelena Poderegin-Harley
Address: 56 Durrels House, Warwick Gardens, London W14 8QB
Telephone: 020 7602 2876
Fax: Same as phone
Unsolicited Manuscripts: Please send synopsis and sample chapter first. Must fit within our subject range.

Honno Welsh Women's Press

Small publishing press dedicated to giving women from Wales the opportunity to see their work in print. Although we do publish longer pieces of fiction and children's books, our emphasis is on anthologies and collections by various writers, so please contact us to be added to our database. The press is registered as a community co-operative, and any profit goes towards the cost of future publications.

Editor(s): Gwenllian Dafydd
Address: Honno Editorial Office, The Theological College, King Street, Aberystywyth SY23 2LT
Telephone: 01970 623 150
Fax: Same as phone
Email: editor@honno.co.uk
Website: www.honno.co.uk
Imprints: Honno Modern Fiction, Honno Children's Books, Honno Autobiography, Honno Classics
Unsolicited Manuscripts: Yes, with a Welsh connection

Hope UK

Drug education leaflets, booklets and prevention manuals published for children and young people and those working/caring for them. Hope UK is a drug education charity which concentrates on prevention issues and includes alcohol and tobacco in its brief.

Editor(s): Martin Perry, George Ruston
Address: 25F Copperfield Street, London SE1 0EN
Telephone: 020 7928 0848
Fax: 020 7401 3477
Email: enquiries@hopeuk.org
Website: www.hopeuk.org

Horizon Scientific Press

Publisher of a wide range of books and journals for the scientific community, mainly in the subjects molecular biology and microbiology. Publisher of The Journal Of Molecular Microbiology And Biotechnology.

Address: PO Box 1, Wymondham, Norfolk NR18 0EH
Telephone: 01953 601106
Fax: 01953 603068
Email: mail@horizonpress.com
Website: www.horizonpress.com
Imprints: Horizon Scientific Press, Horizon Press

How To Books Ltd

The series reference book publisher with three imprints: Pathways, How To, and Essentials. Practical, accessible books in the following subject areas: Business and Management, Computer Basics, Jobs and Careers, Living and Working Abroad, Personal Finance, Self-development, Small Business, Student Handbooks, Successful Writing and Family Reference.

Editor(s): Nikki Read
Address: 3 Newtec Place, Magdalen Road, Oxford OX4 1RE
Telephone: 01865 793 806
Fax: 01865 248 780
Email: info@howtobooks.co.uk
Website: www.howtobooks.co.uk
Imprints: Pathways, Essentials
Parent Company: How To Books Ltd
Payment Details: Royalties paid annually
Unsolicited Manuscripts: & well-structured proposals from qualified and experienced writers welcome

John Hunt Publishing Ltd

Books across the spectrum of Christian publishing, for all denominations and viewpoints. An extensive range of illustrated and novelty children's books. New areas in educational publishing for 2000. Three imprints, O books committed to global spirituality, Hunt & Thorpe for children's titles and John Hunt Publishing Ltd for Christianity.

Editor(s): John Hunt
Address: 46a West Street, New Alresford, Hants SO24 9AU
Telephone: 01962 736880
Fax: 01962 736881
Email: office@johnhunt-publishing.com
Website: www.johnhunt-publishing.com
Imprints: Arthur James, Hunt & Thorpe, John Hunt Publishing Ltd, O books (www.o-books.org)
Payment Details: Various
Unsolicited Manuscripts: Yes

Hutton Press Ltd

Publishers of Yorkshire and Lincolnshire local interest books, and maritime interest books.

Editor(s): Charles Brook
Address: 130 Canada Drive, Cherry Burton, Beverley, HU17 7SB
Telephone: 01964 550573
Fax: 01964 550573
Payment Details: Royalties of between 8/10%
Unsolicited Manuscripts: No

ICSA Publishing Ltd

The official publishing company of the Institute of Chartered Secretaries and Administrators (ICSA). Publishes a range of looseleaf and book products for managers in the private, public and voluntary sectors, including Company Secretarial Practice, The Charities Manual and the One Stop series.

Editor(s): Clare Grist Taylor
Address: 16 Park Crescent, London W1N 4AH
Telephone: 020 7612 7020
Fax: 020 7323 1132
Email: icsa.pub@icsa.co.uk
Website: www.icsapublishing.co.uk
Payment Details: On application
Unsolicited Manuscripts: No

IFLA Offices For UAP And International Lending

Universal availability of publications. International lending. Document delivery. Conference proceedings.

Editor(s): Various
Address: c/o The British Library, Boston Spa, Wetherby, West Yorkshire, LS23 7BQ
Telephone: 01937 546124
Fax: 01937 546478
Email: ifla@bl.uk
Unsolicited Manuscripts: No

I

Impart Books

Impart Books is an independent publisher of educational books in English Language Teaching, Mathematics, Statistics and the Welsh Language, but also publishing books in other fields. They specialise in the generation of books to be published either by an overseas publisher or in collaboration with an overseas publisher, principally in the developing world. Most books are created 'in-house', but they publish some meritorious books written by 'outside' authors. The most significant acheivement of IMPART BOOKS has been the development of VISUAL CLASSROOM TESTING (VCT), an effective but simple and inexpensive aid to classroom teaching. It is expected that VISUAL CLASSROOM TESTING (VCT) will completely revolutionise classroom teaching worldwide during the next few years.

Editor(s): Mr Alick Hartley B.Sc.
Address: Gwelfryn, Llanidloes Road, Newtown, Powys SY16 4HX
Telephone: 01686 623484
Fax: 01686 623784
Email: impart@books.mid-wales.net
Website: www.books.mid-wales.net
Imprints: Impart Books, Gwelfryn Publications (obsolescent)
Payment Details: As agreed
Unsolicited Manuscripts: Yes, after permission obtained

Imperial College Press

Imperial College Press was established in 1995 to produce high-quality books and journals in both printed and electronic formats. It is a joint venture between Imperial College of Science, Technology and Medicine and World Scientific Publishing, bringing together into one company the experience of an internationally-recognised institution of higher education and that of an established science publisher. ICP publishes scholarly books and journals in the physical, earth and life sciences, business and management and medicine for university students, academic researchers and practitioners. The Press gives special emphasis to research areas and educational subjects in which the College has particular strengths. Authors are sought from the College and elsewhere.

Editor(s): Anthony Doyle, Ms G Nair, Katherine Williams, (Assistants) Ellen Haigh, Sasha Henrique
Address: 57 Sheldon Street, Covent Garden, London WC2H 9HE
Telephone: 020 7836 3954
Fax: 020 7836 2002
Email: edit@icpress.demon.co.uk
Website: http://www.icpress.demon.co.uk
Parent Company: World Scientific Publishing Co (PTE) Ltd, Singapore

I

Incorporated Council Of Law Reporting For England & Wales

Not-for-profit publishers of The Law Reports, which are always cited in precedence. Also publishers of The Weekly Law Reports, The Industrial Cases Reports, The Consolidated Index to leading law reports and The Statutes (Public and General Acts and General Synod Measures). All law reports are written by barristers or solicitors who attend the cases reported, and the texts of judgments are judicially approved prior to publication. Circulation is worldwide. A registered charity established in 1865.

Editor(s): Robert Williams
Address: Megarry House, 119 Chancery Lane, London WC2A 1PP
Telephone: 020 7242 6471
Fax: 020 7831 5247
Email: postmaster@iclr.co.uk
Website: www.lawreports.co.uk
Imprints: The Law Reports, The Weekly Law Reports, The Industrial Cases Reports
Unsolicited Manuscripts: N/A

The Industrial Society

The Industrial Society is a non-profit organisation which publishes books and special reports independently. We publish approximately 30 new titles a year in areas such as self-development, business skills, and general management.

Editor(s): Susannah Lear (Books), Debbie Marshall (Video and New Media), Cec Bingham (Subscriptions), Carl Upsall (Head of Publishing)
Address: 48 Bryanston Square, London W1H 2EA
Telephone: 020 7479 2000
Fax: 020 7479 2222
Email: publishing@indsoc.co.uk
Website: www.indsoc.co.uk
Payment Details: Royalty of net receipts
Unsolicited Manuscripts: No

Institute For Fiscal Studies

The Institute For Fiscal Studies is one of Europe's pre-eminent centres of policy research. It is a politically independent registered charity, financed by the Economic and Social Research Council (ESRC), private foundations, research sponsorship, corporate donation and individual membership subscriptions.

IFS research aims to provide clear, economically informed and independent analysis of the major policy issues in microeconomics to the widest possible audience, while at the same time producing academic economics of the highest calibre and renown. To apply the lessons learned in theoretical work usefully to the real issues facing the government and the country, IFS draws on expertise from different areas. Our highly-qualified full-time economists collaborate with tax professionals from law, accountancy and the civil service and with leading academics, both from the UK and abroad.
Address: 7 Ridgmount Street, London WC1E 7AE
Telephone: 020 7291 4800
Fax: 020 7323 4780
Email: mailbox@ifs.org.uk
Website: www.ifs.org.uk
Unsolicited Manuscripts: No

Institute Of Economic Affairs

Books on economic, social, environmental and educational policy issues.

Editor(s): Professor Colin Robinson
Address: 2 Lord North Street, London SW1P 3LB
Telephone: 0207 799 8912
Fax: 0207 799 2137
Email: crobinson@iea.org.uk
Website: http://www.ica.org.uk
Unsolicited Manuscripts: Yes, but mainly commissioned

I
Institute of Food Science & Technology

IFST is the professional qualifying body for food scientists and technologists. It is also an educational charity. It publishes:

Food Science & Technology Today (quarterly), International Journal of Food Science & Technology (bi-monthly, jointly with Blackwell Science), a range of technical guides and monographs for the food industry.
See our website at www.ifst.org for full details.
Editor(s): FSTT - Anne Nash, IJFST - Peter Goodenough
Address: 5 Cambridge Court, 210 Shepherds Bush Road, London W6 7NJ
Telephone: 020 7603 6316
Fax: 020 7602 9936
Email: info@ifst.org
Website: www.ifst.org
Unsolicited Manuscripts: Yes - but see guidance to authors on inside front cover of publications before submitting

The Institute Of Irish Studies, The Queen's University Of Belfast

The aim of the Institute is to encourage interest in and to promote and co-ordinate research in those fields of study which have a particular Irish interest, and it is an important multidisciplinary centre. The publications department reflects the growth and diversity of Irish studies today. The list includes a range of academic or semi-academic books, focused on aspects of Irish studies including archaeology, anthropology, biography, botany, cultural studies, history, history of science, local studies, politics, language, literature, proverbs, religion, transport, women's studies. There are two major series, The Ordnance Survey Memoirs Of Ireland (40 vols) and Northern Ireland Place-names (7vols).

Editor(s): Margaret McNulty
Address: Queen's University Belfast, 8 Fitzwilliam Street, Belfast BT9 6AW
Telephone: 028 9027 3235
Fax: 028 9043 9238
Email: iispubs@qub.ac.uk
Website: http://www.qub.ac.uk/iis/publications.html
Parent Company: The Queen's University of Belfast
Unsolicited Manuscripts: Yes - academic work only. Please write in the first instance.

Institute Of Physics Publishing

One of the world's leading science publishers. The company publishes books, journals and magazines in physics and related subject areas. Within the books programme, IOP produces reference works for industry and academia, research monographs, graduate textbooks, high level undergraduate textbooks, and popular science books. The author base is international. Subjects: astronomy and astrophysics; condensed matter physics; high energy physics; history of physics; materials science; mathematical physics; measurement and instrumentation; medical physics; nuclear physics; optics; plasma physics; sensors and smart materials.

Editor(s): Jim Revill, John Navas, Tom Spicer, Nicki Dennis
Address: Dirac House, Temple Back, Bristol BS1 6BE
Telephone: 0117 930 1146
Fax: 0117 930 1186
Email: nicki.dennis@iop.org
Website: www.bookmarkphysics.iop.org
Parent Company: Institute of Physics
Payment Details: Royalty as agreed, usually 10% of net receipts
Unsolicited Manuscripts: No

The Institution Of Chemical Engineers

IChemE sets out to publish books and journals which allow engineers and scientists to improve their professional skills and performance. Subjects: environment; safety and loss prevention; contract and project management; process design and operation; dust handling; process control; biotechnology; oil, gas and energy. IChemE is the agent in the UK, Europe and Asia for the American Institute Of Chemical Engineers (AIChE).

Editor(s): Various
Address: 165-189 Railway Terrace, Rugby CV21 3HQ
Telephone: 01788 578214
Fax: 01788 560833
Email: jcressey@icheme.org.uk
Website: www.icheme.org
Imprints: IChemE
Payment Details: Royalties on discussion
Unsolicited Manuscripts: No

I

Intellect Books

Intellect is a multidisciplinary publisher tracking contemporary and cultural issues through its books, journals and website. Full details and ordering at www.intellectbooks.com.

Editor(s): Masoud Yazdani, Robin Beecroft, Keith Cameron
Address: Postal: PO Box 862, Bristol BS99 1DE
Office: 6 Thomas Street, Lawrence Hill, Bristol BS5 9JG
Telephone: 0117 955 6811
Fax: Same as phone
Email: robin@intellectbooks.com
Website: www.intellectbooks.com
Payment Details: Standard contract
Unsolicited Manuscripts: Yes

Inter-Varsity Press

Inter-Varsity Press operates as IVP and also under the imprints of Apollos and Crossway. It publishes Christian books which are true to the Bible and which will communicate the Gospel, develop discipleship and strengthen the church for its mission in the world.

Address: 38 De Montfort Street, Leicester LE1 7GP (editorial and design), Norton Street, Nottingham NG7 3HR (production and marketing)
Telephone: 0116 255 1754 (Leics), 0115 978 1054 (Nottm)
Fax: 0116 254 2044 (Leics), 0115 942 2694 (Nottm)
Email: ivp@uccf.org.uk (Leics), ivp@ivpbooks.com (Nottm)
Imprints: IVP, Apollos, Crossway
Parent Company: Universities and Colleges Christian Fellowship
Payment Details: Royalties (variable)
Unsolicited Manuscripts: Please submit outline and sample

I

Intercept Limited

Intercept has over 15 years' publishing expertise in science and technology. We have distribution partnerships with The Natural History Museum (London), The National Research Council Research Press (Canada), The Ray Society and the United Nations Environment Programme. Being part of an international publishing group and our worldwide marketing database mean that we can reach wide audiences. Our subject areas include Biotechnology, Water, the Environment, Natural History, Ecology, Pest Management, Agricultural Science, Zoology, Botany, Geology and Food Science and Technology.

Editor(s): Andrew Cook (Managing Editor)
Address: PO Box 716, Andover, Hampshire SP10 1YG
Telephone: 01264 334748
Fax: 01264 334058
Email: intercept@andover.co.uk
Website: http://www.intercept.co.uk
Parent Company: Technique & Documentation - Lavoisier (Paris, France)
Payment Details: Variable, as agreed between publisher and author
Unsolicited Manuscripts: Accepted

Interlink Publishing Group

Established in 1987, Interlink Publishing is an independent publishing house specialising in: world travel, world literature, world history and politics, health & healthy eating, and poetry.

Editor(s): Michel Moushabek
Address: C/o Roundhouse Publishing Group, Millstone, Limers Lane, Northam, Devon, EX39 2RG
Telephone: 01237 474474
Fax: 01237 474774
Email: round.house@fsbdial.co.uk
Website: www.roundhouse.net
Imprints: Crocodile Books, Olive Branch Press
Payment Details: Royalties twice yearly
Unsolicited Manuscripts: No

I International Maritime Organization (IMO)

IMO is a specialised agency of the United Nations dealing with maritime safety and the prevention and control of marine pollution. IMO's publishing activities include the production and sales of numerous texts (conventions, codes, regulations, recommendations, etc) both in print and in electronic form. IMO has some 250 titles in English; they are translated into French and Spanish, and an increasing number also into Arabic, Chinese and Russian.

Address: 4 Albert Embankment, London SE1 7SR
Telephone: 020 7735 7611
Fax: 020 7587 3241
Email: publications-sales@imo.org
Website: www.imo.org

Internet Handbooks Ltd

The internet continues to grow exponentially. Unique in the UK, Internet Handbooks meet the pressing need for practical easy-to-use guides to help everyone start discovering and enjoying the new possibilties of online information and interactivity. These large-format illustrated paperbacks are aimed at private individuals and families, students at school, college and university, job hunters, people at work, business managers, professional people, firms, local authorities and government - in fact, everyone today. Internet Handbooks show how to acquire the necessary skills, and enjoy everything this amazing medium has to offer. The series now contains around 50 titles published and in preparation, ranging from 'Creating a Home Page on the Internet' to 'Finding a Job on the Internet' (2nd edition) and 'Where to Find It on the Internet' (2nd edition). A fully illustrated catalogue is available, plus a substantial free web site. The books are priced at £9.99 to £12.99 paperback.

Editor(s): Roger Ferneyhough
Address: Unit 5 Dolphin Building, Queen Anne's Battery, Plymouth, PL4 0LP
Telephone: 01752 262626
Fax: 01752 262641
Email: post@internet-handbooks.co.uk
Website: http://www.internet-handbooks.co.uk
Payment Details: Royalties by arrangement
Unsolicited Manuscripts: No

I

IOM Communications

IOM Communications publishes books on materials science and engineering. The books include textbooks and reference works covering metals, ceramics, polymers and composite materials. IOM Communications is a wholly owned subsidiary of The Institute of Materials, the learned and professional body for materials scientists and engineers.

Editor(s): Peter Danckwerts
Address: 1 Carlton House Terrace, London SW1Y 5DB
Telephone: 020 7451 7305
Fax: 020 7839 2289
Email: Bill_Jackson@materials.org.uk
Website: www.materials.org.uk
Parent Company: The Institute of Materials
Payment Details: Royalties on sales
Unsolicited Manuscripts: To Peter Danckwerts

Irish Academic Press

Book publisher interested in following subject areas: Irish history, military history, Irish culture and heritage, arts and literature. Two new series: New Directions In Irish History and Women In Irish History. New manuscript and reprint ideas in the Press' subject areas welcomed.

Editor(s): Linda Longmore
Address: Northumberland House, 44 Northumberland Road, Ballsbridge, Dublin 4, Ireland
Telephone: 353 1 6688244
Fax: 353 1 6601610
Email: info@iap.ie
Website: www.iap.ie
Imprints: Irish Academic Press, Irish University Press
Unsolicited Manuscripts: Yes - send to Editor

I

Iron Press

Since 1973 Iron Press as been publishing contemporary poetry, drama and fiction. It began as a small publisher and retains the philisophy of a small publisher, bringing out only four or five books a year, single collections of work, plus anthologies of new verse and fiction. Iron's outlook is both regional - it encourages authors from its native North-East, national - in its encouragement of writers elsewhere, and international - its poetry anthologies include The Poetry of Perestroika, and Voices of Conscience, 200 suppressed poets from forty countries. No unsolicited mss please, and we're unlikely to take hopeful novices.

Editor(s): Peter Mortimer, Kitty Fitzgerald, Valerie Laws
Address: 5 Marden Terrace, Cullercoats, North Shields, Tyne & Wear NE30 4PD
Telephone: 0191 253 1901
Fax: Same as phone
Email: seaboy@freenetname.co.uk
Website: www.ironpress.co.uk
Payment Details: Negotiable
Unsolicited Manuscripts: No

Isis Publishing Ltd

Publishers of large-print and audio books.

Editor(s): Veronica Babington Smith
Address: 7 Centremead, Osney Mead, Oxford OX2 0ES
Telephone: 01865 250333
Fax: 01865 790358
Email: audiobooks@isis-publishing.co.uk
Imprints: Isis Large Print, Isis Audio Books

Islam International Publications Ltd

Religion and theology, children's books.

Address: Islamabad, Sheephatch Lane, Tilford, Surrey GU10 2AQ
Telephone: 01252 783155
Fax: 01252 783155
Parent Company: Al Shirkatul Islamiyyah

Islamic Texts Society

The Islamic Texts Society publishes books from the Islamic heritage mostly in the form of translations of original Arabic texts. Subjects covered: Qur'an, Hadith, philosophy, science etc.

Editor(s): Fatima Azzam
Address: 22a Brooklands Avenue, Cambridge CB2 2DQ
Telephone: 01223 314387
Fax: 01223 324342
Email: mail@its.org.uk
Website: www.islamictextssociety.org.uk
Imprints: Islamic Texts Society
Payment Details: Royalties 7.5% of net receipts
Unsolicited Manuscripts: Yes

I
ITDG publishing

Publisher and distributor of books and periodicals at practical and policy levels on appropriate technology, Third World development, water and sanitation, agriculture, enterprise development, small-scale construction and manufacture, energy and workshop equipment.

Editor(s): Tony Milner (Managing Director); Helen Marsden (Publisher: Books)
Address: 103-105 Southampton Row, London WC1B 4HL
Telephone: 020 7436 9761
Fax: 020 7436 2013
Email: itpubs@itpubs.org.uk
Website: www.itdgpublishing.org.uk
Imprints: Intermediate Technology Publications
Parent Company: Intermediate Technology Development Group
Unsolicited Manuscripts: Yes

Ithaca Press

Established 1973, publishes academic books, mainly on the Middle East, in the fields of history, politics and international relations, economics, social anthropology, religion and literature. Extensive backlist. Has expanded in recent years to include subjects of more general interest such as women's studies, legal studies and biography. Ithaca Press Paperbacks was launched in 1996 to reach a wider audience, including in particular students of social sciences. Important Ithaca Press series are Middle East Monographs, co-published with St Anthony's College, Oxford; the Oriental Institute Monographs, co-published with the Oriental Institute; and the Durham Middle East Monographs, co-published with the Centre for Islamic and Middle Eastern Studies, University of Durham. Strong links are also maintained with the School of Oriental and African Studies, University of London.

Editor(s): Emma Hawker (Editorial Manager)
Address: 8 Southern Court, South Street, Reading RG1 4QS
Telephone: 0118 959 7847
Fax: 0118 959 7356
Email: enquiries@garnet-ithaca.demon.co.uk
Parent Company: Garnet Publishing Ltd

Jane's Information Group

Jane's Information Group is the leading global information provider for defence, security, transport and law enforcement organisations. Jane's has developed a dynamic range of formats - books, magazines, CD-ROMs, e-mail and online services and secure intranet solutions. Jane's also offers a consultancy service for customers who require a confidential tailor made service to meet their particular needs. Many customers visit the Jane's website, www.janes.com to get Jane's editors' expert views on defence news related issues, view Jane's portfolio of products and download sample pages from the Jane's online catalogue.

Editor(s): Various
Address: Sentinel House, 163 Brighton Road, Coulsdon, Surrey CR5 2YH
Telephone: 020 8700 3700
Fax: 020 8763 1006
Email: info@janes.co.uk
Website: www.janes.com
Parent Company: The Woodbridge Company Ltd
Unsolicited Manuscripts: No

Janus Publishing Company Ltd

Publishing under two imprints, 'Janus' and 'Empiricus', for both subsidised and non-subsidised publications. Art, biography and autobiography, crime, economics, fiction, history, humour, music, medical, military and war, nautical, the occult, philosophy, poetry, politics and world affairs, science, science fiction, self-help, religion and theology, travel.

Editor(s): Sandy Leung
Address: 76 Great Titchfield Street, London W1P 7AF
Telephone: 020 7580 7664
Fax: 020 7636 5756
Email: publishers@januspublishing.co.uk
Website: http://www.januspublishing.co.uk
Imprints: Janus, Empiricus
Parent Company: Junction Books Ltd
Payment Details: Janus - mostly subsidised; Empiricus - no subsidies
Unsolicited Manuscripts: Yes, must be printed and in double space

Jarrold Publishing

Travel guides mostly UK; leisure and heritage titles. All books have a high photographic content and some artwork.

Editor(s): Sarah Letts
Address: Whitefriars, Norwich, Norfolk NR3 1TR
Fax: 01603 662748
Email: sarah.letts@jarrold.com
Parent Company: Jarrold and Sons Ltd
Payment Details: Fees and royalties
Unsolicited Manuscripts: Approach in writing first

A H Jolly (Editorial) Ltd

Both a book publisher and a book packager - putting titles together for other publishers. Encompassing in-house editing, design, photography and pre-press. Non-fiction, illustrated, arts-related.

Address: Yelvertoft Manor, Yelvertoft, Northamptonshire NN6 6LF
Telephone: 01788 823868
Fax: 01788 823915
Email: ahjolly@globalnet.co.uk
Payment Details: By individual arrangement
Unsolicited Manuscripts: Synopsis only

Jordan Publishing Ltd

Jordan Publishing, the UK's largest independent law publisher, have been producing practical legal books for over 100 years. In recent years the Jordans imprint has expanded to cover company law, commercial law, property, agricultural law, charities, private client work, education, personal injury, crime and specialist insolvency titles. Under our Family Law imprint there is an extensive range of journals, law reports and reference works representing the primary source of legal update and information for family lawyers.

Address: 21 St Thomas Street, Bristol BS1 6JS
Telephone: 0117 918 1232
Fax: 0117 918 1406
Email: dchaplin@jordanpublishing.co.uk
Website: www.jordanpublishing.co.uk
Imprints: Jordans, Family Law
Unsolicited Manuscripts: Yes

Richard Joseph Publishers Ltd

Publishers of directories of antiquarian and secondhand book dealers in many countries around the world. Also published are directories of dealers in prints and maps, ephemera and collectables. A few titles also published about secondhand books.

Editor(s): Claire Brumhan
Address: Unit 2, Monks Walk, Farnham, Surrey GU9 8HT
Telephone: 01252 734347
Fax: 01252 734307
Email: rjoe01@aol.com
Website: http://members.aol.com/rjoe01/sheppards.htm
Imprints: Sheppard's
Unsolicited Manuscripts: Not accepted unless directly related

S Karger AG

Founded in 1890, Karger is an independent medical publisher based in Basel, Switzerland. We publish 80 journals and about 60 new books a year, primarily in highly specialised medical research.

Editor(s): Peter Lawson
Address: 58 Grove Hill Road, Tunbridge Wells TN1 1SP
Email: karger@karger.ch
Website: www.karger.com
Imprints: Karger
Parent Company: S Karger AG, Basel
Unsolicited Manuscripts: No

Karnak House

Specialists in African and Caribbean studies only. Subjects published are history, education, linguistics, languages, egyptology, prehistory, anthropology, sociology and politics. Fiction only - no memoirs, biographies or autobiographies.

Editor(s): A S Saakana
Address: 300 Westbourne Park Road, London W11 1EH
Telephone: 020 7243 3620
Fax: Same as phone
Imprints: Karnak House
Unsolicited Manuscripts: Yes but synopsis and sample chapter only, plus SAE

Katabasis

Katabasis publishes English and (translations of) Latin American poetry and prose. Major British publisher of Nicaraguan poetry. We publish the Common Words series of poetry and prose anthologies, whose first 2 titles are Work and Home. Recent and new titles include: The Poetry of Earth, a long essay by Dinah Livingstone; The Moon's Story (poetry) by Adele David and Zapatista Stories by Subcomandante Marcos.

Editor(s): Dinah Livingstone
Address: 10 St Martins Close, London NW1 0HR
Telephone: 020 7485 3830
Fax: Same as phone
Email: katabasis@katabasis.co.uk
Website: http://www.katabasis.co.uk
Unsolicited Manuscripts: No, letter of inquiry

Keepdate Publishing

Traditional and new media publishers. Specialises in regional publications for the North of England.

Editor(s): Managing Editor: Michael Marshall
Address: 21 Portland Terrace, Newcastle Upon Tyne NE2 1QQ
Telephone: 0191 2819444
Fax: 0191 2813105
Email: keepdate@mailgate.newsnorth.com
Website: www.newsnorth.com
Payment Details: By negotiation
Unsolicited Manuscripts: Yes

K
Kegan Paul Ltd
International scholarly publishing house.

Editor(s): Editorial Director: Kaori O'Connor
Address: PO Box 256, 121 Bedford Court Mansions, Bedford Avenue, London WC1B 3SW
Telephone: 020 7580 5511
Fax: 020 7436 8099
Email: books@keganpaul.com
Website: www.keganpaul.com
Unsolicited Manuscripts: Yes

Kenilworth Press Ltd
Leading publisher of instructional equestrian books, including the official books of the British Horse Society, and the famous Threshold Picture Guides.

Editor(s): Lesley Gowers
Address: Addington, Buckingham, MK18 2JR
Telephone: 01296 715101
Fax: 01296 715148
Email: mail@kenilworthpress.co.uk
Imprints: Kenilworth, Threshold
Payment Details: Royalties
Unsolicited Manuscripts: Yes

Kensington West Productions Ltd

Publisher of sports, leisure, photography and business titles. We specialise in large format illustrated books.

Editor(s): Julian West
Address: 5 Cattle Market, Hexham, Northumberland NE46 1NJ
Telephone: 01434 609933
Fax: 01434 600066
Email: info@kensingtonwest.co.uk
Website: www.kensingtonwest.co.uk
Unsolicited Manuscripts: No, please send synopsis

The King's England Press

Formed in 1989 to reprint Arthur Mee's King's England series of 1930s guidebooks to the English counties. Due this year are Surrey and Cambridgeshire. Also available - Notts, Derbys, Durham, Essex, Herts, Lincs, Warwicks, Staffs, Leics & Rutland, West Yorks. Press also publishes children's poetry by Gez Walsh (The Spot On My Bum) and Andrew Collett (Always Eat Your Bogies), also available are Bitey the Veggie Vampire and Wang Fu the Kung Fu Shrew, by Chris White. Plus other books on local history and folklore. See website or send for free catalogue.

Editor(s): Steve Rudd
Address: Camberton House, Goldthorpe Industrial Estate, Goldthorpe, Rotherham S63 9BL
Telephone: 01226 270258
Fax: 01709 897787
Email: sales@kingsengland.co.uk
Website: www.kingsengland.com and www.pottypoets.com

𝒦 Laurence King Publishing

Lawrence King Publishing specialises in books on the history of art, on architecture, and on design for professionals and students.

Editor(s): Lesley Ripley Greenfield: Editorial Director, Philip Cooper: Commissioning Editor (Architecture), Joanne Lightfoot: Commissioning Editor (Design)
Address: 71 Great Russell Street, London WC1B 3BN
Telephone: 020 7831 6351
Fax: 020 7831 8356
Email: enquiries@calmann-king.co.uk
Website: www.laurence-king.com
Imprints: Lawrence King
Parent Company: Calmann & King Ltd
Payment Details: Advance against royalties
Unsolicited Manuscripts: Yes

Jessica Kingsley Publishers

Professional and academic level books on special needs, arts therapies, social work, psychiatry, psychology and practical theology. Books for professionals and parents on autism, Asperger's syndrome and related conditions. An independent company founded in 1987, now publishing over 100 books a year.

Editor(s): Jessica Kingsley, Graham Sleight, Amy Lankaster-Owen
Address: 116 Pentonville Road, London N1 9JB
Telephone: 020 7833 2307
Fax: 020 7837 2917
Email: post@jkp.com
Website: www.jkp.com
Payment Details: Royalties
Unsolicited Manuscripts: No, but proposals for books in our subject areas welcome - send outline, contents and author CV

Kluwer Academic/Plenum Publishers

Plenum Publishing is now part of Kluwer Academic Publishers. The UK company, based in London, provides an editorial base for new journals and books at postgraduate, research and professional levels in life sciences, physical sciences and social sciences.

Editor(s): Ken Derham - Phys, Chem, Maths & Social Sciences, also responsible for KA/PPs Russian journal programme, Joanna Lawrence - biosciences as well as proceedings volumes in all subject areas
Address: Lower Ground Floor, 241 Borough High Street, London, SE1 1GB
Telephone: +44 207 940 7490
Fax: +44 207 940 7495
Email: k.derham @plnum.co.uk, Jo@plenum.co.uk, Mail@plenum.co.uk
Website: www.wkap.nl
Imprints: Kluwer Academic/Plenum Publishers, and prior to 1998 - Plenum Press
Parent Company: Kluwer Academic Publishers
Payment Details: Dependant on project
Unsolicited Manuscripts: Yes

Knockabout Comics

Publishers of graphic novels and comic books for a adult readership. Robert Crumb, Gilbert Shelton, Hunt Emerson, Alan Moore. Also distributors of graphic novels and comic books for all ages.

Publishers of drug information titles.

Editor(s): Tony Bennett, Carol Bennett
Address: Unit 24, 10 Acklam Road, London W10 5QZ
Telephone: 020 8969 2945
Fax: 020 8968 7614
Email: knockcomic@aol.com
Website: www.knockabout.com
Imprints: Knockabout, Hassle Free Press, Fanny
Payment Details: 10% of cover price
Unsolicited Manuscripts: No

Kogan Page

Kogan Page is the UK's leading independent business book publisher. Its long-established and much respected lists span a wide range of subjects, including business management, human resources, finance, international business, European issues, training and education.

Editor(s): Pauline Goodwin, Philip Mudd, Linda Batham
Address: 120 Pentonville Road, London N1 9JN
Telephone: 020 7278 0433
Fax: 020 7837 6348
Email: kpinfo@kogan-page.co.uk
Website: www.kogan-page.co.uk
Imprints: Penton Press
Payment Details: Six monthly
Unsolicited Manuscripts: Yes

Landfall Publications

About 30 books published so far, all with a Cornish interest. Main series is Landfall Walks Books, 14 volumes by Bob Acton giving directions for round walks with copious information on points of interest. Another ongoing series is Exploring Cornish Mines, and industrial archaeology is the focus of several other publications. Also publish books by Viv Acton, including two popular ones about Cornwall during World War 2, plus other local history books by this author and others.

Address: Landfall, Penpol, Devoran, Truro TR3 6NR
Telephone: 01872 862581
Email: bob.acton@virgin.net
Unsolicited Manuscripts: No

Landy Publishing

Publishes local history for Lancashire townships. Also Lancashire dialect poetry.

Address: 3 Staining Rise, Staining, Blackpool FY3 0BU
Telephone: 01253 895678
Fax: Same as phone
Payment Details: By arrangement
Unsolicited Manuscripts: No. Phone or write first

Lapwing Publications

Northern Irish authors living in N.Ireland, UK and EU. Authors should have strong links with Northern Ireland. Small print runs. A5-size pamphlets or metric equivalents, generally saddle-stitched, paper-bound, preferably 48 pages maximum, perfect bound celloglazed.

Editor(s): Dennis Greig, Rene Greig
Address: 1 Ballysillan Drive, Belfast BT14 8HQ
Telephone: 028 90875 134
Imprints: Ha'penny Press
Payment Details: 10% of print run
Unsolicited Manuscripts: Yes, always, up to 20 poems

Law Pack Publishing Ltd

Self-help law, business, management and careers titles. Books, kits, software and forms.

Editor(s): Jamie Ross
Address: 10-16 Cole Street, London SE1 4YH
Telephone: 020 7940 7000
Fax: 020 7940 7001
Email: mailbox@lawpack.co.uk
Website: www.lawpack.co.uk
Imprints: Take Note; Made Easy Guides
Unsolicited Manuscripts: Yes

L
Law Society Publishing

A commercial publishing business existing within The Law Society of England and Wales. Publish practical handbooks, guides and legal reference material designed to enable solicitors and other law practitioners to carry out their work more effectively. Main publishing areas: litigation (including ADR/PI), commerce, employment law, human rights, practice management, IT, professional conduct, property and conveyancing, crime, environmental law, family and social welfare, partnerships, wills and probate and legal reference.

Editor(s): Steven Reed, Angela Atcheson, Ben Mullane
Address: 113 Chancery Lane, London WC1A 1PL
Telephone: 020 7320 5876
Fax: 020 7404 1124
Email: steven.reed@lawsociety.org.uk
Website: www.publishing.lawsociety.org.uk
Imprints: Law Society Publishing
Parent Company: The Law Society of England and Wales
Payment Details: Royalties (negotiable)
Unsolicited Manuscripts: Yes

Lawrence And Wishart Ltd

Independent left publisher, specialising in politics and cultural studies, also publishing in the areas of history and education.

Editor(s): Sally Davison
Address: 99A Wallis Road, London, E9 5LN
Telephone: 020 8533 2506
Fax: 020 8533 7369
Email: editorial@l-w-bks.demon.co.uk
Website: l-w-bks.co.uk
Unsolicited Manuscripts: No

LDA - Part of McGraw-Hill Children's Publishing

Publishers of educational materials for Primary Schools and Special Needs.

Editor(s): Cathy Griffin, Corin Redsell, Lee Humber
Address: Abbeygate House, East Road, Cambridge CB1 1DB
Telephone: 01223 357788
Fax: 01223 460557
Website: www.LDAlearning.com
Imprints: Living and Learning
Parent Company: McGraw-Hill Children's Publishing
Unsolicited Manuscripts: Yes

Learning Materials Ltd

A popular company with teachers, devoted to publishing materials for children with special educational needs, giving excellent support in literacy and numeracy. The majority of books are photocopiable and provide much-needed differentiation within the classroom. In addition to English and mathematics, subjects covered include history, science, thinking skills and life skills. New publications for 2002 include: High Frequency Words, Confusing Letters, Support for Basic Grammars Bks 7 & 8, Support for Basic Spelling Bks 7 & 8 and New Reading & Thinking Bk 6.

Editor(s): Barbara Mitchelhill
Address: Dixon Street, Wolverhampton WV2 2BX
Telephone: 01902 454026
Fax: 01902 457596
Email: Learning.Materials@btinternet.com
Website: http://www.learning.materials.btinternet.com
Payment Details: By negotiation
Unsolicited Manuscripts: Enquire first

L
Learning Together

Practice tests for 9-12 year olds in reasoning (verbal and non-verbal), English, maths and science. Target group is end of Key Stage 2.

Editor(s): Stephen McConkey, Tom Maltman
Address: 18 Shandon Park, Belfast BT5 6NW
Telephone: 028 9040 2086 or 028 9042 5852
Fax: 028 9040 2086 or 028 9042 5852

Legal Action Group

Legal Action Group works with lawyers and advisers to promote equal access to justice. It is committed to improving law and practice, and its publishing programme is put together with this in mind. LAG focuses on the areas that most affect disadvantaged groups, providing practical books and law reports for lawyers at affordable prices.

Editor(s): Publisher: Hannah Casey
Address: 242 Pentonville Road, London N1 9UN
Telephone: 020 7833 7425
Fax: 020 7837 6094
Email: lag@lag.org.uk
Website: www.lag.org.uk
Parent Company: LAG Education and Service Trust Ltd
Payment Details: Royalty based on published price
Unsolicited Manuscripts: Yes - usual format is for synopsis initially

Lennard Publishing

General non-fiction but only where projects are underwritten by sponsorship or a guaranteed order for a large proportion of the print run.

Editor(s): Adrian Stephenson
Address: Windmill Cottage, Mackerye End, Harpenden, Herts AL5 5DR
Telephone: 01582 715866
Fax: 01582 715121
Email: lennard@lenqap.demon.co.uk
Parent Company: Lennard Associates Ltd
Payment Details: By negotiation
Unsolicited Manuscripts: No

Letts Educational

Educational books for use at home and in school for 3-18 year olds. We also publish books to help trainee teachers achieve Qualified Teacher Status.

Address: 414 Chiswick High Road, Chiswick, London, W4 5TF
Telephone: 0208 996 3333
Fax: 0208 742 8390
Email: mail@lettsed.co.uk
Website: www.letts-education.com
Parent Company: Granada Learning
Payment Details: Royalties
Unsolicited Manuscripts: No

John Libbey & Co Ltd

John Libbey & Co Ltd offer a fast, flexible and comprehensive publishing service. The company has achieved a reputation for well produced, timely publications - made available at realistic prices. Many titles are published with leading researchers, professional institutions and pharmaceutical companies, and based on proceeding conferences. Our specialised subjects are; epilepsy, obesity, nutrition, neurology and nuclear medicine. We also publish books and journals in cinema, film and animation. We welcome your inquiries about our company and our products.

Address: PO Box 276, Eastleigh SO50 5YS
Telephone: 023 8065 0208
Fax: 023 8065 0259
Email: johnlibbey@aol.com
Website: www.johnlibbey.com
Imprints: John Libbey, Eurotext

Library Association Publishing

With over 200 titles in print Library Association Publishing is one of the largest publishers worldwide in the specialist field of library and information science. At the forefront of library and information development, Library Association Publishing has a comprehensive list covering all the major areas of professional activity.

Editor(s): Publisher: Helen Carley
Address: 7 Ridgmount Street, London WC1E 7AE
Telephone: 020 7255 0590
Fax: 020 7255 0591
Email: lapublishing@la-hq.org.uk
Website: http://www.la-hq.org.uk/lapublishing
Parent Company: The Library Association
Payment Details: Negotiable
Unsolicited Manuscripts: Yes

Lion Publishing Plc

Publishes Christian books for general readers, both children and adults.

Editor(s): Publishing Directors: Rebecca Winter, Tony Wales, Editors: Morag Reeve, Su Box, Lois Rock
Address: Peter's Way, Sandy Lane West, Oxford OX4 6HG
Telephone: 01865 747550
Fax: 01865 747568
Email: b.passaportis@lion-publishing.co.uk
Website: www.lion-publishing
Payment Details: Royalties paid twice a year
Unsolicited Manuscripts: To Charlotte Stewart

Listen & Live Audio Books

An expanding publisher of audio books on tape and CD, with an impressive list of authors and narrators, including 'The Worst-Case Scenario Survival Handbook' read by Burt Reynolds.

Editor(s): Alfred Martino
Address: C/o Roundhouse Publishing Ltd, Millstone, Limers Lane, Northam, Devon, EX39 2RG
Telephone: 01237 474474
Fax: 01237 474774
Email: round.house@fsbdial.co.uk
Website: www.roundhouse.net
Payment Details: Royalties twice yearly
Unsolicited Manuscripts: No

L

Little Tiger Press

Children's picture books, 4-7 years, pre-school and novelty books 0-4 years.

Editor(s): Alison Morris
Address: 1, The Coda Centre, 189 Munster Road, London SW6 6AW
Telephone: 020 7385 6333
Fax: 020 7385 7333
Email: info@littletiger.co.uk
Imprints: Little Tiger Press
Parent Company: Magi Publications
Payment Details: To be agreed with author
Unsolicited Manuscripts: Yes, welcomed, but please phone first

Little, Brown & Company (UK)

General fiction and non-fiction hardback and paperback. Non-fiction includes - biographies and autobiographies, politics, current affairs, popular science and history. Fiction includes - thrillers, crime, SF and fantasy, women's fiction and literary fiction.

Editor(s): Alan Samson, Barbara Boote, Hilary Hale, Richard Beswick, Lennie Goodings, Julia Charles, Tim Holman
Address: Brettenham House, Lancaster Place, London WC2E 7EN
Telephone: 020 7911 8000
Fax: 020 7911 8100
Email: email.uk@littlebrown.com
Imprints: Little Brown, Warner, Abacus, Virago, Orbit
Parent Company: Time Warner Inc
Payment Details: None
Unsolicited Manuscripts: Prefer not

The Littman Library Of Jewish Civilization

The Littman Library of Jewish Civilization, established in 1965, publishes scholarly works that explain and perpetuate the Jewish heritage. Following the guidelines laid down by its founder, it publishes works of scholarship that reflect objectivity, fresh research, and new insight, and that are as far as possible definitive in their field. The Library also publishes translations of contemporary scholarship originally published in other languages, as well as of Hebrew and Aramaic classics so as to make the Jewish religious and literary heritage more accessible to English-speaking readers.

Editor(s): Connie Webber
Address: PO Box 645, Oxford OX2 0UJ
Telephone: 01235 811622
Fax: Same as phone
Email: editorial@littman.co.uk
Website: www.littman.co.uk
Unsolicited Manuscripts: Yes

Liverpool University Press

Academic and scholarly books in the fields of archaeology, architecture, art and art history, contemporary culture and society, history (all periods and areas of the world), literary criticism (English, American, French, Iberian, Latin American), environmental studies, science fiction criticism, poetry studies, sociology, veterinary science.

Editor(s): Publisher: Robin Bloxsidge
Address: 4 Cambridge Street, Liverpool L69 7ZU
Telephone: 0151 794 2231
Fax: 0151 794 2235
Email: j.m.smith@liv.ac.uk
Website: www.liverpool-unipress.co.uk
Imprints: Liverpool University Press
Parent Company: The University of Liverpool
Payment Details: Royalties paid annually; advances negotiable
Unsolicited Manuscripts: Yes

£
LLP Professional Publishing

Publishers and information providers to the international shipping, transportation, legal, insurance, energy and financial markets. Publish reference and professional books and directories for these markets. 200 backlist titles and up to 30 new titles each year.

Address: 69-77 Paul Street, London EC2A 4LQ
Telephone: 020 7553 1000
Fax: 020 7553 1107
Website: www.informabookshop.com
Parent Company: Informa Group Plc
Unsolicited Manuscripts: To Reference Publishing Division

Locomotives International

Locomotives International publications cover the less familiar aspects of British-built locomoives overseas and overseas railways in general. All gauges are encompassed, with the accent mainly on steam, and particular delight is taken in the rare, obscure, and downright bizarre. Our 'Steam and Rail in ...' series of softbacks focuses on a separate country in each volume and is now being expanded. These and some of our other books are made up of contributions from more than one author and any items for titles not currently in preparation may also be considered for the quarterly 'Locomotives International' magazine.

Editor(s): Paul Catchpole
Address: The Old School House, Arrow, Alcester, Warwickshire B49 5PJ
Telephone: 01789 766332
Fax: 01789 766850
Email: locomotives.international@talk21.com
Website: www.locomotivesinternational.co.uk
Imprints: Locomotives International
Payment Details: Twice yearly
Unsolicited Manuscripts: Yes

Logaston Press

Concentrates on publishing books on history, social history and archaeology concerning central or South Wales, Welsh Borders, and/or West Midlands. Discuss ideas/synopsis first before considering chapters/manuscript.

Editor(s): Andy Johnson, Ron Shoesmith
Address: Logaston, Woonton, Almeley, Herefordshire HR3 6QH
Telephone: 01544 327344
Imprints: Logaston Press
Payment Details: By mutual agreement, normally on publication
Unsolicited Manuscripts: Send outline idea first, manuscript by request only

Y Lolfa

Welsh - language and English - language for adults and children. Children's books: original. Age groups: all. Particular interest in contemporary welsh writing; original series for children; music; books for learners and tourists, politics and general books on Wales. Around 20% of titles are commissioned.

Editor(s): Lefi Gruffudd (General Editor)
Address: Talybont, Ceredigion SY24 5AP
Telephone: 01970 832 304
Fax: 01970 832 782
Email: ylolfa@ylolfa.com
Website: www.ylolfa.com

Lonely Planet Publications

Independent travel guidebook publisher. Over 460 books including regional, country and city guides, first time, pocket, food and restaurant guides, pictorial travel books, atlases, sheet city maps, phasebooks, walking, cycling, wildlife and diving guides, travel literature and books on healthy travel.

Editor(s): Katharine Leck
Address: 10a Spring Place, London NW5 3BH
Telephone: 020 7428 4800
Fax: 020 7428 4828
Email: go@lonelyplanet.co.uk
Website: www.lonelyplanet.com/
Parent Company: Lonely Planet Publications Australia
Payment Details: Dependent on contract
Unsolicited Manuscripts: No

Lothian Books

A general trade publisher of travel, cookery, self-help & new age, and young adult titles.

Editor(s): Peter Lothian
Address: C/o Roundhouse Publishing Ltd, Millstone, Limers Lane, Northam, Devon EX39 2RG
Telephone: 01237 474474
Fax: 01237 474774
Email: round.house@fsbdial.co.uk
Website: www.roundhouse.net
Payment Details: Royalties twice yearly
Unsolicited Manuscripts: No

LTP (Language Teaching Publications)

LTP is an independent publisher specialising in innovative materials for the ELT market. LTP has an exceptional business list and teacher training which continues to grow alongside general English products. Established titles include: Innovations, Idioms Organiser, Teaching Collocation, Business Matters, The Working Week, The Lexical Approach, The LTP Dictionary of Collocations. New titles for 2001 are: English Vocabulary Organiser and Taboos & Issues.

Editor(s): M Lewis, J Hill
Address: 114a Church Road, Hove, East Sussex BN3 2EB
Telephone: 01273 736344
Fax: 01273 775361
Email: ltp@ltpwebsite.com
Website: www.ltpwebsite.com
Unsolicited Manuscripts: Accepted with contents page, rationale, 3 sample units/chapters

Lucis Press Ltd

Lucis Press publishes books of esoteric philosophy, a continuation of the Ageless Wisdom presented as a guide to the merging of spiritual values and goals with the challenges of modern living. The teaching of the Tibetan Master, Djwhal Khul, written by Alice Bailey, encompasses a wide range of subjects including the new psychology of the soul, education, discipleship, astrology, healing, intuition, karma and telepathy. Other author's titles include the Agni Yoga series.

Editor(s): Sarah McKechnie
Address: 3 Whitehall Court, Suite 54, London SW1A 2EF
Telephone: 020 7839 4512
Fax: 020 7839 5575
Email: lucispress@lucistrust.org
Website: www.lucistrust.org/
Parent Company: Lucis Publishing, New York

Lucky Duck Publishing

Specialise in books for teachers and parents which present a positive approach to behaviour management. Our catalogue includes books, videos and teaching materials about self-esteem, bullying, circle time, circle of friends, emotional curriculum, parenting skills and equal opportunities. We have published a number of first-time authors, and provide a supportive editorial service to assist in the production of user-friendly materials. Visit the website for more information.

Editor(s): George Robinson, Barbara Maines
Address: 3 Thorndale Mews, Clifton, Bristol BS8 2HX
Telephone: 0117 9732881
Fax: 0117 9731707
Email: publishing@luckyduck.co.uk
Website: www.luckyduck.co.uk
Payment Details: 10% of net sales
Unsolicited Manuscripts: No

Lund Humphries

Publishers of books on fine art, architecture, decorative arts, design and photography. Specialise in co-publications with museums and galleries. Publishers for the Henry Moore Foundation, and distributors for a number of museums worldwide.

Editor(s): Publishing Director: Lucy Myers
Address: Mecklenburgh House, 11 Mecklenburgh Square, London WC1N 2AE
Telephone: 020 7841 9800
Fax: 020 7837 6322
Email: mecklenburgh@ashgatepub.co.uk
Website: www.ashgate.com, www.lundhumphries.com
Parent Company: Ashgate Publishing Ltd
Unsolicited Manuscripts: Yes

M

Léirmheas

Publishers of Irish historical and political material and some other items of Irish interest (1 book of poetry).

Editor(s): Daltún Ó Ceallaigh
Address: PO Box 3278, Dublin 6, Ireland
Telephone: 353 1 4976944
Email: leir@eircom.net
Website: http://homepage.eircom.net/~mheas
Imprints: Léirmheas

Macmillan Children's Books

Publishes novels, series fiction, picture books, non-fiction (illustrated and non-illustrated), poetry and novelty books in paperback and hardback. No unsolicited material.

Editor(s): Managing Director: Kate Wilson; Full-colour Publishing Director: Alison Green; Black and White Publishing Director: Sarah Davies
Address: 20 New Wharf Road, London, M1 9RR
Telephone: 020 7014 6000
Fax: 020 7014 6001
Website: www.panmacmillan.com
Imprints: Macmillan, Pan, Campbell Books
Parent Company: Macmillan Publishers Ltd
Unsolicited Manuscripts: No unsolicited material

ℳ
Macmillan Online Publishing

Art, music, politics, current affairs, economics, finance, science.

Editor(s): Sara Lloyd, Laura Macy, Jane Turner
Address: The Macmillan Building, 4-6 Crinan Street, London, N1 9XW
Telephone: 020 7883 4000
Fax: 020 7843 4640
Website: www.macmillan.co.uk
Imprints: Grove's Dictionaries
Parent Company: Macmillan Ltd
Payment Details: Vary
Unsolicited Manuscripts: Yes

Macmillan Publishers Ltd

Macmillan Publishers, founded in 1843, publish approximately 1400 titles a year. Unsolicited proposals and synopses are welcome in all divisions of the company, which are: Macmillan Press Ltd, publishing textbooks and monographs; Macmillan Education, publishing international education titles; Macmillan Heineman ELT, publishing ELT titles; Macmillan, publishing biographies, autobiographies, crafts, hobbies, economics, gift books, health and beauty, history, humour, natural history, travel, philosphy, politics and world affairs, psychology, theatre and drama, gardening, cookery, encyclopedias; Pan, publishing fiction and non-fiction paperbacks; Papermac, publishing serious non-fiction; Picador, publishing literary and general fiction and non-fiction; Sidgwick & Jackson, publishing military and war and music; Macmillan Children's Books and Campbell Books, publishing novels, board books, picture books; Macmillan Reference Ltd, publishing works of reference in academic, professional and vocational subjects; Boxtree, publishing books linked to, and about, television, film, popular culture, humour and sport.

Address: 25 Eccleston Place, London SW1W 9NF
Telephone: 020 7881 8000
Fax: 020 7881 8001
Imprints: Macmillan, Pan, Papermac, Sidgwick & Jackson
Parent Company: Holtzbrinck
Payment Details: Royalties are paid annually or twice-yearly depending on contract
Unsolicited Manuscripts: Yes

Magna Large Print Books

Family saga, doctor/nurse, mystery, suspense/adventure, romance, romantic/suspense, westerns, thrillers, general fiction, historical romance and a small amount of non-fiction. Please note: we only publish large-print books which have already been published in ordinary print.

Editor(s): Diane Allen
Address: Magna House, Long Preston, Nr Skipton, North Yorkshire BD23 4ND
Telephone: 01729 840225
Fax: 01729 840683
Imprints: Magna, Dales and Story Sound
Parent Company: The Ulverscroft Group
Unsolicited Manuscripts: No

Mainstream Publishing Co Ltd

Scotland's largest independent company founded over 21 years ago and still wholly owned by its directors. Mainstream specialise in non-fiction with particular emphasis on sport, popular culture, true crime and current affairs.

Editor(s): Bill Campbell (Publisher)
Address: 7 Albany Street, Edinburgh EH1 3UG
Telephone: 0131 557 2959
Fax: 0131 556 8720
Email: enquires@mainstreampublishing.com
Website: www.mainstreampublishing.com
Imprints: Mainstream Sport
Unsolicited Manuscripts: Yes

ℳ
Management Books 2000 Ltd

Management guides, handbooks and directories, covering all types of business book from career development to technical reference. Also interested in general non-fiction titles of particular topical relevance.

Editor(s): Nicholas Dale-Harris, James Alexander
Address: Forge House, Limes Road, Kemble, Cirencester, Gloucester, GL7 6AD
Telephone: 01285 771441
Fax: 01285 771055
Email: m.b.2000@virgin.net
Website: www.mb2000.com
Imprints: Management Books 2000, Mercury Business Books
Payment Details: Advance/Royalties
Unsolicited Manuscripts: Yes

Management Pocketbooks Ltd

Pocket-size (A6 landscape), succinct, factual text, and high visual content distinguish Management Pocketbooks. More than 50 titles in the series, which broadly fall into the following categories: training, personal development, management, sales and marketing, and finance. Flagship The Trainer's Pocketbook has sold over 40,000 copies. The pages of a Pocketbook resemble an overhead transparency: a heading denotes the subject of the page; the text is often presented as bullet-points; acronyms, mnemonics and other memory trigger devices are used; and illustrations are included wherever possible. Thumb logos enable reader to identify the chapter they are reading. Many of the Pocketbook authors are trainers and present their own training materials in a similar way. The books are £6.99 and when discounted (for multiple copies) they can be used as inexpensive course material, either before, during or after the training event. ISBN series prefix 1 870471.

Editor(s): Ros Baynes, Sue Kerr, Adrian Hunt
Address: 14 East Street, Alresford, Hants SO24 9EE
Telephone: 01962 735573
Fax: 01962 733637
Email: sales@pocketbook.co.uk
Website: www.pocketbook.co.uk
Payment Details: 10% of net receipts
Unsolicited Manuscripts: To Ros Baynes

Institute Of Management

Publisher of books, checklists, CD-ROMs, on over 200 management-related topics. I M publishes independently and in association with Hodder & Stoughton and Butterworth Heinemann.

Editor(s): Tricia Bradley
Address: Management House, Cottingham Road, Corby NN17 1TT
Telephone: 01536 204222
Fax: 01536 201651
Email: publications@imgt.org.uk
Website: www.inst-mgt.org.uk

Manchester University Press

Art history, history, theology and religion (Editor: Whittle). Economics and business studies, international law, politics (Editor: Mason). Architecture, design, film and media, foreign language texts, literary studies, music, philosophy and theory, photography (Editor: Frost). We also publish a number of journals.

Editor(s): Alison Whittle (history), Tony Mason (economics), Matthew Frost (humanities)
Address: Oxford Road, Manchester M13 9NR
Telephone: 0161 275 2310
Fax: 0161 274 3346
Email: mup@man.ac.uk
Website: www.manchesteruniversitypress.co.uk
Imprints: Mandolin
Payment Details: Royalties
Unsolicited Manuscripts: Yes

M
Maney Publishing

Maney is one of the few remaining independent publishers of quality in an era of declining production standards and the increasing concentration of publishing in the hands of international conglomerates. Since 1945 Maney has offered academic societies, their editors and authors outstanding service in the publication of their books and journals: that process continues with the development of our journal publishing imprint Maney Publishing and our monograph imprint Northern Universities Press. We publish in the areas of archaeology, architecture, history, decorative arts, literature and language and more recently the biomedical sciences.

Editor(s): Managing Director: Michael Gallico
Address: Hudson Road, Leeds LS9 7DL
Telephone: 0113 249 7481
Fax: 0113 248 6983
Email: maney@maney.co.uk
Website: www.maney.co.uk
Imprints: Northern Universities Press, Maney Publishing
Parent Company: W S Maney & Son Ltd
Unsolicited Manuscripts: Yes

Mango Publishing

Focuses on the Caribbean - especially literature and poetry from Caribbean heritage writers, particularly women. Anything with a Caribbean connection is considered.

Editor(s): Joan Anim-Addo
Address: PO Box 13378, London SE27 0ZN
Email: j.anim-addo@virgin.net
Imprints: Mango Publishing
Payment Details: By arrangement
Unsolicited Manuscripts: Yes

Manson Publishing Ltd

Books for professionals and students in medicine, veterinary medicine, biological and agricultural sciences and earth sciences. All our books are distributed through Blackwell Science Ltd.

Address: 73 Corringham Road, London NW11 7DL
Telephone: 020 8905 5150
Fax: 020 8201 9233
Email: manson@man-pub.demon.co.uk
Website: www.manson-publishing.co.uk
Imprints: Manson Publishing Ltd, The Veterinary Press
Unsolicited Manuscripts: No

Peter Marcan Publications

Publisher of: The Marcan Handbook Of Arts Organisations (5th edition, 2001); and the Greater London History And Heritage Handbook (1999). Also some second-hand/out of print bookselling (Greater London and other UK and overseas metropolitian regions; horticulture).

Editor(s): Peter Marcan
Address: PO Box 3158, London SE1 4RA
Telephone: 020 7357 0368

Marcham Manor Press

Specialist publisher interested in PhD level academic publications in the field of history and church history c1520-1900.

Editor(s): Gervase Duffield
Address: Appleford, Abingdon, Oxon OX14 4PB
Telephone: 01235 848319
Imprints: Marcham Books, Sutton Courtenay Press
Parent Company: Appleford Publishing Group
Unsolicited Manuscripts: Only in our specialist field

M
Maritime Books

Publishers of books on the Royal Navy. Very specialist - mainly reference works and factual accounts. Not autobiographies.

Editor(s): M A Critchley
Address: Lodge Hill, Liskeard PL14 4EL
Telephone: 01579 343663
Fax: 01579 346747
Email: orders.marbooks@virgin.net
Website: www.navybooks.com

Marshalle Publications

Alternative or complementary medicine, biblical diseases and medicines, homeopathy, murder and poisoning by arsenic, history of the Hebrews from 12C BC. History, short stories, Westcountry stories including Tamerton Treacle Mines. Amusing incidents.

Editor(s): Mervyn Madge
Address: Chelfham House, Saltburn Road, Plymouth PL5 1PB
Telephone: 01752 361832

Marston House

Publishers of high quality illustrated seminal books on specialist themes: contemporary ceramics, vernacular architecture, sculpture, specialist horticulture.

Editor(s): Leslie Birks-Hay
Address: Marston House, Marston Magna, Yeovil, Somerset BA22 8DH
Telephone: 01935 851331
Fax: 01935 851372
Email: marston.house@virgin.net
Imprints: Marston House
Parent Company: Alphabet & Image Ltd
Payment Details: Royalty twice yearly according to contract
Unsolicited Manuscripts: No

Martin Books

Food, drink, cookery, beauty, health, homes and interiors, gardening, general leisure, interest.

Editor(s): Susanna Clarke, Anna Hitchin
Address: 88 Regent Street, Cambridge CB2 1DP
Telephone: 01223 448770
Fax: 01223 448777
Parent Company: Simon & Schuster UK Ltd
Unsolicited Manuscripts: No

Association Of Teachers Of Mathematics (ATM)

Mathematics Teaching Journal - 4 issues a year is concerned with classroom approaches to mathematics teaching.

Micromath Journal - 3 issues a year focuses on intergrating ICT into the mathematics classroom.

Every issue contains articles written by teachers from KS1 - 4. Recent issues have contained articles on number and mental mathematics.

The Association of Teachers of Mathematics supports the teaching and learning of Mathematics.

Editor(s): Mathematics Teaching - Helen Williams, Geoff Dunn, Robin Stewart. Micromath - David Wright, Julie Ann Edwards
Address: ATM, 7 Shaftesbury Street, Derby DE23 8YB
Telephone: 01332 346599
Fax: 01332 204357
Email: admin@atm.org.uk
Website: www.atm.org.uk

M
Mathew Price Ltd

Education through delight. Co-edition specialists UK Publisher for fiction and non-fiction for 1 to 10-year-olds. Board books, novelties, picture books and natural history.

Address: The Old Glove Factory, Bristol Road, Sherborne, Dorset DT9 4HP
Telephone: 01935 816010
Fax: 01935 816310
Email: sued@mathewprice.com
Unsolicited Manuscripts: To Sue Davies

Kevin Mayhew Ltd

Non-denominational christian publishing company producing books, music, hymn books, worship resources and church requisites.

Editor(s): Elizabeth Bates (books), Janet Simpson (music)
Address: Maypole Farm, Buxhall, Stowmarket, Suffolk IP14 3BW
Telephone: 01449 737978
Fax: 01449 737834
Email: info@kevinmayhewltd.com
Imprints: Kevin Mayhew, Palm Tree Press
Unsolicited Manuscripts: To music or editorial dept

B McCall Barbour

Publishers of Christian books, greeting cards, calendars and gift items etc. Also wholesale distributors for Bibles, books etc, from various other publishers. British agents for Zondervan Publishers, Living Stories Inc, AMG Publishers, Riverside/World Bibles, Dake's Bibles, Kirkbride Bibles, Sword of the Lord Publishers and Schoettle Publishers as well as Thomas Nelson Bibles and Books. Singspiration Music and Peterson Music also sole distributors. This firm is a family business established in 1900 and is strictly evangelical.

Editor(s): T C Danson-Smith
Address: 28 George IV Bridge, Edinburgh EH1 1ES
Telephone: 0131 225 4816
Fax: Same as phone
Payment Details: By arrangement
Unsolicited Manuscripts: No

Medici Society Ltd

Publishes illustrated children's picture books drawing on the themes of art, nature and biblical stories. Books on art include titles on Monet, Renoir, L S Lowry, J M W Turner, Millais and John Constable.

Address: Grafton House, Hyde Estate Road, London NW9 6JZ
Telephone: 020 8205 2500
Fax: 020 8205 2552
Website: www.medici.co.uk
Unsolicited Manuscripts: No - please send synopsis with illustrations

ℳ

Society For The Study Of Medieval Languages And Literature

Publishes the journal Medium Aevum on subjects in the language and literature of medieval European countries, including English. Also publishes an occasional series under the title Medium Aevum Monographs in the same areas: manuscripts (normal length between 50,000 and 70,000 words) for monographs, are refereed, and a contribution to publication costs (in the region of £500 to £700) is normally required.

Editor(s): H Cooper (English), University College Oxford OX1 4BH; N Palmer (Germanic), St Edmund Hall, Oxford OX1 4DR; E Kennedy (Romance), The White Cottage, Byles Green, Upper Bucklebury, Reading RS7 6SG
Address: Hon Treasurer, SSMLL, Magdalen College, Oxford OX1 4AU
Telephone: 01865 276087
Fax: Same as phone
Email: david.pattison@magd.ox.ac.uk
Website: http://units.ox.ac.uk/departments/modlang/ssmll/
Unsolicited Manuscripts: To editors as appropriate

Mehring Books

Mehring Books produce high quality editions of socialist books and pamphlets. Titles cover a wide range of subjects, from history and philosophy to culture, science and contemporary politics. Recent publications include, 'Art as the cognition of life', by Alexsandr Voronsky - outstanding Marxist literary critic and writer on art, aesthetics and culture. Voronsky was editor of the most important literary journal in the 1920s USSR and an opponent of Stalin. Also '1937 - Stalin's year of terror' by noted Russian historian Vadim Z Rogovin. 'Human BSE - Anatomy of a health disaster', contains submissions by Professor Richard Lacey and the families of nvCJD victims. Also available: 'A State Murder Exposed - The Truth about the Killing of Joy Gardner'. Please visit our website or ask for our free catalogue.

Address: P O Box 1306, Sheffield S9 3UW
Telephone: 0114 2440055
Fax: 0114 2440224
Email: sales@mehringbooks.co.uk
Website: www.mehringbooks.co.uk
Imprints: Mehring Books

Melrose Press Ltd

The International Biographical Centre of Cambridge has been producing a full range of biographical directories for more than thirty years. These directories cover vast interest and geographical areas and are specially designed to provide easy access to detailed biographical information from many varied, prominent individuals. All IBC titles are compiled without political, racial or religious bias and are of genuine international interest.

Editor(s): Jon Gifford
Address: St Thomas Place, Ely, Cambs CB7 4GG
Imprints: International Biographical Centre (IBC)
Unsolicited Manuscripts: Yes biographical data only

Menard Press

Menard Press celebrated its thirtieth birthday in 1999 with a group of new books, including new translations of Rilke and Nerval, and Itinerary, the intellectual autobiography of the great Mexican poet Octavio Paz, its third book by a Nobel Prize winner. Menard Press, which specialises in literary translation (mainly of poetry), rarely publishes texts submitted in the usual way, rather it seeks out work of the kind its faithful readers have come to expect over many years of sporadically intensive activity. Around half of the 150 published books are still in print. In addition to translated poetry and other literary texts it has published major essays on the nuclear issue, and a number of testimonies by survivors of Nazism. Its worldwide trade distributors are Central Books, apart from North America, where Small Press Distribution is used. Five new books are planned for 2001-2002.

Editor(s): Anthony Rudolf
Address: Menard Press (Anthony Rudolf), 8 The Oaks, Woodside Avenue, London N12 8AR
Telephone: 020 8446 5571
Fax: Same as phone
Imprints: Menard Press and Menard Medames
Unsolicited Manuscripts: No

ℳ
Mercat Press

Non-fiction Scottish interest titles, no novels or poetry.

Editor(s): Tom Johnstone, Seán Costello, Catherine Read
Address: 53 South Bridge, Edinburgh EH1 1YS
Telephone: 0131 622 8219
Fax: 0131 557 8149
Email: sean.costello@jthin.co.uk (or) tom.johnstone@jthin.co.uk
Website: www.mercatpress.com
Imprints: Mercat Press
Parent Company: James Thin Ltd
Payment Details: Annual royalty on copies sold
Unsolicited Manuscripts: Yes - preferably sample chapters and synopsis

Mercier Press

Publishers of Irish literature, folklore, history, politics, humour, theology, general non-fiction.

Address: 5 French Church Street, Cork, Ireland
Telephone: +353 21 4275 040
Fax: +353 21 4274 969
Email: books@mercier.ie
Website: www.mercier.ie
Imprints: Marino Books, 16 Hume Street, Dublin 2, Ireland. Publishers of fiction, children's fiction, current affairs, health, mind and spirit, general non-fiction
Parent Company: Mercier Press
Unsolicited Manuscripts: Synopsis and sample chapters preferred

The Merlin Press

The Merlin Press publishes books in the humanities and social sciences, including the Annual Socialist Register.

Editor(s): A Zurbrugg
Address: P O Box 30705, London WC2E 8QD
Telephone: 020 7836 3020
Fax: 020 7497 0309
Email: tz@merlinpress.co.uk
Website: www.merlinpress.co.uk
Imprints: Greenprint
Payment Details: Royalties on copies sold
Unsolicited Manuscripts: No

Merrell Publishers Ltd

Publishers of books on fine art, decorative art, photography, architecture, textiles and design.

Editor(s): Julian Honer
Address: 42 Southwark Street, London SE1 1UN
Telephone: 020 7403 2047
Fax: 020 7407 1333
Email: mail@merrellpublishers.com
Imprints: Merrell
Unsolicited Manuscripts: All correspondence to Hugh Merrell, Publisher

Merrick & Day

Merrick & Day publish a specialist range of curtain making and design books for professional curtain makers, interior designers and anyone with an interest in soft furnishings.

Address: Redbourne Hall, Redbourne, Gainsborough, Lincs DN21 4JS
Telephone: 01652 648814
Fax: 01652 648104
Email: sales@merrick-day.com
Website: www.merrick-day.com
Imprints: Merrick & Day

Merton Priory Press Ltd

A small independent publisher of academic and mid-market British history, especially local history and industrial history. About six new titles a year. Proposals from young academic historians seeking publication of their first book welcome.

Editor(s): Philip Riden
Address: 67 Merthyr Road, Whitchurch, Cardiff CF14 1DD
Telephone: 029 2052 1956
Fax: 029 2062 3599
Email: merton@dircon.co.uk
Imprints: Merton Priory Press
Parent Company: Independent
Payment Details: Royalties half-yearly, normally 10% retail
Unsolicited Manuscripts: Please send synopsis first

Methodist Publishing House

Popular religious hymn books, serious theology, religious music and drama, Bible study material and the DISCIPLE Bible study course.

Editor(s): Brian Thornton, Susan Hibbins
Address: 20 Ivatt Way, Peterborough PE3 7PG
Imprints: Foundery Press
Parent Company: The Methodist Church
Payment Details: Subject to negotiation
Unsolicited Manuscripts: Yes

Metro Publishing Ltd

General non-fiction publisher in categories including biography/autobiography, military, popular science, reference, cookery, health, popular psychology, self-help, giftbooks. Recent titles include Lynda Lee-Potter's Class Act, Can Reindeer Fly?, Little Book of Not Smoking, Real Fast Vegetarian Food. Also distributes the highly illustrated Carroll & Brown list - covering mind, body, spirit areas and subjects including cookery, health, giftbooks, parenting and self-help. Titles include Simon Brown's Face Reading, The Angelic Year, Get Fit, Feel Fantastic.

Address: 19 Gerrard Street, London W1V 7LA
Telephone: 020 7734 1411
Fax: 020 7734 1811
Email: metro@metro-books.com
Imprints: Metro Books, Richard Cohen Books
Payment Details: Royalties 6-monthly
Unsolicited Manuscripts: Yes with SAE to Peter Day

ℳ
Micelle Press

Technical books and monographs on the science of cosmetics, toiletries, fragrances, detergents and emulsions, and the ingredients and techniques used in the preparation of these products. Natural materials - their sources and applications.

Editor(s): Janet Barber
Address: 10-12 Ullswater Crescent, Weymouth, Dorset DT3 5HE
Telephone: 01305 781574
Fax: Same as phone
Email: tony@wdi.co.uk
Website: www.wdi.co.uk/micelle
Imprints: Micelle Press
Payment Details: By negotiation
Unsolicited Manuscripts: Send synopsis or sample chapter first

Midland Publishing

Aviation and railways.

Address: 4 Watling Drive, Hinckley, LE10 3EY
Telephone: 01455 254490
Fax: 01455 254495
Email: midlandbooks@compuserve.com
Parent Company: Ian Allan Group Ltd
Unsolicited Manuscripts: No

Midnag (Mid Northumberland Arts Group)

Publishing programme centres on literature and visual arts.

Editor(s): Managing Editor: G S Payne
Address: Pick Sharpeners' Shop, Woodhorn Colliery Museum, Ashington, Northumberland NE63 9YF
Telephone: 01670 853962
Fax: 01670 810958
Imprints: MidNag
Parent Company: Mid Northumberland Arts Group
Payment Details: On application
Unsolicited Manuscripts: No

Milestone Publications

Milestone Publications is the publishing and bookselling division of Goss & Crested China Ltd. We only publish books on Goss & Crested china and English heraldic porcelain.

Editor(s): Nicholas Pine
Address: 62 Murray Road, Horndean, Waterlooville, Hants PO8 9JL
Telephone: 023 9259 7440
Fax: 023 9259 1975
Email: info@gosschinaclub.demon.co.uk
Website: www.gosschinaclub.co.uk
Imprints: Milestone, Milestone Publications
Parent Company: Goss & Crested China Ltd
Unsolicited Manuscripts: Should never be sent

ℳ
Miller's Publications Ltd

Miller's Antiques Price Guide, Miller's Collectables Price Guide, Miller's Collectors Cars Price Guide, Miller's Classic Motorcycles Price Guide. Antique and Collectables reference books and directories.

Editor(s): Elizabeth Norfolk, Madeleine Marsh, Mick Walker, Dave Selby
Address: The Cellars, 5 High Street, Tenterden, Kent TN30 6BN
Telephone: 01580 766411
Fax: 01580 766100
Email: firstnamesurname@millers.uk.com
Website: www.millers.uk.com
Parent Company: Octopus Publishing Group Ltd

Harvey Miller Publishers

History of art, reference works; particularly medieval art and history, and 17th century studies.

Editor(s): Johan Van der Beke
Address: 2 Byron Mews, London NW3 2NQ
Telephone: 020 7284 4359
Fax: 020 7267 8764
Email: johan.van.der.beke@brepols.com
Website: www.brepols.com
Parent Company: Brepols Publishers
Unsolicited Manuscripts: No

J Garnet Miller Ltd
Plays and theatre books.

Address: 10 Station Road, Industrial Estate, Colwall WR13 6RN
Telephone: 01684 540154
Fax: Same as phone
Parent Company: Cressrelles Publishing Co
Unsolicited Manuscripts: Yes

Mind Publications
Mental health, self-help, psychiatric drug information, complementary therapies, advocacy and mental health legislation.

Editor(s): Anny Brackx
Address: Granta House, 15-19 Broadway, Stratford, London E15 4BQ
Telephone: 020 8221 9660
Fax: 020 8221 9681
Email: a.brackx@mind.org.uk
Parent Company: Mind
Unsolicited Manuscripts: No

ℳ
Minerva Press Ltd

Founded in 1992, the Minerva imprint dates back to 1792. Publishes fiction and non-fiction; biography, poetry, children's and religious books. Specialises in new authors who may be asked to contribute towards the cost of publication; publishes around 250 titles a year. No 'adult' or sexually explicit material. Unsolicited manuscripts, synopses and ideas for books welcome.

Address: 6th Floor, 1 Cavendish Place, London W1B 2HS
Telephone: 020 7580 4114
Fax: 020 7580 9256
Email: mail@minerva-press.co.uk
Website: www.minerva-press.co.uk
Parent Company: Hybeck Holdings Ltd
Payment Details: Royalties twice-yearly
Unsolicited Manuscripts: Yes

University Press of Mississippi

UPM publish a broad range of scholarly, academic and general interest titles encompassing: art & photgraphy, film, popular culture, biography, literature & literary critism, music, American history and civil rights.

Editor(s): Craig Gill
Address: C/o Roundhouse Publishing Ltd, Millstone, Limers Lane, Northam, Devon, EX39 2RG
Telephone: 01237 474474
Fax: 01237 474774
Email: round.house@fsbdial.co.uk
Website: www.roundhouse.net
Imprints: Banner Books
Payment Details: Royalties twice yearly
Unsolicited Manuscripts: No

Mitchell Beazley

Antiques, the arts, crafts, interior design, architecture, gardening, sex and health, wine, cookery and reference books.

Address: 2-4 Heron Quays, London E14 4JP
Telephone: 020 7531 8400
Fax: 020 7531 8650
Website: www.mitchell-beazley.co.uk
Parent Company: Octopus Publishing Group Ltd

Monarch Books

We publish about 35 Christian books per year, ranging from theology and apologetics to psychology, biography, the spiritual life and education. We do not handle fiction, poetry or children's literature. Most of our books are from UK authors and we welcome new authors and ideas.

Editor(s): Tony Collins
Address: Concorde House, Grenville Place, London NW7 3SA
Telephone: 020 8959 3668
Fax: 020 8959 3678
Email: monarch@angushudson.com
Imprints: Monarch
Payment Details: We pay full royalties
Unsolicited Manuscripts: Yes

ℳ
Moorley's Print & Publishing Ltd

All following the Christian faith only: drama scripts; school assemblies; adult verse; children's recitations; prayers and meditations; humorous monologues; Bible study notes for small groups. Commissioned publications undertaken on most subjects.

Editor(s): John R Moorley
Address: 23 Park Road, Ilkeston, Derbyshire DE7 5DA
Telephone: 0115 932 0643
Fax: 0115 932 0643
Email: info@moorleys.co.uk
Imprints: Moorley's, Pawprint Music
Payment Details: Royalties on sales
Unsolicited Manuscripts: No - prior correspondence required

Motor Racing Publications Ltd

Specialist publishers of well-researched and highly illustrated books for competition, performance and classic car enthusiasts, including marque and model histories, biographies and technical and practical books. Subjects published range from Mini to Rolls-Royce, Jeep to Land Rover, MG to Porsche and Cylinder Head Modification to Turbocharging. Publishing proposals welcomed for 'How To' books on competition and road car tuning and modification. Editorial, production and complete publishing service offered to companies or individuals requiring corporate, promotional or personal books.

Editor(s): John Blunsden and John Plummer
Address: Unit 6, The Pilton Estate, 46 Pitlake, Croydon CR0 3RY
Telephone: 020 8681 3363
Fax: 020 8760 5117
Email: mrp.books@virgin.net
Website: www.oberon.co.uk/mrp
Imprints: MRP and The Fitzjames Press
Parent Company: Motor Racing Publications Ltd
Payment Details: Royalties paid twice yearly
Unsolicited Manuscripts: Accepted but initial contact with synopsis recommended

MP Press

Provide publishing/typesetting service for potential authors/projects connected with cricket - history, biography, statistical. Works thus far published: 'Tragic White Roses' Biography of Yorkshire cricketers Alonzo Drake and Major Booth. 'A Century of Headingley Tests 1899-1999' by Paul E Dyson.

Address: 32 Louden Road, Scholes, Rotherham, South Yorkshire S61 2SU
Telephone: 0114 2450119
Fax: Same as phone
Email: mppress@supanet.com
Payment Details: Work on 50/50 costing to cover printing etc where work would not normally be produced
Unsolicited Manuscripts: Only on request after initial enquiry

Multi-Sensory Learning

Special needs titles including a fully structured, integrated and cumulative literacy skills programme.

Editor(s): Philippa Attwood
Address: Earlstrees Court, Earlstrees Road, Corby, Northants NN17 4HH
Telephone: 01536 399003
Fax: 01536 399012
Email: firstbest9@aol.com
Parent Company: First And Best In Education
Payment Details: Royalties
Unsolicited Manuscripts: No

M
Multilingual Matters Ltd

Academic publishers in the fields of applied linguistics, translation studies and tourism. Also parents and teachers' guides and general information on bilingualism.

Address: Frankfurt Lodge, Clevedon Hall, Victoria Road, Clevedon BS21 7HH
Telephone: 01275 876519
Fax: 01275 871673
Email: info@multilingual-matters.com
Website: www.multilingual-matters.com
Imprints: Channel View Publications

John Murray (Publishers) Ltd

School books, success study books, history, biography, travel, art and architecture, politics, current affairs, war and military.

Editor(s): Grant McIntyre, Caroline Knox, Gail Pirkis
Address: 50 Albemarle Street, London W1S 4BD
Telephone: 020 7493 4361
Fax: 020 7499 1792
Payment Details: Royalties paid twice-yearly
Unsolicited Manuscripts: No

National Museum of Wales

The National Museums and Galleries of Wales (NMGW) exist for the advancement of education of the public, through a general knowledge of the archaeology, art, biodiversity, geology and social and industrial history of Wales. It comprises eight museums - National Museum and Gallery, which houses art, archaeology, geology, zoology and botany; The Museum of Welsh Life, featuring over forty buildings from historic periods in Wales and holding collections of national, social and cultural interests; Roman Legionary Museum Caerleon, Segontium Roman Museum, Welsh Slate Museum, Museum of the Welsh Woollen Industry Dre-Fach Felindre, Turner House Gallery Penarth and Big Pit National Mining Museum of Wales. NMGW regularly publishes academic and popular books in these subject areas.

Editor(s): Elin ap Hywel
Address: National Museum and Gallery, Cathays Park, Cardiff CF10 3NP
Telephone: 029 2057 3248
Fax: 029 2022 6938
Email: post@nmgw.ac.uk
Website: www.nmgw.ac.uk
Imprints: National Museums and Galleries of Wales
Unsolicited Manuscripts: No

Peter Nahum At The Leicester Galleries Ltd

Illustrated art books and pamphlets. Example of titles: Burne-Jones, The Pre-Raphaelites And Their Century; Michael Rothenstein's Boxes; Fairy Folk In Fairy Land (William Allingham's fairy poem illustrated by Peter Nahum); Burne-Jones - A Quest For Love.

Editor(s): Peter Nahum
Address: 5 Ryder Street, London SW1Y 6PY
Telephone: 020 7930 6059
Fax: 020 7930 4678
Email: peternahum@leicestergalleries.com
Parent Company: The Leicester Galleries

N
National Academy Press

Publishes the reports issued by the National Academy of Science, the National Academy of Engineering, the Institute of Medicine and the National Research Council, all operating under a charter granted by the Congress of the United States of America. Subjects: science, technology, engineering, medicine and health as well as publishing popular trade books under its imprint Joseph Henry Press

Address: PO Box 317, Oxford, OX2 9RU
Telephone: 01865 865466
Fax: 01865 862763
Email: nap@oppuk.co.uk
Website: www.nas.edu
Imprints: Joseph Henry Press
Parent Company: National Academy Press
Unsolicited Manuscripts: No

The National Archives Of Scotland

The National Archives of Scotland preserves and makes available the historical records of Scotland. Its collections span the 12th - 21st centuries and range from the records of Scottish government prior to the Union of 1707 and the new Scottish Parliament court and legal records, local authority and church records, private archives, family papers, records of institutions, businesses and industrial firms as well as thousands of maps and plans. Our publications are designed to make the holdings of the NAS more accessible to amateur and professional searchers alike. They include indexes and texts of the older groups of records, educational publications for schools, guides for specific researchers and source lists. Many are published under the NAS imprint, others have been published by The Stationery Office and its predecessor, HMSO.

Address: HM General Register House, Edinburgh EH1 3YY
Telephone: 0131 535 1314
Fax: 0131 535 1360
Email: research@nas.gov.uk
Website: www.nas.gov.uk
Unsolicited Manuscripts: We do not accept unsolicited manuscripts

The National Assembly For Wales

The Statistical Directorate in the National Assembly for Wales produces a range of statistical publications covering topics such as population, education, agriculture, transport, local government finance, road accidents, health, housing and social services. For a copy of the leaflet 'Statistical Publications', that provides a list of the publications that are produced, along with the expected publication dates and prices, please telephone the National Assembly for Wales at the number below.

Address: Statistical Directorate, Publications Unit, Cathays Park, Cardiff CF10 3NQ
Telephone: 029 2082 5054
Fax: 029 2082 5350
Email: stats.pubs@wales.gsi.gov.uk
Imprints: Statistical Directorate
Parent Company: National Statistics
Unsolicited Manuscripts: No

National Children's Bureau

NCB promotes the well-being of all children and young people across every aspect of their lives. NCB advocates the participation of children and young people in all matters affecting them. NCB challenges disadvantage in childhood.

NCB is one of the leading publishers in the field of children's services, with a wide range of books, reports, training and development resources and videos to support professionals, parents, and children and young people. Subjects include child development, parenting programmes, sex education, nursery care and education, and special needs.
Address: 8 Wakley Street, London EC1V 7QE
Telephone: 020 7843 6000
Fax: 020 7278 9512
Website: www.ncb.org.uk
Imprints: National Children's Bureau Enterprises
Parent Company: NCB
Unsolicited Manuscripts: No

N
National Coaching Foundation (NCF)

The NCF publishes material in various formats for the education and information of sports coaches. Most material produced is distributed by Coachwise, the trading arm of the NCF, but also by governing bodies of sport. The NCF welcomes authors writing on sports science or coaching issues in generic or sports-specific contexts. The NCF also commissions authors with special interest in these areas for in-house projects.

Editor(s): Bill Galvin, Anne Simpkin, Nicola Cooke
Address: 114 Cardigan Road, Headingley, Leeds LS6 3BJ
Telephone: 0113 2744802
Fax: 0113 2755019
Email: mdrake@coachwise.ltd.uk
Website: www.ncf.org.uk
Parent Company: National Coaching Foundation
Payment Details: Negotiable
Unsolicited Manuscripts: To Bill Galvin, Head of Publications

National Council for Voluntary Organisations (NCVO)

Produces books for the voluntary sector. Major publications include: Voluntary Agencies Directory 2000 - over 2800 contact details for UK voluntary organisations. Good Guide Series - Good Employment Guide, Good Financial Management Guide, Good Trustee Guide. Also a range of publications covering the voluntary sector in subject areas such as Europe, Trusteeship and Rural and the new Voluntary Sector Almanacs series.

Address: Hamilton House, Earlstrees Court, Earlstrees Road, Corby NN17 4AX
Telephone: 01536 399016
Fax: 01536 399012
Email: HHmailing@aol.com
Website: www.ncvo-vol.org.uk
Imprints: NCVO Publications
Parent Company: NCVO
Unsolicited Manuscripts: No thank you

National Extension College (NEC)

Distance learning courses, NVQ training materials, open learning packs, training resources, consultancy and staff development packs. NEC is a self-financing educational trust and is one of the UK's most successful open learning providers.

Address: The Michael Young Centre, Purbeck Road, Cambridge CB2 2HN
Telephone: 01223 400200
Fax: 01223 313586
Email: info@nec.ac.uk
Website: www.nec.ac.uk
Imprints: NEC
Unsolicited Manuscripts: No

National Library Of Scotland

Publishes bibliographies, facsimiles, catalogues, literary and historical books mainly of Scottish interest. Tends to publish in partnership with commercial publishing houses.

Editor(s): Head of Public Programmes: Kenneth Gibson
Address: George 1V Bridge, Edinburgh EH1 1EW
Telephone: 0131 226 4531
Fax: 0131 622 4803
Email: enquiries@nls.uk
Website: www.nls.uk
Unsolicited Manuscripts: Send outline and covering letter in first instance

National Portrait Gallery

Publishers of books on art, biography and cultural history; exhibition catalogues and educational material; as well as posters, postcards and unusual gifts and stationery.

Editor(s): Publishing Manager: Position not yet filled; Sales and Marketing: Pallavi Vadhia; Senior Editor: Anjali Bulby; Editor: Susie Foster
Address: Publications Department, 2 St Martin's Place, London WC2H 0HE
Telephone: 020 7312 2482 or 020 7306 0055 ext 253
Fax: 020 7306 0092
Email: publications@npg.org.uk
Website: www.npg.org.uk

National Trust

Publishers of full colour illustrated books on social history, art and architecture, gardening, cookery, landscape and countryside and books for children.

Address: 36 Queen Anne's Gate, London, SW1H 9AS
Telephone: 0207 222 9251
Fax: 0207 222 5097
Website: www.nationaltrust.org.uk
Unsolicited Manuscripts: No

The Natural History Museum - Publishing Division

Popular natural history, academic and scholarly; biology and zoology; fine art and art history; geography and geology; scientific and technical.

Editor(s): Head of Publishing: Jane Hogg; Editorial Manager: Trudy Brannan; Production Manager: Lynn Millhouse
Address: Cromwell Road, London SW7 5BD
Telephone: 020 7942 5304
Fax: 020 7942 5010
Email: publishing@nhm.ac.uk
Website: www.nhm.ac.uk/publishing/
Imprints: The Natural History Museum
Unsolicited Manuscripts: No

Need2Know

Need2Know publishes a distinctive series of self-help non-fiction for the general reader. Subjects fall within the consumer/health/personal relationship areas. Current titles include A Parent's Guide To Dyslexia, Make The Most Of Your Retirement, The Facts About The Menopause, Make The Most Of Being A Carer, It's Up To You - Your Blueprint For A Better Life and The Green Guide to Better Living. We are open to ideas and proposals for new titles, especially from experts/practitioners in their subject.

Editor(s): James Feeke
Address: Remus House, Coltsfoot Drive, Woodston, Peterborough PE2 9JX
Telephone: 01733 898103
Fax: 01733 313524
Email: andrew@forwardpress.co.uk
Website: www.forwardpress.co.uk
Parent Company: Forward Press Ltd
Payment Details: Advance, 15% royalties
Unsolicited Manuscripts: Yes, please include postage for return

Neil Wilson Publishing Ltd

NWP has reorganised into 4 main imprints to cover specific categories. Angels' Share publishes books on Whisky, including history, leisure, biography etc and alcoho-related subjects as well as food and cookery. The Inn Pin covers outdoor pursuits such as hillwalking and climbing. Vital Spark publishes humour and NWP will cover general non-fiction such as history, reference and true crime.

The 11:9 fiction imprint (backed by the National Lottery New Directions fund) is managed by NWP and publishes contemporary Scottish fiction.
Editor(s): Neil Wilson
Address: 303a The Pentagon Centre, 36 Washington Street, Glasgow G3 8AZ
Telephone: 0141 221 1117
Fax: 0141 221 5363
Email: info@nwp.sol.co.uk
Website: www.nwp.co.uk, www.theinnpin.co.uk, www.vitalspark.co.uk, www.angelshare.co.uk, www.11-9.co.uk
Imprints: NWP, Angels' Share, Vital Spark, The Inn Pin, 11:9
Payment Details: Royalties twice-annually
Unsolicited Manuscripts: Yes

Network Educational Press Ltd

The company focuses its activity on the quality of teaching and learning in mainstream education, working with teachers and their managers in three ways: publishing high-quality, accessible and practical books; producing quality educational conferences; providing in-service training for teachers. All these activities draw upon current practical research, particularly that on how the brain functions, and then present the outcomes in ways that can be applied directly to the classroom. Examples of titles: Accelerated Learning In Practice (Smith); Accelerated Learning In The Classroom (Smith); Effective Learning Activities (Dickinson); Raising Boys' Achievement (Pickering); Effective Provision For Able And Talented Children (Teare); Making Pupil Data Powerful (Pringle and Cobb); Improving Personal Effectiveness for Managers in Schools (Johnston); Best Behaviour (Relf et al); Imagine That... (Bowkett); Effective Careers Education and Guidance (Edwards and Barnes); The Effective School Governor (Marriott); Closing the Learning Gap (Hughes); Lessons are for Learning (Hughes); The alps approach (Accelerated Learning in the Primary School) (Smith and Call). The Learners Revolution (Dryden and Vos); Wise-up (Claxton).

Editor(s): Gina Walker, Carol Thompson, Chris Griffin, Carol Etherington, Jan Baiton, Anne Oppenheimer
Address: Box 635, Stafford ST16 1BF
Telephone: 01785 225515
Fax: 01785 228566
Email: enquiries@networkpress.co.uk
Website: www.networkpress.co.uk
Imprints: School Effectiveness Series, Accelerated Learning Series, Educational Personal Management Series, Visions of Education Series
Unsolicited Manuscripts: Yes, considered

New City

Publishers of religious books.

Editor(s): Callan Slipper
Address: 57 Twyford Avenue, London W3 9PZ
Telephone: 020 8993 6944
Fax: Same as phone
Email: newcity@care4free.net
Unsolicited Manuscripts: To Editor

New Clarion Press

New Clarion Press is an independent UK publisher of books on history, politics and social policy written from a radical and reforming perspective.

Editor(s): Chris Bessant
Address: 5 Church Row, Gretton, Cheltenham GL54 5HG
Telephone: 01242 620623
Fax: Same as phone
Email: newclarionpress.co.uk
Website: www.newclarionpress.co.uk
Payment Details: Usually by royalty
Unsolicited Manuscripts: Synopsis in first instance

New European Publications Limited

New European Publications Limited was founded in 1987 to publish the Journal New European which is now published in association with MCB University Press in Bradford. NEP publishes World Review (Ed by Sir Richard Body MP). It consists of articles by authors writing on the themes of their own books. NEP also publishes books, mainly on European subjects, both independently and with other publishers, but also likes to branch out into fields which happen to interest its directors.

Editor(s): Sir Richard Body, John Coleman
Address: 14-16 Carroun Road, London SW8 1JT
Telephone: 020 7582 3996
Imprints: NEP
Parent Company: New European Publications Limited
Unsolicited Manuscripts: Authors should consult us before sending mss

New Fiction

The New Fiction imprint was launched in 1992 to provide a platform for the work of short story writers and promote it to a wider audience. Editorial Criteria: We are looking for stories that are well-written and provide a 'good read'. The following questions, which we ask ourselves when considering stories for publication, will give you an idea of the specific things we look for. Beginning: Does the story start at an interesting point in the action, that encourages the reader's curiosity and emotions? Characterisation: Are the characters believable? Are they revealed by what they do and say rather than explanation from the author? Content: Does the story keep your attention? If the story is based on fact - are the facts right? If applicable, does the story fulfil the criteria of the genre? Dialogue: Is the dialogue natural? Does the way a character says something fit that character? Writing: Does the writing convey meaning clearly and concisely? Ending: Is the ending believable, satisfying and logical in the context of the story? Contact the address below for submission guidelines.

Editor(s): Heather Killingray
Address: New Fiction, Remus House, Coltsfoot Drive, Woodston, Peterborough PE2 9JX
Telephone: 01733 898101
Fax: 01733 313524
Website: www.forwardpress.co.uk
Parent Company: Forward Press Ltd
Payment Details: Royalties 7.5% of total sales receipts, as calculated 1 year after publication, providing sales target is met, will be split equally between authors published in the book

N
New Holland Publishers (UK) Ltd

International co-edition publishers of illustrated books on natural history, travel, cookery, needlecrafts and handicrafts, interior design, DIY and gardening. Our International travel andwildlife programme covers numerous destinations and includes: travel guides, diving, climbing and golf guides; large format wildlife and 'wild places' titles.

Editor(s): Yvonne McFarlen - Publishing Director, Rosemary Wilkinson - Publishing Manager, Jo Hemmings - Publishing Manager
Address: Garfield House, 86 - 88 Edgeware Road, London, W2 2EX
Telephone: 020 7724 7773
Fax: 020 7724 6184
Email: postmaster@nhpub.co.uk
Website: www.newhollandpublishers.com
Imprints: New Holland, Struik, Southern, Zebra
Parent Company: Millennium Entertainment Group Africa (MEGA)
Payment Details: By negotiation
Unsolicited Manuscripts: Yes

New Island Books

Founded in 1992, New Island Books has successfully continued the innovative and often polemical tradition of its predecessor, The Raven Arts Press. Publishers of fiction, biography, drama and current affairs, titles include The Truth About the Irish by Terry Eagleton and Are You Somebody? by Nuala O' Faolain.

Editor(s): Managing Editor: Ciara Considine, Executive Editor: Dermot Bolger
Address: New Island Books Ltd, 2 Brookside, Dundrum Road, Dublin 14, Ireland
Telephone: +3531 2986867
Fax: +3531 2987912
Email: brookside@iol.ie
Imprints: New Island Books
Payment Details: Own standard contract / royalties paid twice yearly
Unsolicited Manuscripts: Fiction/Non-Fiction - synopsis and sample of writing plus SAE

New Living Publishers

Pentecostal publisher. Only publishing books written by Terry Atkinson. Evangelical, Fundamental and Pentecostal.

Editor(s): Steve Martin
Address: 164 Radcliffe New Road, Whitefield, Manchester M45 7TU
Telephone: 0161 7661166
Fax: Same as phone
Email: theway@newlivingpublishers.co.uk
Website: www.newlivingpublishers.co.uk
Unsolicited Manuscripts: No

New Playwrights' Network

Publishes plays for amateur performance.

Editor(s): L G Smith
Address: 10 Station Road, Colwall, Herefordshire WR13 6RN
Telephone: 01684 540154
Fax: Same as phone

N
New World Press

High-quality general non-fiction and educational books, covering literature, science, culture, philosopy, spirituality. Write to Sales Department for current lists. Bi-monthly journal New World covering similar subjects and short stories. In addition to the scope of books indicated, a new bi-monthly magazine with cutting-edge essays on science, philosophy, culture and spirituality.

Editor(s): Matt Fopson
Address: PO Box 919, Sutton SM2 6ZU
Telephone: 020 8643 3967
Fax: 020 8286 0468
Email: editor@nwpress.co.uk
Website: nwpress.co.uk
Imprints: New World, Knightscross
Unsolicited Manuscripts: No unsolicited mss. Typewritten synopses considered; please allow 6-8 weeks for a response

Nexus Special Interests

Hobby and leisure in the core subject areas of modelling, model engineering, radio control modelling, workshop practice, home brewing and military modelling.

Address: Nexus House, Azalea Drive, Swanley, Kent BR8 8HU
Telephone: 01322 660070
Fax: 01322 616309
Parent Company: Highbury House Communications
Payment Details: Standard authors' contract advance and royalties
Unsolicited Manuscripts: Yes

NIACE

NIACE publishes books, training packs, directories and journals aimed at academics, policy-makers and practitioners in adult education. Our aim is to inform policy and practice for adult learning by publishing well-researched material, presented in an accessible and attractive format. Our staff development and training packs are photocopiable. Proposals for publication should be sent to Virman Man, Senior Publications Officer.

Editor(s): Senior Publications Officer: Virman Man
Address: 21 De Montfort Street, Leicester LE1 7GE
Telephone: 0116 204 4200
Fax: 0116 285 4514
Email: enquiries@niace.org.uk
Website: www.niace.org.uk

NMS Publishing Ltd

Scottish history and culture, biography, Scottish literary anthologies, international art, archaeology, geology, museum studies science and technology.

Editor(s): Lesley Taylor
Address: Royal Museum, Chambers Street, Edinburgh EH1 1JF
Telephone: 0131 247 4026
Fax: 0131 247 4012
Email: publishing@nms.ac.uk
Website: www.nms.ac.uk
Payment Details: Royalties
Unsolicited Manuscripts: Synopsis and sample chapter only

N
No Exit Press

Leading independent publisher of crime and noir fiction.

Address: 18 Coleswood Road, Harpenden, Herts AL5 1EQ
Telephone: 01582 761264
Fax: 01582 712244
Email: info@noexit.co.uk
Website: www.noexit.co.uk
Unsolicited Manuscripts: No

North York Moors National Park Authority

Publish booklets on walking in the North York Moors as well as booklets on local history and natural history of interest to visitors to the area. Also publish planning documents and strategies relevant to the area and research papers relating to archaeology, the environment, etc.

Editor(s): Jill Renney
Address: The Old Vicarage, Bondgate, Helmsley, York YO62 5BP
Telephone: 01439 770657
Fax: 01439 770691
Email: j.renney@northyorkmoors.npa.gov.uk
Website: www.northyorkmoors-npa.gov.uk

Northcote House Publishers Ltd

Established in 1985, publishes up to 30 titles each year in the fields of: literary criticism (Writers and their Work series); education and education management (Resources In Education); careers and self-development (Starting Out...); and a small number of educational dance and drama titles. In addition to the above, a series of studies of specific works of literature is in preparation, aimed at A level and higher education students in both English and Modern Languages.

Editor(s): Brian Hulme
Address: Horndon House, Horndon, Tavistock, Devon PL19 9NQ
Telephone: 01822 810066
Fax: 01822 810034
Email: northcotehouse@virgin.net
Imprints: Writers and their Work
Parent Company: Northcote House Publishers Ltd
Payment Details: Annual royalty by contract
Unsolicited Manuscripts: Well argued proposals in the above subjects with good marketing credentials welcome

Nottingham University Press

Agriculture, medicine, geography, food science, law, sports and engineering. Other subject areas also considered.

Editor(s): D J A Cole
Address: Manor Farm, Main Street, Thrumpton, Nottingham NG11 0AX
Telephone: 0115 9831011
Fax: 0115 9831003
Email: editor@nup.com
Website: www.nup.com
Imprints: Castle Publications
Unsolicited Manuscripts: Yes

NTC Publications Ltd

Specialises in publications for business professionals, particularly in economics, finance, advertising, marketing and the media. NTC publishes a wide range of business books, reports, journals, magazines and industry forecasts and surveys.

Editor(s): David Roberts
Address: Farm Road, Henley-On-Thames, Oxon RG9 1EJ
Telephone: 01491 411000
Fax: 01491 418600
Email: info@ntc.co.uk
Imprints: ADMAP, NTC Research, NTC Publications, World Advertising Research Center, NTC Economic & Financial Publishing
Parent Company: Information Sciences Ltd
Payment Details: Royalties/Contract subject to agreement
Unsolicited Manuscripts: Yes

Oak Tree Press

Ireland's leading publisher of business and professional titles. Specialising in management, human reources, accountancy and marketing.

Editor(s): David Givens - Commissioning Editor
Address: Merrion Building, Lower Merrion Street, Dublin 2, Ireland
Telephone: 353 1 6761600
Fax: 353 1 6761644
Email: oaktreep@iol.ie
Website: www.oaktreepress.com
Parent Company: Cork Publishing Ltd
Unsolicited Manuscripts: Proposals and sample chapter

Oakwood Press & Oakwood Video Library

Established 1931. Family-owned company specialising in transport topics - buses, trams, canals, and especially railways. Producing books of interest to railway historians and enthusiasts alike. Catalogue available.

Editor(s): Various, contact name: Jane Kennedy - Proprietor
Address: PO Box 13, Usk NP15 1YS
Telephone: 01291 650444
Fax: 01291 650484
Email: oakwood-press@dial.pipex.com
Website: www.oakwood-press@dial.pipex.com
Unsolicited Manuscripts: Yes

Oasis Books

Oasis Books publishes pamplets and small limited edition books of poetry and innovative prose, not novels, usually 16 to 40 pages in length.

Editor(s): Ian Robinson
Address: 12 Stevenage Road, Fulham, London SW6 6ES
Telephone: 020 7736 5059
Payment Details: Copies usually
Unsolicited Manuscripts: For the foreseeable future it is best to write a letter of enquiry.

Oberon Books
Theatre books, play texts and translation of plays.

Editor(s): James Hogan, Torben Betts, Dan Steward
Address: 521 Caledonian Road, London N7 9RH
Telephone: 020 7607 3637
Fax: 020 7607 3629
Email: oberon.books@btinternet.com
Website: www.oberonbooks.com
Imprints: Oberon Modern Playwrights, Absolute Classics
Unsolicited Manuscripts: Yes

OCLC Europe, The Middle East & Africa

The Dewey Decimal Classification systems (DDC) is a general knowledge organisation tool that is continuously revised to keep pace with knowledge. The system was conceived by Melvil Dewey in 1873 and first published by Forest Press, which in 1888 became a division of OCLC Online Computer Library Center, Inc. The Dewey Decimal Classification is published in two editions, full and abridged. The Classification is kept up-to-date between editions through monthly posting of new and changed entries on the Dewey home page, and annual publication of additions and corrections in Dewey Decimal Classification Additions, Notes and Decisions (DC&). The full edition is also published in an enhanced electronic version, Dewey for Windows. Each update disc of Dewey for Windows incorporates the changes announced in DC&.

Editor(s): Editor: Joan S Mitchell, Assistant Editors: Julianne Beall, Winton E Matthews Jr, Gregory R New
Address: OCLC Europe, 7th Floor, Tricorn House, 51-53 Hagley Road, Edgbaston, Birmingham B16 8TP
Telephone: 0121 456 4656
Fax: 0121 456 4680
Email: europe@oclc.org
Website: www.oclc.org/europe
Imprints: Forest Press, Albany, New York, 1996
Parent Company: OCLC INC

The Octagon Press

Philosophy, psychology, Sufism, eastern classics and travel. We do not accept any manuscripts which we have not ourselves commissioned under any circumstances.

Editor(s): G R Schrager
Address: PO Box 227, London N6 4EW
Telephone: 020 8348 9392
Fax: 020 8341 5971
Email: octagon@octagonpress.com
Website: www.octagonpress.com
Unsolicited Manuscripts: No

Old Bailey Press

Old Bailey Press publishes a comprehensive range of law books for students and practitioners alike. Publications include Cracknell's Statutes; 150 Leading Cases Series; 101 Questions and Answers Series, Suggested Solutions Series, The Law in Practice Series and the Practitioner's Handbook, a compendium of recent developments in the areas of mainstream legal practice.

Editor(s): Vanessa Osborne
Address: 200 Greyhound Road, London W14 9RY
Telephone: Enquiries: 020 7386 9047 Orders: 020 7381 7407
Fax: 020 7386 0952
Email: obp@hltpublication.co.uk
Website: www.oldbaileypress.co.uk
Imprints: Old Bailey Press/HLT Publications
Parent Company: The HLT Group Ltd

Ollav Healer Publications

Self-publishing company with the following publications: A Path Directed (Life of James Cassidy, WW1 veteran and Belfast City missionary 1892-1970); Cousins (local history booklet); Clarendon, Belfast (locally set historical fiction); Circumstantial Evidence (evidence supporting biblical facts).

Editor(s): D Cassidy
Address: 9 Brunswick Park, Bangor, Co Down BT20 3DR
Telephone: 028 9147 3362
Unsolicited Manuscripts: No

Omnibus Press

The world's largest publisher of books about music, ranging from biographies to picture books and from classical and jazz to rock and pop. Distributors for Gramophone, RED, Firefly, Rogan House and others.

Editor(s): Chris Charlesworth
Address: 8-9 Frith Street, London W1V 5TZ
Telephone: 020 7434 0066
Fax: 020 7434 3310
Email: music@musicsales.co.uk
Website: omnibuspress.com
Imprints: Omnibus Press/Wise Publications/Ozone/Bobcat/Amsco
Parent Company: Music Sales Ltd
Unsolicited Manuscripts: To Chris Charlesworth

On Stream Publications Ltd

Publishers of non-fiction books including food and wine, health, academic, local history and commissioned commercial company histories and promotional literature. Editing and proof-reading services for books not published by us and design service for books and promotions.

Editor(s): Roz Crowley
Address: Cloghroe, Blarney, Co Cork, Ireland
Telephone: 353 214385798
Fax: Same as phone
Email: info@onstream.ie
Website: www.onstream.ie
Imprints: Forum Publications
Parent Company: On Stream Publications Ltd
Payment Details: Royalites paid twice yearly
Unsolicited Manuscripts: No

Oneworld Publications

An independent publishing house specialising in books on world religions, comparative religion, mysticism, philosophy, history, psychology and inspirational writing. Large enough to benefit from worldwide distribution we are also small enough to ensure that we publish only quality titles by authors who are leaders in their field.

Editor(s): Editorial Board
Address: 185 Banbury Road, Oxford OX2 7AR
Telephone: 01865 310597
Fax: 01865 310598
Email: info@oneworld-publications.com
Website: www.oneworld-publications.com
Payment Details: Advance and rate to be agreed on each case
Unsolicited Manuscripts: Enquire by letter first

Onlywomen Press Ltd

The radical edge of feminist, lesbian literature: fiction, political theory, poetry, literary criticism, lesbian romance and crime novels.

Editor(s): Apply first to company as a whole
Address: 40 St Lawrence Terrace, London W10 5ST
Telephone: 020 8354 0796
Fax: 020 8960 2817
Email: onlywomen_press@compuserve.com
Website: www.onlywomenpress.com
Imprints: Zest (lesbian romance), onlywomencrime (lesbian crime novels), Liaison (feminist theory and research)
Payment Details: By publishing contract
Unsolicited Manuscripts: Yes, see submission guidelines on our website or write to request a copy

Open Gate Press

Founded in 1988 by a group of psychoanalysts, social psychiatrists and artists to provide a forum for psychoanalytic social studies - a branch of psychoanalysis which Freud hoped would be a major contribution to the 'liberation of humanity from the pathology of civilisations'. Despite some attempts since Freud's time to apply psychoanalysis to social problems, his hopes have not been fulfilled, and the raison d'etre of Open Gate Press is to remedy this. The company publishes a series Psychoanalysis And Society as well as writings by experts in various fields of the social sciences, with the objective of arousing the interest of a wide public. The aim of the publishers is also to bring life to the increasingly moribund state of philosophy. Finally, the publishers are keen to promote debate on a wide variety of environmental issues.

Editor(s): Jeannie Cohen, Elisabeth Petersdorff
Address: 51 Achilles Road, London NW6 1DZ
Telephone: 020 7431 4391
Fax: 020 7431 5129
Email: books@opengatepress.co.uk
Website: www.opengatepress.co.uk
Imprints: Open Gate Press, Centaur Press, Linden Press
Parent Company: Open Gate Press
Payment Details: Royalties twice-yearly
Unsolicited Manuscripts: Synopses and ideas for books welcome

Open University Press

Subjects published in the areas of health and social welfare, counselling and psychotherapy, psychology, gender studies, sociology, cultural studies, politics, criminology, education and higher education.

Editor(s): Jacinta Evans
Address: Celtic Court, 22 Ballmoor, Buckingham MK18 1XW
Telephone: 01280 823388
Fax: 01280 823233
Email: enquiries@openup.co.uk
Website: www.openup.co.uk
Imprints: Open University Press
Unsolicited Manuscripts: No

Orchard Books

Children's fiction : board books, picture books, gift books. Young and older fiction.

Editor(s): Francesca Dow - Publishing Director
Address: 96 Leonard Street, London EC2A 4XD
Telephone: 020 7739 2929
Fax: 020 7739 2318
Email: ob@wattspub.co.uk
Parent Company: The Watts Publishing Group Ltd
Payment Details: By negotiation
Unsolicited Manuscripts: Yes - Synopsis and 1 chapter only + SAE

Oriel Stringer

Publishers of ornithological books covering the breeding biology of wild birds and their nesting sites.

Editor(s): M J Dawson
Address: 66 Tivoli Crescent, Brighton BN1 5ND
Telephone: 01273 723413

Orion Children's Books

Fiction, age range 0-14+.

Editor(s): Publisher: Judith Elliott
Address: Orion House, 5 Upper St Martin's Lane, London WC2H 9EA
Telephone: 020 7240 3444
Fax: 020 7379 6158
Imprints: Orion Children's Books, Dolphin Paperbacks
Parent Company: Orion Publishing Group
Unsolicited Manuscripts: No

Osborne Books Ltd

Publishers of business education and accounting texts for secondary and tertiary sectors under the Osborne Books imprint. Also publishers of local history and general historical books under the Osborne Heritage imprint.

Editor(s): Michael Fardon
Address: Unit 1b, Everoak Estate, Bromyard Road, St Johns, Worcester WR2 5HN
Telephone: 01905 748071
Fax: 01905 748952
Email: books@osbornebooks.co.uk
Website: www.osbornebooks.co.uk
Imprints: Osborne Books, Osborne Heritage
Payment Details: By negotiation
Unsolicited Manuscripts: To Editor

Osprey Publishing Ltd

Illustrated military history from around the world, covering the all-time greatest battles of land and air from antiquity to the present day. Osprey's series driven books detail weaponry, uniforms, military aviation, providing a reference source for historians, enthusiasts, wargamers and modellers.

The bimonthly Osprey Military Journal features illustrated articles spanning a wide range of military topics, as well as regular sections on culture, news and reviews. Osprey is also responsible for a range of innovative websites. History's major events come to life at www.essentialhistory.com. Find out all about Osprey books at www.ospreypublishing.com, or all about Osprey Military Journal at www.ospreymilitaryjournal.com.
Founded 1969, became independent from Reed Elsevier in 1998.
Address: Elms Court, Chapel Way, Botley, Oxford OX2 9LP
Telephone: 01865 727022
Fax: 01865 727017
Email: info@ospreypublishing.com
Website: www.ospreypublishing.com
Imprints: Men at Arms, Elite, Campaign, New Vanguard, Warrior, Order of Battle, Essentials, Aircraft of the Aces, Combat Aircraft
Payment Details: royalties paid twice a year
Unsolicited Manuscripts: No, detailed synopses only

Peter Owen

Literary (non-genre) adult fiction list, including work in translation. Biographies and memoirs of writers, artists, celebrities, etc. Only very rarely do we publish memoirs of lesser-known people. We also publish general non-fiction including history, literary criticism, arts subjects (not highly illustrated), social science, current affairs, philosophy, psychology and entertainment. Note that all manuscripts or, preferably, synopses and sample chapters, should be accompanied by return postage. No poetry.

Editor(s): Antonia Owen
Address: 73 Kenway Road, London SW5 0RE
Telephone: 020 7373 5628
Fax: 020 7373 6760
Email: admin@peterowen.com
Website: www.peterowen.com
Unsolicited Manuscripts: Only with prior request and SAE

Oxfam Publishing

Publishes and distributes books and other resource materials for development practitioners, policy makers, academics, schools, children and young people, as part of its programme of advocacy, education and information.

Editor(s): Kate Kilpatrick
Address: 274 Banbury Road, Oxford OX2 7DZ
Telephone: 01865 311311
Fax: 01865 312600
Email: publish@oxfam.org.uk
Website: www.oxfam.org.uk/publications.html
Imprints: Oxfam Publishing, Oxfam Education
Parent Company: Oxfam GB
Payment Details: Various
Unsolicited Manuscripts: No

Oxford University Press

A department of the University of Oxford. Furthers the University's objective of excellence in research, scholarship and education by publishing worldwide. It is the world's largest university press, publishing more than 4,000 titles a year. It has a presence in more than 50 countries, employing some 3,700 staff. Turnover in 1999/2000 was £324 million.

Address: Great Clarendon Street, Oxford OX2 6DP
Telephone: 01865 556767
Fax: 01865 556646
Email: enquiry@oup.co.uk
Website: www.oup.com
Parent Company: University of Oxford

Paragon House

Paragon House publish trade books, scholarly research, textbooks, and reference works in the areas of general philosophy, ethics, contemporary values, religion, social thought, women's studies, social sciences, and interdisciplinary studies.

Editor(s): Laureen Enright
Address: c/o Roundhouse Publishing Ltd, Millstone, Limers Lane, Northam, Devon, EX39 2RG
Telephone: 01237 474474
Fax: 01237 474774
Email: round.house@fsbdial.co.uk
Website: www.roundhouse.net
Payment Details: Royalties twice yearly
Unsolicited Manuscripts: No

P
Parkway Publishing

Books on Middle East, mainly Egypt. Non-fiction: facsimile editions of famous travel books. Examples: 1000 Miles Up The Nile by Amelia Edwards; Letters From Egypt by Florence Nightingale; Sultans in Splendour by Philip Mansel.

Address: Unit 3, Taylors Yard, 67 Aldenbrook Road, London SW!2 8AD
Telephone: 020 8772 3300
Fax: 020 8772 3309

Parthian Books

New Welsh fiction and drama in English. Translations of the Welsh Language Fiction. Previous titles include Work, Sex & Rugby; One Woman, One Voice; Fuse; Cardiff Cut

Editor(s): Richard Davies
Address: 53 Colum Road, Cardiff CF10 3EF
Telephone: 029 2034 1314
Fax: Same as phone
Email: parthianbooks@yahoo.co.uk
Website: www.parthianbooks.co.uk
Payment Details: 10% net sales
Unsolicited Manuscripts: No. Synopsis with sample chapters

PASS Publications
(Private Academic & Scientific Studies Ltd)

Publish a series of 10 books for GCE A level in pure mathematics, comprehensively covering the syllabus of most examination boards. They uniquely include (in Part 2) complete solutions to all exercises at the end of each chapter. Can be purchased separately or as a set (set price £95). Publish detailed solutions for the Edexel exams (1994 and continuing) in pure mathematics, mechanics and statistics; produced every year in September for the January and June exams. Also available for technicians are Electrical And Electronic Principles 1 & 2 (£12.95, £14.95) and Engineering Maths (2 books, £9.95 for both). Modular Textbooks, Pure Mathematics. P1, P2, P3, P4 (£13.95, £15.95, £14.95, £18.95 respectively) for 12 copies of P1, or P2, or P3 or P4 50% discount. In the year 2001, will publish New Editions for the modules P1 and P2 to conform with the new syllabus distribution P1, P2, P3. Also will publish GCSE Maths book. Make the grade at GCSE, Higher Tier. A comprehenshive easy to follow revision book with ample worked examples and examination tips by an examiner ISBN :1 872084 769 £12.95, special discount for schools.

P1 New Textbook published ISBN: 1 872684 67x, £7.95
P2 New Textbook to be published ISBN: 1 872684 726, £7.95
P3 New Textbook to be published ISBN: 1 872684 777, £7.95
Questions and full solutions for P2 New and P3 New to published for Edexcel examinations:
P2 New, ISBN: 1 872684 831, £6.95
P3 New, ISBN: 1 872684 882, £7.95

Editor(s): Anthony Nicolaides
Address: 11 Baring Road, London SE12 0JP
Telephone: 020 8857 4085
Fax: 020 8857 9427
Website: www.passpublications.com

P
PasTest

Publishers of revision books for undergraduate and postgraduate medical examinations. Coverage includes:

Undergraduate exams, MRCP 1 and MRCP 2, MRCPCH 1 and MRCPCH 2, MRCS Papers 1 and 2, MRCGP, DCH, DRCOG, MRCOG, FRCA and PLAB.
Editor(s): Sue Harrison
Address: Egerton Court, Parkgate Estate, Knutsford, Cheshire WA16 8DX
Telephone: 01565 752000
Fax: 01565 650264
Email: books@pastest.co.uk
Website: www.pastest.co.uk
Payment Details: Royalty or one off fee
Unsolicited Manuscripts: Yes

Paupers' Press

Publish booklets containing 10,000-15,000-word essays, mostly on literary criticism. Occasionally produce full-length books - but only to accommodate an exceptional manuscript. Publish up to 6 new titles a year, which are distributed in the US by Maurice Bassett. Also operate as a centre for Colin Wilson studies, publishing his work and essays on it by well-known Wilson scholars. Examples of titles: Sex And The Intelligent Teenager by Colin Wilson; Witchcraft And Misogyny by Samantha Giles; Woody Allen's Trilogy Of Terror by Christina Byrnes; So Far So Linear: responses to the work of Jeanette Winterson by Christopher Pressler; Fighting Fictions: the novels of B S Johnson by Nicolas Tredell. We also distribute selected titles for the US publishers Borgo Press and Robert Briggs Associates.

Editor(s): Colin Stanley
Address: 27 Melbourne Road, West Bridgford, Nottingham NG2 5DJ
Telephone: 0115 9815063
Fax: Same as phone
Email: stan2727uk@aol.com
Website: http://members.aol.com/stan2727uk/pauper.htm
Imprints: Paupers' Press
Unsolicited Manuscripts: No. Write in first instance outlining content of essay

Pavilion Books Limited

A substantial and varied list of high quality colour illustrated non-fiction books geared to international co-edition markets. Subjects covered include cookery, gardening, interiors, children's art, photography, travel, biography, humour and gift books.

Editor(s): Publisher: Vivien James
Address: London House, Great Eastern Wharf, Parkgate Road, London SW11 4NQ
Telephone: 020 7350 1230
Fax: 020 7350 1261
Email: info@pavilionbooks.co.uk
Website: www.pavilionbooks.co.uk
Parent Company: C & B Publishing Plc
Payment Details: Negotiable
Unsolicited Manuscripts: Yes - in writing only

Pavilion Publishing (Brighton) Ltd

Publishers of innovative, accessible training materials for health and social care. Areas of interest include mental health, learning disabilities, children and young people and staff development. Many packs cross-refernced to NVQ care levels II and III. We also publish a growing range of journals that look at the issues of putting research into practice.

Editor(s): Edwina Rowling, Justine Heathcote, Jo Hathaway, Julia Brennan
Address: The Ironworks, Cheapside, Brighton BN1 4GD
Telephone: 01273 623222
Fax: 01273 625526
Email: info@pavpub.co.uk
Website: www.pavpub.com
Imprints: Pavilion Publishing
Payment Details: Standard royalty
Unsolicited Manuscripts: Yes

PBN Publications

Publish transcripts of local (Sussex) archives which are of particular interest to family and local historians. Publications are either in book form or on microfiche.

Address: 22 Abbey Road, Eastbourne BN20 8TE
Telephone: 01323 731206

Pearson Education

See website home page.

Address: Pearson Education, Edinburgh Gate, Harlow, Essex CM20 2JE
Telephone: 01279 623623
Fax: 01279 431059
Email: firstname.lastname@pearsoned-ema.com
Website: www.pearsoned-ema.com
Imprints: Longman, Addison-Wesley, Financial Times Prentice Hall, Prentice Hall
Parent Company: Pearson Plc
Payment Details: On request
Unsolicited Manuscripts: Yes

J M Pearson & Son (Publishers) Ltd

Founded 1981; specialise in canal and railway related materials; all titles produced in-house.

Address: Tatenhill Common, Burton-on-Trent DE13 9RS
Telephone: 01283 713674
Fax: Same as phone
Email: jmpearson@jmpearson.co.uk
Website: www.jmpearson.co.uk
Unsolicited Manuscripts: No

Peartree Publications

Christian musicals and educational piano music.

Editor(s): Roger M Stepney
Address: 61 Peartree Lane, Little Common, Bexhill-On-Sea, East Sussex TN39 4RQ
Unsolicited Manuscripts: No

Peepal Tree Press

Peepal Tree is an independent publisher of Caribbean and black British fiction, literary criticism and history.

Editor(s): Jeremy Poynting
Address: 17 Kings Avenue, Leeds LS6 1QS
Telephone: 0113 2451703
Fax: 0113 2459616
Email: hannah@peepal.demon.co.uk
Payment Details: Usually 10% of net receipts
Unsolicited Manuscripts: Yes

Pen and Sword Books Ltd

Publisher's of Military History covering all periods from pre First World War to post Second World War. Topics include biographies, battleground guides, reference an regimental histories. Also publishes local history (Yorkshire).

Address: 49 Church Street, Barnsley S70 2AS
Telephone: 01226 734 555
Fax: 01226 734 438
Website: www.pen-and-sword.co.uk
Imprints: Leo Cooper, Wharncliffe Publishing
Payment Details: Royalties are paid twice a year
Unsolicited Manuscripts: In the first instance please send a synopsis.

P
Penhaligon Page

Penhaligon Page provides a showcase for today's poets. It incorporates the diverse styles and structures that the poetry world encounters. We are giving you the chance to become part of our voice, and join together with other poets. Poems no longer than 30 lines on any theme are considered.

Editor(s): Nathalie Nightingale
Address: Penhaligon Page Ltd, Remus House, Coltsfoot Drive, Woodston, Peterborough PE2 9JX
Telephone: 01733 898104
Fax: 01733 313524
Imprints: Poetry Today, Eden Press
Parent Company: Penhaligon Page Ltd
Unsolicited Manuscripts: Yes

Pentathol Publishing

No new material needed at present.

Editor(s): A E Cowen
Address: PO Box 92, 40 Gibson Street, Wrexham LL13 7NS
Unsolicited Manuscripts: No

The Pentland Press Limited

The Pentland Press welcomes new, unknown authors. We specialise in books the large publishing houses deem uncommercial. Small enough to retain a traditional family approach but large enough to publish over one hundred books every year. We are always interested to hear from authors who have written books in the following areas: autobiography, naval, military, aviation, biography, history, politics, religion, philosophy, self-help, literature, poetry and fiction. A preliminary letter is required before submitting manuscripts.

Address: 1 Hutton Close, South Church, Bishop Auckland, Durham DL14 6XB
Telephone: 01388 776555
Fax: 01388 776766
Email: manuscripts@pentlandpress.co.uk
Website: pentlandpress.co.uk
Unsolicited Manuscripts: Yes

Peridot Press Ltd

Peridot Press publishes easy-to-read, regularly updated reference books and websites including The Gap-Year Guidebook, The Gap-Year Website and The Specialist Speakers Directory. Main readers are students, parents and schools. We do not usually take unsolicited manuscripts but we employ people for short-term research and database work.

Address: 2 Blenheim Crescent, London W11 1NN
Telephone: 020 7221 7404
Website: www.gap-year.com
Imprints: Peridot

℘
Permanent Publications

Publishers of Permaculture Magazine and specialist books on environmental issues, sustainable design and permaculture.

Editor(s): Madeleine Harland
Address: The Sustainability Centre, East Meon, Hants GU32 1HR
Telephone: 01730 823311
Fax: 01730 823322
Email: info@permaculture.co.uk
Website: www.permaculture.co.uk
Imprints: Permanent Publications
Parent Company: Hyden House Ltd
Unsolicited Manuscripts: No

Perpetuity Press

Specialist journals, books and guides in the field of security, risk management, crime prevention, policing and community safety. Subjects covered in our publications include: crime against businesses; security and risk management; crises and disaster management; computer security; business continuity planning; CCTV; financial risk; retail crime; robbery; fraud; civil recovery; staff dishonesty; abuse and violence within the workplace; contigency planning. Journals include: Security Journal, Risk Management: An International Journal and Crime Prevention and Community safety: An International Journal. New in 2002 are Security Law Bulletin and Security in Practice. Recent books include: Human Error - by Design? Private Security, Crime at Work Volumes One and Two, Learning from Disasters: a Management Approach, Zero Tolerance Policing, Public Order Policing, Crime and Security: the Risk to Safe shopping and Commercial Robbery. Practitioner Guides to: Investigating Using the Internet; Executive Protection; Information Security Management; Security Surveys; Business Continuity Management and Fire Safety Management.

Editor(s): Karen Gill
Address: PO Box 376, Leicester LE2 1UP
Telephone: 0116 221 7778
Fax: 0116 221 7171
Email: info@perpetuitypress.co.uk
Website: www.perpetuitypress.co.uk
Unsolicited Manuscripts: Yes

The Perseus Books Group

The Perseus Books Group was created with the belief that an innovative and aggressive new model of publishing can fill a void in today's marketplace and allow works of quality to be published both profitably and well. Devoted entirely to supporting and fostering such works, each Perseus Books Group imprint is editorially independent and individually focused, and all are committed to publishing books that matter. Together the Group publishes for all serious adult readers across all disciplines and subjects.

Address: PO Box 317, Oxford, OX2 9RU
Telephone: 01865 865466
Fax: 01865 862763
Email: perseus@oppuk.co.uk
Website: www.perseusbooksgroup.com
Imprints: Basic Books, Basic Civitas Books, Counterpoint Press, Perseus Publishing, PublicAffairs, Westview Press
Unsolicited Manuscripts: No

Petroc Press

Educational books and other media for doctors, GPs, junior doctors in training as well as qualified professionals.

Editor(s): P L Clarke
Address: Gemini House, 162 Craven Road, Newbury RG14 5NR
Telephone: 01635 522651
Fax: 01635 36294
Email: petroc@librapharm.com
Website: www.librapharm.co.uk
Imprints: Petroc Press
Parent Company: Librapharm Ltd
Payment Details: Royalties paid annually
Unsolicited Manuscripts: Yes

Phaidon Press Ltd

Publishes books on art, architecture, design, photography, decorative arts, fashion and music.

Editor(s): Publisher: Amanda Renshaw
Address: Regent's Wharf, All Saints Street, London N1 9PA
Telephone: 020 7843 1000
Fax: 020 7843 1010
Email: feedback@phaidon.com
Unsolicited Manuscripts: No

Pharmaceutical Press

Publishes information on all aspects of medicine for an international audience of pharmacists, GPs, nurses and other health professionals.

Editor(s): Paul Weller
Address: 1 Lambeth High Street, London SE1 7JN (Orders to: PO Box 151, Wallingford, Oxon OX10 8QU)
Telephone: 020 7735 9141
Fax: 020 7735 5085
Email: pweller@rpsgb.org.uk
Website: www.pharmpress.com
Parent Company: Royal Pharmaceutical Society of Great Britain
Unsolicited Manuscripts: Yes

Phillimore & Co Ltd

British local and family history, genealogy, heraldry and institutional history.

Editor(s): Noel Osborne, Simon Thraves
Address: Shopwyke Manor Barn, Chichester, West Sussex PO20 6BG
Telephone: 01243 787636
Fax: 01243 787639
Email: bookshop@phillimore.co.uk
Website: www.phillimore.co.uk
Payment Details: Royalties by negotiation
Unsolicited Manuscripts: Yes with return postage

Piatkus Books

Founded 1979 by Judy Piatkus. The company is customer-led and is committed to publishing excellent non-fiction and top quality fiction, both commercial and literary. Specialises in publishing books and authors 'who we feel enthusiastic and committed to as we like to build for long-term author success as well as short-term!' Publishes fiction, biography and autobiography, health, mind body and spirit, popular psychology, self-help, business and management, cookery, and other books that tempt us. We do not publish childrens or science fiction books. In 1996 launched a list of mass-market non-fiction and fiction titles. About 175 titles a year (60 of which are fiction).

Editor(s): Non-fiction: Gill Bailey, Fiction: Judy Piatkus, Gillian Green
Address: 5 Windmill Street, London W1T 2JA
Telephone: 020 7631 0710
Fax: 020 7436 7137
Email: info@piatkus.co.uk
Website: www.piatkus.co.uk
Parent Company: Independently owned
Payment Details: Royalties are paid twice yearly
Unsolicited Manuscripts: Piatkus are expanding their range of books and welcome synopses and first 3 chapters

Pica Press

The Pica Press imprint was founded by Christopher Helm, and the first titles were published in 1995. Pica Press specialises in high-quality bird and natural history books, aimed at both amateur birdwatchers and professional ornithologists. Only 8-10 titles are published annually, but in five years the company has built up a solid international reputation as one of the leading publishers of natural history books. Several titles have won awards, and several others have been shortlisted, or selected as best examples of their genre. Most titles are co-published in North America and some have been translated into German, French and Dutch.

Editor(s): Nigel Redman
Address: The Banks, Mountfield, Nr Robertsbridge TN32 5JY
Telephone: 01580 880561
Fax: 01580 880541
Email: nigel.redman@pica-press.co.uk
Parent Company: Helm Information Ltd
Payment Details: Advances against royalties and flat fees
Unsolicited Manuscripts: Yes

Picador

Outstanding international fiction and non-fiction, travel, current affairs, history, science, humour, literary fiction, literary biography. In hardback and paperback.

Editor(s): Publisher: Peter Straus; Deputy Publisher: Maria Rejt; Senior Editorial Director: Ursula Doyle; Senior Editor: Richard Milner; Editor: Mary Mount
Address: 25 Eccleston Place, London SW1W 9NF
Parent Company: Macmillan
Unsolicited Manuscripts: No

Piccadilly Press

Children's picture books, very simple character-based storybooks (very limited range) for ages 2-6 years. Teenage books (10-15 years old) fiction and non-fiction, fast paced and humorous. Parenting Books a series on 'how to help your child'.

Editor(s): Judith Evans
Address: 5 Castle Road, London NW1 8PR
Telephone: 020 7267 4492
Fax: 020 7267 4493
Payment Details: Depending on the ms
Unsolicited Manuscripts: Yes, but not the whole ms, letter and chapter will be OK

Pira International

Pira International is the leading independent centre for research, consultancy, publishing, training and information services for the pulp and paper, packaging, printing and publishing industries. Pira's publishing division produces an extensive range of titles covering the packaging, pulp and paper, prepress and printing, and graphic communications and publishing industries. Pira publications provide you with everything you need to know, ranging from market analysis and information, to details of the latest technology and techniques. Pira reviews give details of the latest industrial developments and our conference proceedings bring you up to date with what experts in the field are currently thinking. Alternatively, if its market analysis and financial information you require, Pira market reports provide incisive information and are accompanied by Pira's independent commentary.

Editor(s): Michael Hancock
Address: Randalls Road, Leatherhead, Surrey KT22 7RU
Telephone: 01372 802000
Fax: 01372 802079
Email: publications@pira.co.uk
Website: www.piranet.com
Unsolicited Manuscripts: Ingmar Folkmans

P
Pisces Angling Publication

Books on fishing. Titles include My Way With The Pole by Tom Pickering and Colin Dyson (£12.95 hardback; £9.95 softback) and Fantastic Feeder Fishing by Archie Braddock (£9.95).

Address: 8 Stumperlowe Close, Sheffield S10 3PP
Telephone: 0114 2304038

Pitkin Unichrome Ltd

Highly illustrated souvenir guides for the tourist industry, specialising in cathedrals, churches, historic cities, great events and famous people.

Editor(s): Managing Editor: Shelley Grimwood; Editor: Gill Knappett
Address: Healey House, Dene Road, Andover SP10 2AA
Telephone: 01264 409200
Fax: 01264 334110
Email: guides@pitkin-unichrome.com
Website: www.britguides.com
Parent Company: Johnsons News Group
Unsolicited Manuscripts: No

The Playwrights Publishing Company

One-act and full length plays, comedy and drama, for amateur groups, professional and schools - reading fee charged - SAE required.

Editor(s): Tony and Liz Breeze
Address: 70 Nottingham Road, Burton Joyce, Nottinghamshire NG14 5AL
Telephone: 01159 313356
Email: playwrightspublishingco@yahoo.com
Imprints: Ventus Books
Unsolicited Manuscripts: With reading fee (£15 one act/£30 full length)

Plexus Publishing Limited

Publishers of high quality illustrated books with an emphasis on the following subjects: biography, popular music, rock 'n' roll, popular culture, art, photography and cinema.

Editor(s): Sandra Wake
Address: 55A Clapham Common Southside, Clapham, London SW4 9BX
Telephone: 020 7622 2440
Fax: 020 7622 2441
Email: plexus@plexusuk.demon.co.uk
Website: www.plexusbooks.com
Unsolicited Manuscripts: Yes

Pluto Press Ltd

Pluto Press, established in 1970, is one of the UK's leading independent publishers. We are committed to publishing the best critical writing across the social sciences and humanities. Our authors include Noam Chomsky, Sheila Rowbotham, Pierre Bourdieu, Jean Baudrillard, Hal Foster, Augusto Boal, Susan George, Israel Shahak, Antonio Gramsci, Frantz Fanon and bell hooks. Pluto Press currently publishes over 60 titles a year and has an extensive backlist of over 400 titles. We have global profile supported by our team of representatives and agents. Warehouses in the UK, USA, Canada, Australia and South Africa ensure rapid delivery of our books anywhere in the world.

Editor(s): Roger van Zwanenberg, Anne Beech
Address: Pluto Press, 345 Archway Road, London N6 5AA
Telephone: 020 8348 2724
Fax: 020 8348 9133
Email: pluto@plutobks.demon.co.uk
Website: www.plutobooks.com
Unsolicited Manuscripts: Yes

The Poetry Business

A small independent literary publisher of contemporary poetry and fiction. List includes Michael Schmidt, Dorothy Nimmo and Michael Laskey. Run an annual book and pamphlet competition - apply for details. Also publish The North magazine: new poetry, reviews and articles.

Editor(s): Peter Sansom, Janet Fisher
Address: The Studio, Byram Arcade, Westgate, Huddersfield HD1 1ND
Telephone: 01484 434840
Fax: 01484 426566
Email: edit@poetrybusiness.co.uk
Imprints: Smith/Doorstop Books
Payment Details: Royalties
Unsolicited Manuscripts: Sample 12 poems only please

Poetry Now

Publishes anthologies of more modern verse, likes to deal with topical, provocative issues but will also consider poetry on any subject. New poets always welcome, there are no entry fees and we publish a wide range of poetry. Poetry Now also publishes a quarterly magazine featuring workshops, competition news, profiles and articles of interest. In each issue there is also poetry published on five different subjects, changing each issue. We are always looking for guest editors (must have had poetry published), article writers, etc. If you contact us by email, please include postal address.

Editor(s): Managing Editor: Heather Killingray, Editors: Nathalie Nightingale
Address: Remus House, Coltsfoot Drive, Woodston, Peterborough PE2 9JX
Telephone: 01733 898101
Fax: 01733 313524
Email: poetrynow@forwardpress.co.uk
Website: www.forwardpress.co.uk
Imprints: Poetry Now, Strongwords (16-24 year olds), Women's Words (Female poets only)
Parent Company: Forward Press Ltd
Payment Details: Small payments for magazine material published, plus Top 100 Poets of the Year competition for anthologies: with £3,000 first prize
Unsolicited Manuscripts: Single poems only

Polar Publishing

Design, print and produce quality sports publications (football, cricket). Catalogue available.

Editor(s): Julian Baskcomb, Julia Byrne
Address: 9-17 Tuxford Road, Hamilton Business Park, Leicester LE4 9TZ
Telephone: 0116 274 4774
Fax: 0116 274 4775
Email: juliabyrne@polargroup.co.uk, julianbaskcomb@polargroup.co.uk
Imprints: Polar Publishing
Parent Company: Polar Print Group Ltd
Payment Details: Individual agreements
Unsolicited Manuscripts: Yes

The Policy Press

Public policy and governance. Social welfare and social exclusion. Social care and disability. Issues for older people. Family policy, child welfare and domestic violence. Healthcare and health inequalities. Labour markets, training and lifelong learing. Housing and construction. Area regeneration. Policy and politics journal.

Editor(s): Dawn Louise Rushen
Address: 34 Tyndall's Park Road, Bristol BS8 1PY
Telephone: 0117 954 6800
Fax: 0117 973 7308
Email: tpp@bristol.ac.uk
Website: www.policypress.org.uk
Unsolicited Manuscripts: Will only accept proposals

P
Politicio's Publishing

Specialist publisher of political books. Sister company of Politicio's Bookstore and Politico's Design

Editor(s): Sean Magee, Iain Dale
Address: 8 Artillery Row, London, SW1P 1RZ
Telephone: 0207 828 0010
Fax: 0207 828 8111
Email: publishing@politicos.co.uk
Website: www.politicospublishing.co.uk
Unsolicited Manuscripts: Yes

Polity Press

Polity is a leading global publisher in the social sciences and humanities. We publish some of the best authors in these fields and we have an outstanding list of textbooks for students. Our aim is to combine the publication of original, cutting-edge work of the highest quality with the development of a systematic programme of textbooks and coursebooks which will be valuable for students and scholars in further and higher education.

The Polity list is particularly strong in the areas of sociology, politics and social and political theory. We also have strong and rapidly expanding lists in a range of other fields including gender studies, media and cultural studies, philosophy, literature, history, geography and anthropology.

Editor(s): David Held, John Thompson, Louise Knight, Sally-Ann Spencer
Address: 65 Bridge Street, Cambridge CB2 1UR
Telephone: 01223 324315
Fax: 01223 461385
Email: polity@dial.pipex.com
Website: www.polity.co.uk
Unsolicited Manuscripts: Unsolicited proposals only - no manuscripts

Polygon

New fiction, Scottish culture, Gaelic, guides/travel, folklore.

Editor(s): Commissioning Editor: Alison Bowden
Address: 22 George Square, Edinburgh EH8 9LF
Fax: 0131 662 0053
Website: www.eup.ed.ac.uk
Parent Company: Edinburgh University Press
Unsolicited Manuscripts: Yes

Polygon at Edinburgh

An academic/trade imprint - cultural and intellectual non-fiction. Scottish language, literature and culture; Scottish history and politics; celtic and folklore.

Editor(s): Alison Bowden - Non-fiction all areas, Nicola Carr - Scottish history and politics
Address: 22 George Street, Edinburgh EH8 9LF
Fax: 0131 662 0053
Website: www.eup.ed.ac.uk
Parent Company: Edinburgh University Press
Unsolicited Manuscripts: Yes

P
Pomegranate Europe Ltd

Pomegranate Europe is renowned for publishing an extensive range of quality paper products. The prolific variety of images include classic and contemporary, fresh and popular, artists and photographers. The extent of subjects are equally dynamic and diverse. From culture and nature to leisure and humour. Our excellent standard of images, from source to print, is maintained through collaboration with the world's major institutions, libraries and galleries.

Editor(s): Katie Burke
Address: Fullbridge House, Fullbridge, Maldon, Essex CM9 4LE
Telephone: 01621 851 646
Fax: 01621 852 426
Email: sales@pomeurope.co.uk
Website: www.pomegranate.com
Parent Company: Pomegranate Communications

Populace Press

Small independent publisher specialising in children's titles. We serve as a springboard for career authors, and also encourage one-off writers of all ages. Publications are not restricted to book format only; as a new publisher we look to the Internet as an excellent medium for future development of storytelling.

Editor(s): Mary Cooke
Address: 31 Malmesbury Road, Chippenham, Wilts SN15 1PS
Telephone: 01249 461131
Fax: Same as phone
Email: populacepress@mailhost.net
Website: www.mailhost.net/~populacepress
Payment Details: No advances. Quarterly for 1st eighteen months, then annual royalties
Unsolicited Manuscripts: Yes

David Porteous Editions

Non-fiction publishers of high quality colour illustrated books on hobbies and leisure pursuits for the UK and international markets. Subjects include watercolour painting, papercrafts, cross stitch, salt dough, papier mache and other crafts.

Address: PO Box 5, Chudleigh, Newton Abbot, Devon TQ13 0YZ
Telephone: 01626 853310
Fax: 01626 853663
Website: www.davidporteous.com
Payment Details: Royalties
Unsolicited Manuscripts: No - letter/synopsis first

Portland Press

Portland Press is the wholly owned publishing subsidiary of the Biochemical Society. It is a not-for-profit publisher of journals and books in the cellular and molecular life sciences. The surplus from sales of its publications are returned to the scientific community via the activities of the Biochemical Society.

Address: Commerce Way, Colchester, CO2 8HP
Telephone: 01206 796351
Fax: 01206 799331
Email: editorial@portlandpress.com
Website: www.portlandpress.com
Parent Company: Biochemical Society
Unsolicited Manuscripts: No

P
Power Publications

Publishers of local history, cycle guides, pub walking guides, pub guides and penstemons.

Editor(s): Mike Power/Gill Coombes
Address: 1 Clayford Avenue, Ferndown, Dorset BH22 9PQ
Telephone: 01202 875223
Fax: Same as phone
Email: powerpublications@freeserve.co.uk
Payment Details: 7.5% nett sales
Unsolicited Manuscripts: Yes

T & A D Poyser

Books on ornithology and natural history for the general and advanced reader.

Editor(s): Andrew S Richford
Address: Harcourt Place, 32 James Town Road, London NW1 7BY
Telephone: 020 7424 4251
Fax: 020 7424 4253
Email: andy_richford@harcourt.com
Website: www.academicpress.com
Imprints: T and A D Poyser, Poyser Natural History
Parent Company: Academic Press
Payment Details: Variable royalty scales
Unsolicited Manuscripts: No

Praxis Books

A small press, producing only one or two titles per year. Shared costs, shared proceeds. Proposals will be considered - enclose 2-3 sample chapters and full synopsis, plus ideas as to how the book might be marketed. Assessment service details on request. No new fiction.

Editor(s): Rebecca Smith
Address: Crossways Cottage, Walterstone, Herefordshire HR2 0DX
Email: 100543.3270@compuserve.com
Website: www.beckysmith.demon.co.uk
Imprints: Praxis Books
Payment Details: Shared costs, shared proceeds
Unsolicited Manuscripts: Yes, with return postage

PRC Publishing Ltd

Book packagers of general illustrated non-fiction.

Editor(s): Martin Howard
Address: Kiln House, 210 New Kings Road London SW6 4NZ
Telephone: 020 7736 5666
Fax: 020 7736 5777
Email: martin.howard@prcpub.com
Website: www.prcpub.com
Parent Company: Chrysalis Books
Payment Details: Usually flat fee but occasionally royalty
Unsolicited Manuscripts: Yes

P
Prentice Hall

Publishes books and CD-ROMS for teaching and learning English as a foreign language at all levels. Particular strengths are business English, English for specific purposes and English for academic purposes.

Address: Campus 400, Maylands Avenue, Hemel Hempstead HP2 7EZ
Telephone: 01442 881891
Fax: 01442 882288
Email: orders@prenhall.co.uk
Website: www.pheurope.co.uk

Prestel Publishing Ltd

Publishers of books on art, architecture, photography, ethnographic art, decorative arts.

Editor(s): Philippa Hurd
Address: 4 Bloomsbury Place, London WC1A 2QA
Telephone: 020 7323 5004
Fax: 020 7636 8004
Email: editorial@prestel-uk.co.uk
Parent Company: Prestel Verlag
Unsolicited Manuscripts: Yes

Prim-Ed Publishing Ltd

Prim-Ed Publishing specialises in producing an extensive range of high quality, photocopiable resources, for all areas of the primary curriculum. Written by teachers, for teachers, these titles are designed to cut preparation time whilst maintaining a high level of content quality and task value. Clear instructions, page layouts and relevant graphics are features of our titles which help to stimulate increased motivation, interest and concentration.

Available products in the Prim-Ed range include Numero, and Values Education. Numero is a fun, mathematical card game, that is ideal for developing and reinforcing the mental calculationwork required by the National Curriculum. Values Education is a photocopiable 14-book series that promotes core values abd develops self-esteem through PSE and citizenship, using language, discussion and group-working skills. Suitable for ages 5-14 years.

A range of interactive literacy and numeracy CD-ROMs, merit stickers and refernce titles are also available.

Address: 4th floor tower court Foleshill Enterprise Park Courtaulds Way Coventry CV6 5NX
Telephone: 08700131208
Fax: 08700131209
Email: sales@prim-ed.com
Website: www.prim-ed.com

℘ Prion Books Ltd

Prion (previously known as Multimadia Books) publishes books on Humour, Drink, literary and historical reprints, books on pubs and literary travel, popular culture etc.

Editor(s): Andrew Goodfellow
Address: Imperial Works, Perren Street, London NW5 3ED
Telephone: 020 7482 4248
Fax: 020 7482 4203
Email: books@prion.co.uk
Website: prionbooks.com
Imprints: Prion
Parent Company: Red Lion
Payment Details: Standard royalties, twice yearly
Unsolicited Manuscripts: Only with s.a.e and outlines/extracts only. Not by e-mail.

Pritam Books

Books on teaching Pujabi, Urdu, English for the speakers of Punjabi for school and FE colleges. Punjabi and Urdu bilingual dictionaries in english: Sikhism, Indian Musical Instruments, Phrase book (in English, Punjabi, Hindustani, Bengali).

Address: 102 Sandwell Road, Handsworth, Birmingham B21 8PS
Telephone: 0121 523 7429
Email: dbbhogal@netscapeonline.co.uk

Profile Books Ltd

Profile was founded five years ago to publish stimulating non-fiction. We aim to publish in a wide range of subjects including politics, current affairs, history, travel and popular science. We also publish all The Economist Books and have done so since we started.

In 2002 we will be publishing about 50 books - a sufficiently small number that everyone in the company can be involved in every book - but large enough to ensure that we are effective.

Though Profile is small, through our experience and clever outsourcing, we hope we can publish more effectively and more nimbly than some of the bigger companies. We set out to publish fast, paying careful attention to what is special about each book.

We are distributed in the UK by Random House who are part of the largest publisher in the world and currently sold by Signature Book Representation. We have similar arrangements overseas.

All our titles are available everywhere from all good bookshops and online from amazon.co.uk. Our US and foreign rights are handled through leading literary agents. In five we have sold rights in 15 languages.

Editor(s): Andrew Franklin, Martin Lui, Peter Carson
Address: 58a Hatton Garden, London EC1N 8LX
Telephone: 020 7404 3001
Fax: 020 7404 3003
Email: info@profilebooks.co.uk
Website: www.profilebooks.co.uk
Imprints: Profile Books, The Economist Books
Parent Company: Profile Books
Payment Details: Advances against royalties. Royalties are paid twice yearly in the uaual way. We have a minimum terms agreement contract.
Unsolicited Manuscripts: No, never without a letter outlining the subject and what is special about the book first.

℘ Prospero Books

Prospero is a self-publishing company helping authors to publish their own books in both the traditional printed form and on-line, by providing all the expertise and services needed to convert a manuscript into a finished book. Manuscripts can be on any subject, and books are produced to a professional standard in the format and quantity chosen by the author. Advice is given on sales, marketing and publicity.

Editor(s): Hester Rice
Address: 46 West Street, Chichester, West Sussex PO19 1RP
Telephone: 01243 782700
Fax: 01243 786300
Email: prospero@summersdale.com
Website: www.prospero-books.com
Payment Details: Authors fund production of their books, own all copies and retain 100% of any income
Unsolicited Manuscripts: Yes

Psychology Press

This imprint was created specifically to serve the needs of researchers, professionals and students concerned with the science of human and animal behaviour. It publishes at all levels, including primary research journals, monographs, professional books, student texts and credible scientifically valid popular books. Psychology Press intends to publish psychology in its broadest sense, encompassing work of psychological significance by people in related areas, such as biology, neuroscience, linguistics, sociology, artificial intelligence, as well as the work of mainstream psychologists. Its publications will be of interest to any discipline which is concerned in any way with the science of human and animal behaviour.

Address: 27 Church Road, Hove, East Sussex BN3 3FA
Telephone: 01273 207 411
Fax: 01273 205 612
Email: information@psypress.co.uk
Website: www.tandf.co.uk/homepages/pphome.htm
Parent Company: Taylor & Francis Ltd

Guild Of Pastoral Psychology

We publish booklets of lectures given to the Guild of Pastoral Psychology. The content is concerned with the depth psychology of C G Jung and spirituality and religion in its widest aspect. The pamphlets reflect the views and ideas of scholars and analysts since the Guilds inception in 1937. £2-£3 plus postage. Only lectures given to the Guild are considered. List of pamphlets can be sent.

Editor(s): Guild Committee
Address: 164 Ilbert Street, London W10 4QD
Telephone: 020 8964 1559
Fax: Same as phone
Email: diana@grace-jones.freeserve.co.uk
Website: www.guildofpastoralpsychology.org.uk
Unsolicited Manuscripts: No

The Psychotherapy Centre

An established therapy, training, referral and publishing centre, helping people to understand themselves, live their lives more effectively, and resolve their emotional problems, relationship behaviour and psychogenetic conditions. Some of its numerous publications, such as 'Emotional Problems: Different Ways Of Dealing With Them'; 'Enjoy Parenthood' and 'Selecting A Psychotherapist' are written in-house by the practitioners. For some others, such as 'Group Therapy: We Tried It', or 'Two Therapies And After', well-written, accurate, informative and interesting write-ups of personal experiences are welcome - there is likely to be payment if the publication takes off and becomes a best-seller.

Address: 67 Upper Berkley Street, London W1H 7QX
Telephone: 020 7723 6173
Unsolicited Manuscripts: Quality accounts of personal experiences of problems and therapies are considered

P
Public Record Office

The Public Record Office is the national archives of the United Kingdom. Publishes a wide range of historical titles; specialities are family history, military history, primary source material and academic titles.

Editor(s): Jane Crompton, Sheila Knight
Address: Kew, Richmond, Surrey TW9 4DU
Telephone: 020 8392 5206
Fax: 020 8392 5266
Email: bookshop@pro.gov.uk
Website: www.pro.gov.uk/
Imprints: Public Record Office, PRO Publications
Unsolicited Manuscripts: To Jane Crompton

PublicAffairs LTD

Launched in the autumn of 2001, PublicAffairs Ltd, is a new UK imprint made up of select quality non-fiction titles. This radical and exciting list encompasses journalism, history, biography and social criticism.

Address: PO Box 317, Oxford, OX2 9RU
Telephone: 01865 860960
Fax: 01865 862763
Email: info@theperseuspress.com
Unsolicited Manuscripts: No

Central Publishing Ltd

A family run company offering all the processes involved in publication as individual services - from manuscript appraisal and editing to publication, promotion, marketing, invoicing and dispatch.

Also considers publication under traditional publishing contract terms where significant potential sales figures can be proven.

Titles presently in publication include 'Please Play On' a biography of John McEnroe, by James Harbridge; 'T.E. Lawrence - Unravelling The Enigma' a biography by Dr Andrew Norman; 'Minor Intervention' a sci-fi novel by Robert Bennick; 'Quality Tennis' an instruction book by Mariana Diaz Oliva and James Harbridge.

Specialises in short-run book production for the self-publisher, with run lengths from as little as 100.

Editor(s): Jayne Sykes
Address: Royd Street Offices, Royd Street, Milnsbridge, Huddersfield, HD3 4QY
Telephone: 01484 641678
Fax: 01484 641687
Email: sales@centralpublishing.co.uk
Website: www.centralpublishing.co.uk
Payment Details: Quarterly
Unsolicited Manuscripts: Yes

The Publishing Training Centre At Book House

Publish training materials, and offer a mail order service (Book Publishing Books) for training materials and books about publishing. Also offer a wide range of courses on all aspects of the publishing industry. Most are available in London and Oxford although some can be studied via distance learning. Courses cover the following broad subject areas: editorial; computing; electronic publishing; journals publishing; management; marketing; production; rights and contracts. Basic Proofreading, Basic Editing and Effective Copywriting are all available by distance learning. Course guide or mail order catalogue available on application.

Editor(s): John Whitley
Address: 45 East Hill, Wandsworth, London SW18 2QZ
Telephone: 020 8874 2718
Fax: 020 8870 8985
Email: publishing.training@bookhouse.co.uk
Website: www.train4publishing.co.uk
Unsolicited Manuscripts: No

Puff Adder Books

Puff Adder Books are epublishers. The website is an online bookstore selling a range of writer's guides, fiction and children's eBooks. It also provides guidance for those seeking to be ePublished including information about contract, copyright and royalties and has links to other resource sites for writers. It has a thriving writing community at Author Network (HYPERLINK http://www.author-network.com).

Editor(s): Karen Scott - Managing Editor; Diana Hayden - Assistant Editor
Address: 35A Lower Park Road, Brightlingsea, Colchester, Essex, CO7 0JX
Telephone: 01206 303607
Fax: 01206 303607
Email: books@puff-adder.com
Website: www.puff-adder.com
Imprints: Young Puff Adders
Parent Company: Author Network (www.author-network.com)
Payment Details: 45% paid quarterly
Unsolicited Manuscripts: Yes

Puffin Books

Children's list, publishing in virtually all fields including fiction, non-fiction, poetry, picture books and media-related titles, for ages from 6 months to 16 years.

Editor(s): Managing Director: Philippa Milnes-Smith, Publishing Director: Penny Morris
Address: 27 Wrights Lane, London W8 5TZ
Telephone: 020 7416 3000
Fax: 020 7416 3099
Email: firstname.lastname@Penguin.co.uk
Website: www.puffin.co.uk
Imprints: Puffin (PB), Hamish Hamilton Children's (HB), Viking Children's (HB)
Parent Company: Penguin
Unsolicited Manuscripts: No

Pumpkinseed Productions

Started in 2000 with publication of its first book 'Hampstead memories' (memoirs of 60 Hampstead residents, with stories from 1914-1970). Future publications: photography books, children's illustrated books, personal reminiscences from storytellers of all ages.

Editor(s): Ellen Emerson
Address: PO Box 29760, London NW3 1FH
Fax: 020 7431 3142
Email: mail@pumpkinseedproductions.com
Website: www.pumpkinseedproductions.com
Unsolicited Manuscripts: No

Quadrille

Founded in 1994 with the objective of creating a small list of innovative books with serious front list potential while simultaneously establishing a core backlist. Publishes high-quality illustrated non-fiction in the chosen fields of cookery, gardening, interiors, crafts, magic and health.

Address: 5th Floor, Alhambra House, 27-31 Charing Cross Road, London WC2H 0LJ
Telephone: 020 7839 7117
Fax: 020 7839 7118
Email: enquiries@quadrille.co.uk
Unsolicited Manuscripts: Non-fiction synopses and ideas welcome

Quadrillion Publishing Ltd

Publisher of mass-market illustrated non-fiction titles. Subject areas: cookery, crafts, popular history, gardening, pop culture, transport, gift. Some 100 new titles published each year. Own list and distribution in US (with sales and marketing) based in New York. Published in US under CLB imprint. Also publish an extensive children's list under the Zig-Zag imprint; subjects: reference and early-learning series for ages 2-12. Pepperpot is a gift and stationery range distributed under the Pepperpot Island brand in the UK and US.

Address: Godalming Business Centre, Woolsack Way, Godalming, Surrey GU7 1XW
Telephone: 01483 426277
Fax: 01483 426947
Email: wss@quad-pub.co.uk
Imprints: CLB, Zig-Zag, Pepperpot
Payment Details: Outright purchase of copyright; flat fee: additional payment for foreign rights sales
Unsolicited Manuscripts: Synopsis and covering letter only

Quartet Books Ltd

Literary fiction, literature in translation, popular non-fiction, literary and music biography, music - popular, rock and jazz.

Editor(s): Jeremy Beale, Stella Kane
Address: 27 Goodge Street, London W1P 2LD
Telephone: 020 7636 3992
Fax: 020 7637 1866
Email: quartetbooks@easynet.co.uk
Imprints: Robin Clark
Parent Company: Namara Group
Payment Details: Royalties paid twice yearly
Unsolicited Manuscripts: Yes

Quartz Editions

Publishers and packagers of highly illustrated books for the international children's market in the main. Predominantly non-fiction and educational. Most titles are in extensive series.

Address: Premier House, 112 Station Road, Edgware HA8 7BJ
Telephone: 020 8951 5656
Fax: 020 8381 2588
Imprints: Quartz

Queen Anne Press

Sporting yearbooks, official coaching manuals and sponsored sports titles.

Editor(s): Adrian Stephenson
Address: Windmill Cottage, Mackerye End, Harpenden, Herts AL5 5DR
Telephone: 01582 715866
Fax: 01582 715121
Email: queenanne@lenqap.demon.co.uk
Parent Company: Lennard Associates Ltd
Payment Details: By negotiation
Unsolicited Manuscripts: No

Quiller Publishing Ltd

Founded in January 1981, Quiller has a high reputation for non-fiction - art books, travel, sport, biography, food and drink, architecture amongst other subjects. As a paricular niche, Quiller Press publishes for companies, organisations and charities and has developed sophisticated direct selling techniques. For more information send for catalogue and/or leaflet giving details of past projects and our modus operandi. Distribution is through Airlife in Shrewsbury and representation to the book trade is through Airlife. Overseas we are represented in USA, Australia, Europe, Scandinavia and other parts of the world via dedicated book distributors.

Editor(s): J J Greenwood, A Johnston
Address: Wykey House, Wykey, Shrewsbury, SY4 1JA
Telephone: 01939 261 616
Fax: 01939 261 606
Email: info@quillerbooks.com
Imprints: Quiller Press, Swan Hill Press
Payment Details: Royalties
Unsolicited Manuscripts: Yes

Radcliffe Medical Press Ltd

Publishers of high quality management and clinical books and electronic media for primary and secondary care. Radcliffe has an unrivalled list of practical books for general practitioners, dealing with the many management and organisational issues they face in the rapidly changing National Health Service. In addition, we publish titles on specific clinical areas, and thoughtful works on varied topics such as patients' rights, euthanasia, public health and child welfare.

Editor(s): Gillian Nineham, Jamie Etherington, Liz Walker
Address: 18 Marcham Road, Abingdon, Oxon OX14 1AA
Telephone: 01235 528820
Fax: 01235 528830
Email: contact.us@radcliffemed.com
Website: www.radcliffe-oxford.com
Unsolicited Manuscripts: Yes

Ragged Bears Publishing Ltd

Publisher's of quality children's books and book related products.

Editor(s): Henrietta Stickland
Address: Milborne Wick, Sherborne, Dorset DT9 4PW
Telephone: 01963 251018
Fax: 01963 250889
Email: info@raggedbears.co.uk
Website: www.raggedbears.co.uk
Unsolicited Manuscripts: Yes

Ransom Publishing Ltd

Ransom Publishing is a young innovative multimedia publisher who develop their own titles and license in titles developed by overseas partners. Ransom has developed a reputation for publishing high quality multimedia titles of strong educational value in both formal education and the home environment, covering a wide range of subjects for children and adults. Ransom market and distribute their products in the major world markets for multimedia and license their titles for translation and localisations in many countries and in many languages. Ransom are one of the fastest growing multimedia publishers in the UK. They are unusual in that thay have a strong base in both educational markets and consumer (retail) markets, plus direct marketing arm which supports trade sales.

Editor(s): Contact Managing Director
Address: Ransom House, Unit 1, Brook Street, Watlington OX4 5PP
Telephone: 01491 613711
Fax: 01491 613733
Email: Ransom@Ransompublishing.co.uk
Website: www.ransom.co.uk

Ravenswood Publications Ltd

Niche publisher for the academic and practitioner markets in public service finance, management and law. Current area of specialist interest is local authority leisure and recreation management. Authors will be required to contribute to the marketing database for their publication. At present publishing in hard copy only, but open to offers on electronic output. PLS is mandated for collection of photocopy fees and for digitisation of printed materials.

Address: 35 Windsor Road, London N7 6JG
Telephone: 020 7272 5032
Fax: Same as phone
Email: denise.naylor@virgin.net
Unsolicited Manuscripts: Contact first to check subject, or send CV only

Reader's Digest Children's Publishing Ltd

Early learning, information and reference (0-12 years). Very strong emphasis on novelty formats and unusual editorial approaches. Innovative production techniques and book-plus-toy formats are features. No picture storybooks.

Editor(s): Managing Editor: Cathy Jones
Address: King's Court, Parsonnage Lane, Bath BA1 1ER
Telephone: 01225 473204
Fax: 01225 460942
Email: info@readersdigest.co.uk
Website: jill.eade@readersdigest.co.uk
Imprints: Reader's Digest Children's Books
Parent Company: Reader's Digest
Unsolicited Manuscripts: No

Reading And Language Information Centre

The Reading and Language Information Centre specialises in short, practical publications on matters of topical interest to teachers.

Editor(s): Viv Edwards
Address: The University of Reading, Bulmershe Court, Reading, Berks RG6 1HY
Telephone: 0118 931 8820
Fax: 0118 931 6801
Email: reading-centre@reading.ac.uk
Website: www.ralic.reading.ac.uk
Payment Details: 7½% royalties.
Unsolicited Manuscripts: No

Reaktion Books

Reaktion Books publishes beautifully produced and innovative books in the fine arts, architecture, design, film, photography, history, cultural studies, Asian Studies, literary studies and travel writing.

Editor(s): Michael Leaman - Editorial Director, Peter Dent - Commission
Address: 79 Farringdon Road, London EC1M 3JW
Telephone: 020 7404 9930
Fax: 020 7404 9931
Email: info@reaktionbooks.co.uk
Website: www.reaktionbooks.co.uk
Unsolicited Manuscripts: Yes

Reardon Publishing (The Cotswold Publisher)

A family-run publishing house founded in 1976, producing publications related to the Cotswold area. Reardon Publishing also acts as a distributor for other publishers and so we are able to offer a wide range of Cotswold books, maps, walking cards, videos and postcards in our specialised subjects of walking, driving, cycling, folklore and tourism in both the Cotswolds and associated counties. Titles include, for example, The Cotswold Way Guide, Video And Map, Cotswold Rideabout, The Haunted Cotswolds, Cotswold Driveabout.

Editor(s): Nicholas Reardon, Peter T Reardon
Address: 56 Upper Norwood Street, Leckhampton, Cheltenham GL53 0DU
Telephone: 01242 231800
Website: www.reardon.co.uk
Imprints: Walkabout, Driveabout, Rideabout, Walkcards
Payment Details: Royalties paid twice-yearly
Unsolicited Manuscripts: Yes, with return postage

Reflections Of A Bygone Age

Books using old picture postcards as illustrations highlighting localities and themes including local history, transport, sport, politics plus Picture Postcard Annual and Postcard Collecting: a beginner's guide to picture postcard collecting. Also Collect Modern Postcard catalogues (3 editions).

Editor(s): B G Lund
Address: 15 Debdale Lane, Keyworth, Notts NG12 5HT
Telephone: 0115 937 4079
Fax: 0115 937 6197
Email: reflections@argonet.co.uk
Website: www.postcard.co.uk/ppm

Research Studies Press Ltd

Research Studies Press Ltd is an independent British publisher. We publish mostly academic and professional books in growing areas of science and technology, principally in the fields of engineering (particularly electronic, electrical, mechanical and materials engineering), computing, botany and forestry.

Editor(s): Giorgio Martinelli
Address: 16 Coach House Cloisters, 10 Hitchin Street, Baldock, Herts SG7 6AE
Telephone: 01462 895060
Fax: 01462 892546
Email: vaw@rspltd.demon.co.uk
Website: www.research-studies-press.co.uk
Unsolicited Manuscripts: No (all m/s are approved by series editors)

Rex Natura (Ltd) Of The Rex Foundation Wildlife Charitable Trust

Small specialist publisher producing select, high quality natural history books, non-fiction and wildlife adventure romance, and related field sketches artwork, drawn from zoological fact and fieldwork observation, and resulting predominantly from the research of the foundation mainly undertaken in Africa and Asia. All highly individualistic and richly illustrated titles - with both artwork and photography - Rex Natura's mission is the dissemination of 'good news' natural history; aiming to inspire and inform in equal measure the public on wildlife, environment and conservation.

Editor(s): L Godsall Bottriell, P Bottriell, P K Onslow Makabuzi
Address: PO Box 141, Aylesbury, Bucks HP22 6YT
Telephone: 01525 217001
Fax: 01296 625299
Email: LenaGod@king-cheetah.freeserve.co.uk
Website: www.king-cheetah.com
Parent Company: The Rex Foundation
Unsolicited Manuscripts: No

RIBA Publications

RIBA Publications is a leading architecture and construction publisher and bookseller in the UK. We specialise in practice management titles, legal and professional reference books, as well as being the publisher for the JCT Ltd building contracts. In addition to our growing list of practice and professional titles. RIBA Publications publish monographs and picture pocketbooks on leading architecture and construction practitioners, and the Royal Institute of British Architects (RIBA) collections.

Editor(s): Mark Lane, Matthew Thompson
Address: Construction House, 56-64 Leonard Street, London EC2A 4LT
Telephone: 020 7251 7100
Fax: 020 7608 2375
Email: markl@ribabooks.com, editor@ribap.fsnet.co.uk
Website: www.ribabookshop.com, www.architecture.com
Parent Company: RIBA Companies Ltd
Unsolicited Manuscripts: Yes

Richard Kay (Publications)

Publishes books the majority of which have a Lincolnshire association; also a few with a more general historical interest, and a few titles of medico-political and economico-political concern. Books in and about Lincolnshire dialect including a 10,000-word dictionary. Life in Lincolnshire and Vernacular History series. Local history - academic and nostalgic.

Editor(s): Richard Allday
Address: 80 Sleaford Road, Boston, Lincolnshire PE21 8EU
Telephone: 01205 353231
Email: rebecca@richardkay.freeserve.co.uk
Imprints: Richard Kay, History Of Boston Project
Payment Details: Royalties where appropriate paid annually
Unsolicited Manuscripts: Initial letter preferred

Richmond House Publishing Co Ltd

Publishes British Theatre Directory, Artistes and Agents and a London Theatre/Concert hall seating plan guide. The first two books are for theatrical reference used by colleges, schools, companies, media and the profession.

Editor(s): British Theatre Directory/Seating Plan Guide - Spencer Block, Artistes and Agents - Charlotte Humphrey
Address: Douglas House, 3 Richmond Buildings, London W10 3HE
Telephone: 020 7437 9556
Fax: 020 7287 3463
Email: sales@rhpco.demon.co.uk
Website: www.rhpco.uk

RICS Books

RICS Books is the commercial publishing arm of the Royal Institution of Chartered Surveyors and is the leading supplier of published material to the surveying, construction, property and related professions. RICs Books publishes a wide selection of products from RICS best practice titles to specially commissioned books. New legislation, regulations and frequently encountered areas of practice and procedure are covered.

Address: Surveyor Court, Westwood Business Park, Coventry CV4 8JE
Telephone: 020 7222 7000
Fax: 020 7334 3851
Email: mailorder@rics.org.uk
Website: www.ricsbooks.org.uk
Parent Company: RICS Business Services
Unsolicited Manuscripts: Yes - to Product Development Manager

Roadmaster Publishing

Publishers of Motoring and Car Histories, Commercial Vehicles and local interest books about Kent and South East Area.

Editor(s): Malcolm Wright
Address: PO Box 176, Chatham, Kent ME5 9AQ
Telephone: 01634 862843 (answerphone)
Fax: 01634 201555
Imprints: Roadmaster Publishing
Payment Details: Usually 10% of retail sales cover price 7.5% paper editions
Unsolicited Manuscripts: Yes, but only in above areas of interest please

Robson Books

Publishers of general non-fiction, biographies, sport, politics, humour, military, showbusiness.

Editor(s): Jeremy Robson - Publisher
Address: 10 Blenheim Court, Brewery Road, London N7 7NY
Telephone: 020 7700 7444
Fax: 020 7700 4552
Email: robson@chrysalisbooks.co.uk
Website: www.robsonbooks.com
Imprints: Robson Books
Parent Company: Chrysalis Plc
Payment Details: Normal royalties
Unsolicited Manuscripts: Synopsis and couple of chapters preferred to complete manuscripts - must have SAE

Society For The Promotion Of Roman Studies

Leading organisation in the UK for those interested in the study of Rome and the Roman Empire. Its scope is wide, covering Roman history, archaeology, literature and art down to about AD700. It has a broadly-based membership, drawn from over forty countries and from all ages and walks of life. The Society publishes two journals, the Journal Of Roman Studies, which contains articles and book reviews dealing with the Roman world in general, and Britannia, which has articles and reviews specifically on Roman Britain; also two monograph series - the JRS and Britannia monographs.

Editor(s): M D Goodman (JRS), L J F Keppie (Britannia)
Address: Senate House, Malet Street, London WC1E 7HU
Telephone: 020 7862 8727
Fax: 020 7862 8728
Email: romansoc@sas.ac.uk
Website: http://www.sas.ac.uk/icls/roman/
Imprints: Society for the Promotion of Roman Studies

ℛ Rosedene Publisher

We publish in-house only. Titles are Time Tested Alternative Remedies, Making Something From Nothing, The Big Search - Overland Journey To India And Back To Great Britain.

Address: Rosedene Health Food Farm, Buller Hill, Redruth, Cornwall TR16 6SS
Telephone: 01209 219075
Email: rosedene@rosedene2000.free-online.co.uk

Rough Guides Ltd

Rough Guides are publishers of travel, music and reference books. Rough Guide now publish over 150 travel guides to countries and cities from Alaska to Zimbabwe. They also publish a range of music reference books, including the much respected Rough Guide to World Music. Other music titles include guides to Opera, Rock, Country, Techno, Blues, House and Soul. Rough Guides are continually adding to their breadth of topics and now publish guidebooks to subjects as diverse as pregnancy, football, restaurants, musical instruments, unexplained phenomena and the best-selling Rough Guide to the Internet.

Address: 62-70 Shorts Gardens, London WC2H 9AH
Telephone: 020 7556 5000
Fax: 020 7556 5050
Email: mail@roughguides.co.uk
Website: www.roughguides.com

Roundhouse Publishing Ltd

Distributors of a broad range of non-fiction titles to the UK and European booktrade through our network of trade sales representatives.

Editor(s): Alan Goodworth
Address: Millstone, Limers Lane, Northam, Devon EX39 2RG
Telephone: 01237 474 474
Fax: 01237 474 774
Email: round.house@fsbdial.co.uk
Website: www.roundhouse.net
Imprints: Roundhouse, Roundhouse Reference Books, Roundabout, Pencil Press
Payment Details: Royalties twice-yearly
Unsolicited Manuscripts: No

The Rowman & Littlefield Publishing Group

The Rowman & Littlefield Publishing Group is one of the largest and fastest growing international, independent publishers. The company publishes in virtually all fields in the humanities and social sciences. While celebrating its 25th anniversary in 2000, it published more than 1,000 new academic, reference and general interest books. More than 20,000 new books have been published since the company was founded in 1975. It remains a privately held, independent corporation 26 years later.

Address: PO Box 317, Oxford, OX2 9RU
Telephone: 01865 865466
Fax: 01865 862763
Email: randl@oppuk.co.uk
Website: www.rlpgbooks.com
Imprints: Rowman & Littlefield Publishers, AltaMira Press, Lexington Books, University Press of America
Unsolicited Manuscripts: No

ℜ Rowton Press Ltd

Leading publisher for horse-racing titles - also publishes sports books.

Address: PO Box 10, Oswestry Salop SY10 8WU
Telephone: 01691 679111
Fax: 01691 679114
Email: odds.on@btinternet.com
Payment Details: By arrangement
Unsolicited Manuscripts: Yes

Royal College Of General Practitioners

The Royal College Of General Practitioners (RCGP) is the academic organisation in the UK for general practitioners. Its aim is to encourage and maintain the highest standards of general medical practice and act as the voice of general practitioners on education, training and standard issues. Under its Royal Charter the College is entitled to 'diffuse information on all matters affecting general medical practice' and as a consequence has developed a long and prestigious list of publications. The College is justifiably proud of its varied titles, which range from the latest research and ideas in contemporary medicine to practical guidelines for dealing with specific medical conditions. By identifying new and topical areas of interest, the College has remained at the forefront of medical publishing.

Editor(s): Dr Rodger Charlton, Editor - College Publications
Address: 14 Princes Gate, Hyde Park, London SW7 1PU
Telephone: 020 7581 3232
Fax: 020 7225 3047
Email: info@rcgp.org.uk
Website: www.rcgp.org.uk

Royal College Of Psychiatrists

The Royal College of Psychiatrists' publishing proramme aims to advance the science and practice of psychiatry, promote study and research and increase public knowledge of psychiatry.

Editor(s): Professor Greg Wilkinson
Address: 17 Belgrave Square, London SW1X 8PG
Telephone: 020 7235 2351
Fax: 020 7259 6507
Email: publications@rcpsych.ac.uk
Website: www.rcpsych.ac.uk
Imprints: Royal College of Psychiatrists, Gaskell
Payment Details: 10% royalty on retail price
Unsolicited Manuscripts: Yes

The Royal Institute Of International Affairs

The RIIA, also known as Chatham House, was founded in 1920 and is a research and membership organisation functioning independently of government and vested interests. It is impartial and holds no collective opinion on any aspect of international affairs. Its resident research fellows, specialised information resources and range of publications, conferences and meetings span the fields of international politics, economics, security and energy/environmental issues. Publications include scholarly monographs, discussion papers, briefings, co-publications, as well as a quarterly and a monthly journal. Publications have a worldwide reputation for quality, accessibility and topicality.

Editor(s): Margaret May (Books etc); Journals eds: Graham Walker (The World Today), Caroline Soper (International Affairs)
Address: Chatham House, 10 St James's Square, London SW1Y 4LE
Telephone: 020 7957 5700
Fax: 020 7957 5710
Email: contact@riia.org
Website: www.riia.org
Imprints: Chatham House Papers (with Continuum/Pinter), International Affairs (quarterly journal - Blackwells), The World Today (monthly magazine - RIIA)
Unsolicited Manuscripts: only for journals: contact relevant editor

Royal Society Of Chemistry

An internationally renowned publisher, the RSC produces a range of high quality, competitively priced books on chemistry and allied subjects. These range from texts for undergraduates and graduates, through to reviews, handbooks and conference proceedings.

Address: Thomas Graham House, Science Park, Milton Road, Cambridge CB4 0WF
Telephone: 01223 420066
Fax: 01223 423429
Email: books@rsc.org
Website: www.rsc.org
Unsolicited Manuscripts: May be sent to the Publisher, Print Products at the Cambridge address

The Rubicon Press

The Rubicon Press specialises in ancient history (principally Egyptology); history (Kings and Queens of Britain); nineteenth century travel; biography and literature. All written by academics for the general reader, and illustrated.

Editor(s): Anthea Page, Robin Page
Address: 57 Cornwall Gardens, London SW7 4BE
Telephone: 020 7937 6813
Fax: Same as phone
Email: RobinRub@aol.com
Imprints: The Rubicon Press
Payment Details: Royalties
Unsolicited Manuscripts: Yes if relevant to our areas of publication

Rudolf Steiner Press

The works of Rudolf Steiner translated into English, and other authors whose work is related to Steiner's ideas. Also, books which contain new research and ideas of a spiritual and scientific nature. No fiction, poetry or children's books.

Editor(s): S Gulbekian
Address: Hill House, The Square, Forest Row, East Sussex, RH18 5ES
Telephone: 01348 824433
Website: www.rudolfsteinerpress.com
Imprints: Sophia Books
Unsolicited Manuscripts: No

Russell House Publishing Ltd

RHP's books and training manuals are designed to help anyone studying or working in these areas to develop their thinking and practice: social policy, social care, helping children and families, work with young people, activities for training and work with young people, combating social exclusion, striving for safer communities, working with offenders. Although principally focussed on policy and practice in the UK, we also publish the journal Social Work In Europe, and other comparative works.

Address: 4 St George's House, Uplyme Road Business Park, Lyme Regis DT7 3LS
Telephone: 01297 443948
Fax: 01297 442722
Email: help@russellhouse.co.uk
Payment Details: Royalties
Unsolicited Manuscripts: Yes if relevant to our areas of publication

The Rutland Press

Publishers of the RIAS Illustrated Architectural Guides to Scotland series; monographs; technical; Scottish urban design.

Address: 15 Rutland Square, Edinburgh EH1 2BE
Telephone: 0131 229 7545
Fax: 0131 228 2188
Email: rutland@rias.org.uk
Website: www.rias.org.uk
Parent Company: Royal Incorporation of Architects in Scotland
Unsolicited Manuscripts: No

Ryland Peters & Small

Publishers of high quality illustrated books and stationery aimed at an international market. Subject areas include cookery, gardening and interior design.

Editor(s): Alison Starling - Publishing Director
Address: Kirkman House, 12-14 Whitfield Street, London W1T 2RP
Telephone: 020 7436 9090
Fax: 020 7436 9790
Email: info@rps.co.uk
Website: www.rylandpeters.com
Unsolicited Manuscripts: No

The Salariya Book Company

Children's illustrated non-fiction; mainly history, science and natural history.

Editor(s): Karen Barker Smith, Stephanie Cole
Address: 25 Marlborough Place, Brighton BN1 1UB
Telephone: 01273 603306
Fax: 01273 693857/621619
Email: salariya@salariya.com
Website: http:/www.salariya.com
Unsolicited Manuscripts: Concepts for ages 3-12 considered, SAE essential

Saltire Society

The Saltire Society's publications aim to raise awareness of Scottish topical issues, historical facts, poetry and the languages of Scotland. They also commemorate famous Scots such as - Walter Scott, Thomas Carlyle, Robert Burns, Andrew Fletcher.

They are aimed at the general reader as well as academics and are modestly priced.
Editor(s): Saltire Society Publications Committee
Address: 9 Fountain Close, 22 High Street, Edinburgh EH1 1TF
Telephone: 0131 556 1836
Fax: 0131 557 1675
Email: saltire@saltire.org.uk
Website: www.saltire-society.demon.co.uk
Payment Details: Agreed percentage per year, calculated to 31st March
Unsolicited Manuscripts: Yes - If on a Scottish topic

S

Sandhill Press Ltd

Specialise in publishing books of local interest to Northumberland.

Editor(s): Beryl Sanderson
Address: 17 Castle Street, Warkworth, Morpeth, Northumberland NE65 0UW
Telephone: 01665 712483
Fax: 01665 713004
Email: sandhill@thebookhouse.demon.co.uk
Website: www.thebookhouse.demon.co.uk
Unsolicited Manuscripts: No

Sangam Books Limited

One of the major strengths of the Sangam Books list is its quantity of titles reflecting India, from its long history, art and culture, its philosophy and religion, to its current affairs and contemporary public figures, Islam, Hinduism, Sikhism and Buddhism are studied, as are temples and classical dance. Publishes books on Sociology, Scientific and Technical and on Indian fiction.

Editor(s): Mr Anthony de Souza
Address: 57 London Fruit Exchange, Brushfield Street, London E1 6EP
Telephone: 020 7377 6399
Fax: 020 7375 1230
Email: sangambks@aol.com
Imprints: Orient Longman, Universities Press, Vikas Books Ltd, UBS Publisher
Parent Company: Orient Longman Ltd, India
Unsolicited Manuscripts: No

Saqi Books

Saqi Books specializes in high quality books on a wide range Middle East related subjects. Areas of intrest include art and architure, politics, history, gender studies, fiction, poetry and literary studies. We also publish illustrated books.

Editor(s): Mai Ghoussoub, Sarah Al-Hamad
Address: 26 Westbourne Grove, London W2 5RH
Telephone: 020 7221 9347
Fax: 020 7229 7492
Email: saqibooks@dial.pipex.com
Website: www.saqibooks.com
Imprints: Echoes, Islamic College for Advanced Studies
Parent Company: Arab Books Ltd
Unsolicited Manuscripts: Yes

Save The Children

Save the Children publishes a wide range of materials for policy-makers, academics and practitioners working with children in the UK and overseas. We also produce curriculum resources for use in primary settings. Free catalogues available.

Editor(s): Managing editor: Ravi Wickremasinghe
Address: 17 Grove Lane, London SE5 8RD
Telephone: 020 7703 5400
Fax: 020 7708 2508
Email: publications@scfuk.org.uk
Website: www.savethechildren.org.uk
Imprints: Save the Children
Unsolicited Manuscripts: Yes

S
SAWD Books
Local interest books, also cookery, gardening and general non-fiction.

Editor(s): Allison Wainman, David Wainman
Address: Plackett's Hole, Bicknor, Sittingbourne, Kent ME9 8BA
Telephone: 01795 472262
Fax: 01795 422633
Email: wainman@sawd.demon.co.uk
Parent Company: Sawd Publications
Payment Details: Royalties bi-annually
Unsolicited Manuscripts: Synopses considered

Alastair Sawday Publishing
Small independent publishers who specialise in accommodation guides. Countries covered: Britain, France, Spain, Portugal, Italy and Ireland. Also Paris Hotels.

Address: The Home Farm Stables, Barrow Court lane, Barrow Gurney, Bristol, BS48 3RW
Telephone: 01275 464891
Fax: 01275 464887
Email: info@sawdays.co.uk
Website: www.sawdays.co.uk

SB Publications

Local history, pictorial local history books, travel guides (GB only) - walking and touring, pictorial transport history, (especially railway and maritime), mythology, unknown, unusual, ghosts and legends. All books should be based on events in the UK.

Editor(s): Stephen Benz, Brigid Chapman, Judy Moore
Address: 19 Grove Road, Seaford, East Sussex BN25 1TP
Telephone: 01323 893498
Fax: 01323 893860
Email: sales@sbpublications.swinternet.co.uk
Website: www.sbpublications.swinternet.co.uk
Imprints: Bergunn
Payment Details: Royalties, 10% of selling price; paid annually no advances
Unsolicited Manuscripts: Synopsis with SAE enclosed

Scandinavia Connection

English-edition Scandinavian books about Scandinavian countries published in Scandinavia and distributed by the Scandinavia Connection in London. Books on Norway, on Iceland, on Finland, on Denmark, on Sweden. Also maps, videos and CD's.

Address: 26 Woodsford Square, London W14 8DP
Telephone: 020 7602 0657
Fax: 020 7602 8556
Email: books@scandinavia-connection.co.uk
Website: www.scandinavia-connection.co.uk
Imprints: KOM, Cappelen, B&B Norway, Norta Books, Index Publishing, Mal og Menning, Forlagid, Dreifingarmidstodin, Borgen, Aschehoug, Nyt Nordisk, Atlantis, ICA, J-P Lahall, Otava.
Parent Company: Max Morgan-Witts Productions Ltd
Unsolicited Manuscripts: No

S

Scarthin Books

Local studies with a wider scholarly appeal; specialised monographs written for the educated layman.

Editor(s): David Mitchell
Address: The Promenade, Scarthin, Cromford, Derbyshire DE4 3QF
Telephone: 01629 823272
Website: www.scarthinbooks.com
Imprints: Family Walks
Payment Details: Royalties quarterly
Unsolicited Manuscripts: Unsolicited synopses considered

Scholastic Children's Books

Children's books publisher. High quality fiction and original individual titles; best-selling non-fiction; picture books; pre-school and licensed titles.

Address: Commonwealth House, 1-19 New Oxford Street, London WC1A 1NU
Telephone: 020 7421 9000
Fax: 020 7421 9001
Website: www.scholastic.co.uk
Imprints: Point, Hippo, Scholastic Press
Parent Company: Scholastic USA
Unsolicited Manuscripts: Admin for fiction/non-fiction/pre-school dept

Association For Science Education

The Association for Science Education (ASE) is the professional body for those involved in science education at all levels, from pre-school to higher education. The ASE has a lively publishing arm. 'Written by teachers for teachers', is a slogan of which the ASE can justly br proud. Written by individual members, working groups and committees, as specially commissioned projects and joint ventures with industry, ASE publications often arise as direct responses to topical issues and developments.

Editor(s): Various
Address: ASE, College Lane, Hatfield, Herts AL10 9AA
Telephone: 01707 283000
Fax: 01707 266532
Email: info@ase.org.uk
Website: www.ase.org.uk
Payment Details: No payments to authors
Unsolicited Manuscripts: Yes

Science Museum Publications

History of science and technology, public understanding of science, museology, railway history, photographic history, reference and museum guide books.

Editor(s): Ela Ginalska
Address: Exhibition Road, London SW7 2DD
Fax: 020 7942 4362
Email: publicat@nmsi.ac.uk
Website: www.nmsi.ac.uk/publications
Imprints: Science Museum, NRM, NMPFT
Parent Company: NMSI Trading Ltd
Payment Details: Fee arranged with author
Unsolicited Manuscripts: Yes

SCM-Canterbury Press Ltd

Hymn and worship-song books for churches, schools, colleges, hospitals and similar institutions. Wide range of titles on liturgy and worship, prayer and spirituality, reference, Bible study, ministry and mission, theology and doctrine, biography, church music, and multi-faith educational books and other resources. Divisions of SCM-Canterbury Press Ltd are SCM Press - philosophy, theology and ethics from an open perspective; Canterbury Press Norwich - general religious books, liturgical, major Christian hymn books, prayer books and pilgrimage guides; Religious and Moral Education Press (RMEP) - regious, personal and social education books for primary, middle and secondary schools and colleges (including assembly material) and teachers/administrative books. Also G J Palmer & Sons Ltd, publisher of Church Times weekly newspaper (ideas welcome, but no mss); The Sign and Home Words - monthly nationwide parish magazine inserts; Hart advertising - offering specialist advertising service to religious and charitable organisations.

Editor(s): Alex Wright (SCM Press), Christine Smith (Canterbury Press), Mary Mears (RMEP)
Address: St Mary's Works, St Mary's Plain, Norwich, Norfolk NR3 3BH
Telephone: 01603 612914
Fax: 01603 624483
Email: admin@scm-canterburypress.co.uk
Website: www.scm-canterburypress.co.uk, www.churchtimes.co.uk
Imprints: SCM Press, Canterbury Press Norwich, Religious and Moral Education Press (RMEP)
Parent Company: Hymns Ancient and Modern Ltd
Payment Details: By negotiation
Unsolicited Manuscripts: By negotiation

Scottish Braille Press

Printers and publishers of braille and producers of audio, large print, tactile diagrams and material on disc for visually handicapped persons.

Address: Craigmillar Park, Edinburgh EH16 5NB
Telephone: 0131 662 4445
Fax: 0131 662 1968
Email: scot.braille@dial.pipex.com
Website: www.scottish-braille-press.org
Parent Company: The Royal Blind Asylum and School

Scottish Children's Press

Scottish Children's Press publish books for children by 1) Scottish authors, 2) People resident in Scotland, or 3) About Scottish themes.

Editor(s): Avril Gray
Address: Unit 13d Newbattle Abbey Business Annexe, Newbattle Road, Dalkeith EH22 3LJ
Telephone: 0131 660 4757 (editorial only), 0131 660 4666 (orders only)
Fax: 0131 660 6414
Email: info@scottishbooks.com
Website: www.scottishbooks.com
Imprints: Scottish Children's Press
Parent Company: S C P Children's Ltd
Payment Details: As per individual contract
Unsolicited Manuscripts: No, please telephone for submission guidelines

Scottish Cultural Press

Scottish Cultural Press publish books by 1) Scottish authors, 2) People resident in Scotland, or 3) About Scottish themes.

Editor(s): Avril Gray
Address: Unit 13d Newbattle Abbey Business Annexe, Newbattle Road, Dalkeith EH22 3LJ
Telephone: 0131 660 6366 (editorial only), 0131 660 4666 (orders only)
Fax: 0131 660 6414
Email: info@scottishbooks.com
Website: www.scottishbooks.com
Imprints: Scottish Cultural Press
Parent Company: S C P Publishers Ltd
Payment Details: As per individual contract
Unsolicited Manuscripts: No, please telephone before sending anything

S
Scottish Library Association

The Scottish Library Association is the professional body representing librarians in Scotland. Its publishing programme includes work on librarianship which are aimed at the profession, as well as bibliographies, scottish interest, local and national history materials for the wider market.

Editor(s): Various
Address: Scottish Library Association, Scottish Centre For Information And Library Services, 1 John Street, Hamilton ML3 7EU
Telephone: 01698 458888
Fax: 01698 458899
Email: sla@slainte.org.uk
Website: www.slainte.org.uk
Imprints: Scottish Library Association
Unsolicited Manuscripts: Accepted only if consistent with subject areas described above

Scripture Union

Publisher of Bible reading notes, children's group resources, general Christian adult books and children's fiction, picture books and assembly resources.

Editor(s): Publishing Manager: John Ball
Address: Queensway House, 207-209 Queensway, Bletchley, Milton Keynes MK2 2EB
Telephone: 01908 856000
Fax: 01908 856111
Email: info@scriptureunion.org
Website: www.scripture.org.uk
Unsolicited Manuscripts: Synopsis and sample chapters to John Ball

S

Seafarer Books

Books on traditional sailing, mainly narrative.

Editor(s): Patricia Eve
Address: 102 Redwald Road, Rendlesham, Woodbridge, Suffolk IP12 2TE
Telephone: 01394 420789
Fax: 01394 461314
Email: info@seafarerbooks.com

Search Press Ltd

Publishes a wide selection of hobby books, all highly illustrated in full colour, covering a wide range of subjects including crafts, painting, drawing, papercrafts, decorative arts, embroidery, silk painting and organic gardening.

Editor(s): Editorial Director: Roz Dace
Address: Wellwood, North Farm Road, Tunbridge Wells, Kent TN2 3DR
Telephone: 01892 510850
Fax: 01892 515903
Email: searchpress@searchpress.com
Website: www.searchpress.com
Imprints: Search Press
Unsolicited Manuscripts: No

Martin Secker & Warburg

Literary fiction and general non-fiction.

Editor(s): Geoff Mulligan, David Milner
Address: Random House, 20 Vauxhall Bridge Road, London SW1V 2SA
Telephone: 0207 8408400
Parent Company: Random House
Unsolicited Manuscripts: No

S
Self-Counsel Press

As our name implies, we are an expanding publisher of self-help business books - titles that explore and explain sometimes complex ideas and issues, not with professional jargon, but with language that everyone can understand.

Editor(s): Diana Douglas
Address: C/o Roundhouse Publishing Ltd, Millstone, Limers Lane, Northam, Devon, EX39 2RG
Telephone: 01237 474474
Fax: 01237 474774
Email: round.house@fsbdial.co.uk
Website: www.roundhouse.net
Payment Details: Royalties twice yearly
Unsolicited Manuscripts: No

Seren

General literary publisher specialising in writing in the English language from Wales. Publishing around 30 new titles a year, the list includes poetry, fiction, biography, drama, criticism and art. Most books have a direct connection to Wales through author (birth or residence) or subject matter, though Seren also publishes Border Lines, a series of introductory biographies of writers, artists and composers who lived, worked and found inspiration on both sides of the English-Welsh border. Seren is the imprint of Poetry Wales, a quarterly magazine publishing the best in poetry from Wales and the world.

Editor(s): Amy Wack (poetry/drama), Mick Felton (fiction/biography/criticism/art), John Powell Ward (Border Lines)
Address: First Floor, 38-40 Nolton Street, Bridgend CF31 3BN
Telephone: 01656 668018
Fax: 01656 649226
Email: seren@seren.force9.co.uk
Parent Company: Poetry Wales Press Ltd
Payment Details: By negotiation
Unsolicited Manuscripts: With SAE for return

Serpent's Tail Ltd

Inspired by Continental paperback original publishing houses and founded in 1986 to give a voice to writers outside the mainstream. During its first year Serpent's Tail published 12 books, 6 of which were translations. Now publishing 40 books a year, including original British and American fiction, music and popular culture books, crime fiction, tranlations and short story anthologies.

Address: 4 Blackstock Mews, London N4 2BT
Telephone: 020 7354 1949
Fax: 020 7704 6467
Email: info@serpentstail.com
Website: www.serpentstail.com
Payment Details: No payment involved re manuscripts
Unsolicited Manuscripts: After query

Severn House Publishers Limited

Hardcover fiction by well-known authors primarily for library publication.

Editor(s): Hugo Cox
Address: 9-15 High Street, Sutton, Surrey SM1 1DF
Telephone: 020 8770 3930
Fax: 020 8770 3850
Email: editorial@severnhouse.com
Website: www.severnhouse.com
Payment Details: Standard royalty terms
Unsolicited Manuscripts: No, via agents only please

S
Shaw & Sons Limited

Shaw & Sons publish a list of over sixty books covering a wide range of subjects for professionals at various depths, from definitive loose-leaf works to simple quick-reference guides. These texts are predominantly for legal and local government professionals but also include topics for businesses and environmental agencies. At the forefront of Shaw's book list are annual directories. These include the renowned Shaw's Directory of Courts in the United Kingdom, which is used by thousands of solicitors, government departments and other agencies each year. Shaw's Local Government Directory is the most comprehensive and best value reference work of its kind, and Shaws have recently taken over publication of the Varsity Directory of Investigators and Process Servers and the 'bible' of the probation service, the NAPO Probation Directory. Shaws are always interested in considering new books for publication and prospective authors should write to the Managing Editor with a synopsis of their proposals.

Editor(s): Crispin Williams
Address: Shaway House, 21 Bourne Park, Bourne Road, Crayford, Kent DA1 4BZ
Telephone: 01322 621100
Fax: 01322 550553
Email: publications@shaws.co.uk
Website: www.shaws.co.uk
Imprints: Shaw
Unsolicited Manuscripts: Yes - to Crispin Williams

Sheaf Publishing Ltd

Local interest books, non-fiction only.

Address: 191 Upper Allen Street, Sheffield S3 7GW
Telephone: 0114 273 9067
Unsolicited Manuscripts: No, ideas and synopses welcome, particularly concerning local history

Sheffield Academic Press Ltd

Founded in 1976. Originally known as JSOT Press. Now the leading academic publisher of biblical titles. Recently expanded its list to include archaeology, European studies, literary studies, history and culture, languages, scientific, professional and reference.

Address: Mansion House, 19 Kingfield Road, Sheffield S11 9AS
Telephone: 0114 2554433
Fax: 0114 2554626
Email: admin@sheffac.demon.co.uk
Website: www.sheffieldacademicpress.com
Imprints: Sheffield Academic Press, JSOT Press, Almond Press
Unsolicited Manuscripts: Manuscripts, synopses, ideas and proposals welcome. No fiction

Sheffield Hallam University Press

Sheffield Hallam University Press is the publishing company within Sheffield Hallam University and has been operating successfully for 21 years. It produces a diverse range - computer packages, video training packs, CDs, loose leaf training packs, practical tools, books, journals, series and games. It produces and publishes materials from within SHU and also externally. It has now broadened into mainstream academic publishing and publishes materials from other institutions with links to Sheffield Hallam University. Whilst work is not commissioned, authors are drawn from many other educational institutions.

Editor(s): Monica Moseley
Address: Adsetts Centre, City Campus, Sheffield S1 1WB
Telephone: 0114 225 4702
Fax: 0114 225 4478
Email: shupress@shu.ac.uk or m.mosley@shu.ac.uk
Website: www.shu.ac.uk/shupress/
Imprints: SHU Press
Parent Company: Sheffield Hallam University
Unsolicited Manuscripts: No

S
Sheldon Press

Publishers of health and self-help books for the popular market. Our health books are written for non-experts, and include titles such as Fertility - a natural approach, Coping with Thyroid Problems and Curing Arthritis The Drug-free Way. Our self-help books are written for a similar readership, and include Coping with Anxiety and Depression, How To Improve Your Confidence and The Good Stress Guide. Our new series of books on natural remedies such as cider vinegar, garlic and antioxidants sets out the real benefits of these products. All our books are reliable, no-nonsense reference books for the general reader.

Editor(s): Joanna Moriarty, Liz Marsh
Address: Holy Trinity Church, Marylebone Road, London NW1 4DU
Telephone: 020 7643 0382
Fax: 0207 6430391
Email: director@sheldonpress.co.uk
Payment Details: By negotiation
Unsolicited Manuscripts: Please send a synopsis and sample chapter

Sheldrake Press

Publishers of highly illustrated non-fiction. Subjects include travel, history, railways, architecture and interior design, cookery, music, gift stationery, art and reference. Titles include the Wild Guides, The Victorian House Book, The Kate Greenaway Baby Book and Amsterdam: Portrait of a City.

Editor(s): J S Rigge
Address: 188 Cavendish Road, London SW12 0DA
Telephone: 020 8675 1767
Fax: 020 8675 7736
Email: mail@sheldrakepress.demon.co.uk
Website: www.sheldrakepress.demon.co.uk
Parent Company: Sheldrake Holdings Ltd
Payment Details: Subject to negotiation
Unsolicited Manuscripts: Check first by telephone

Shepheard-Walwyn (Publishers) Ltd

We publish in three broad areas - all non-fiction: books originated in calligraphy; history, political economy and philosophy, not in a narrow academic sense, but to help us understand where we are and how, by understanding better, things might be improved; books of Scottish interest.

Editor(s): Anthony Werner
Address: Suite 604, The Chandlery, 50 Westminister Bridge Road, London SE1 7QY
Telephone: 020 7721 7666
Fax: 020 7721 7667
Email: books@shepheard-walwyn.co.uk
Website: www.shepheard-walwyn.co.uk
Payment Details: Royalties are paid six-monthly or yearly depending on market potential of book
Unsolicited Manuscripts: Yes, but with return postage - synopsis preferred

Shetland Times Publishing

Publish books on local interest subjects.

Address: Prince Alfred Street, Lerwick, Shetland ZE1 0EP
Telephone: 01595 693622
Fax: 01595 694637
Email: publishing@shetland-times.co.uk
Website: www.shetland-books.co.uk
Imprints: The Shetland Times Ltd
Parent Company: The Shetland Times Ltd

S

Short Books

Short Books publishes Guides to EFL (English as a Foreign language) institutions worldwide, and also EFL course works for distance learning on the Internet.

Editor(s): Katharine Mendelsohn
Address: 18 Quarry Road, Winchester, Hants SO23 0JG
Telephone: 01962 855068
Fax: 01962 855068
Email: Sales@shortbooks.co.uk
Website: www.eflweb.co.uk
Imprints: Short Books
Parent Company: digitalbrain plc
Payment Details: Fees or royalties
Unsolicited Manuscripts: No

Shropshire Books

Publish books and leaflets about Shropshire to help residents and visitors explore and understand the county. Main subject areas covered so far are walking, cycling, history, archaeology, transport, folklore, wildlife, architecture, agriculture, gardens, literature and many more. Complete booklist available.

Editor(s): Helen Sample
Address: The Annexe, Shirehall, Abbey Foregate, Shrewsbury SY2 6ND
Telephone: 01743 255043
Fax: 01743 255050
Email: helen.sample@shropshire-cc.gov.uk
Website: http://www.shropshirebooks.co.uk
Parent Company: Shropshire County Council
Unsolicited Manuscripts: Send to Editor

Sigma Press

Walking, cycling, outdoor leisure, local history, sport, dance, travel guides and folklore.

Editor(s): Graham Beech
Address: 1 South Oak Lane, Wilmslow, Cheshire SK9 6AR
Telephone: 01625 531035
Fax: 01625 536800
Email: info@sigmapress.co.uk
Website: www.sigmapress.co.uk
Imprints: Sigma Leisure
Payment Details: By royalty
Unsolicited Manuscripts: No

Simon & Schuster Ltd

Founded in 1986, Simon & Schuster publish non-fiction; reference, music, travel and biography, fiction; mass market paperbacks, literary fiction and children's books.

Editor(s): Clare Ledingham, Martin Fletcher, Helen Gummer
Address: Africa House, 64-78 Kingsway, Holborn, London WC2B 6AH
Telephone: 0207 3161900
Email: amanda.harris@simonandschuster.co.uk
Imprints: Earthlight, Pocket Books, Scribner, Touchstone, Simon & Schuster, Simon & Schuster Children's Books
Parent Company: Viacom

S

Charles Skilton Ltd

General book publishers including reference, fine art, architecture and fiction.

Editor(s): James Hughes
Address: 2 Caversham Street, London SW3 4AH
Telephone: 020 7351 4995
Fax: Same as phone
Imprints: Luxor Press, Albyn Press, Fortune Press
Parent Company: Skilton
Payment Details: By negotiation
Unsolicited Manuscripts: Introductory letter required first

Skoob Russell Square

Well known poetry, Far Eastern literature, esoterica and occult. We will not be taking in any new material for the foreseeable future, for conventional publication. We do operate 'co-operative publishing' agreements, however these involve the author or institution in the cost, please apply for details.

Editor(s): Mark Lovell
Address: 10 Brunswick Centre London WC1N 1AE
Telephone: 0207 2788760
Fax: 0207 2783137
Email: books@skoob.com
Imprints: Skoob Seriph, Skoob Esoterica, Skoob Pacifica
Unsolicited Manuscripts: For co-operative publishing, please get in touch first

SLG Press

Short pamphlets and books about the spiritual life, prayer, and things which help towards a greater understanding of Christian tradition.

Editor(s): Sister Isabel Mary SLG
Address: Convent of The Incarnation, Fairacres, Oxford OX4 1TB
Telephone: 01865 721301
Fax: 01865 790860
Imprints: Fairacres Publications, SLG Press
Parent Company: SLG Charitable Trust Limited
Payment Details: No royalties, author receives 5% of the print run in lieu
Unsolicited Manuscripts: Yes but no poetry please

Smith Settle Ltd

Local and regional history (Yorkshire and North of England); general interest; fine and limited editions; customs and folklore; outdoor and leisure.

Editor(s): Ken Smith, Mark Whitley
Address: Ilkley Road, Otley, West Yorkshire LS21 3JP
Telephone: 01943 467958
Fax: 01943 850057
Email: sales@smith-settle.co.uk
Imprints: Westbury Academic Publishing, Yorkshire Journal
Payment Details: By negotiation
Unsolicited Manuscripts: Yes but send synopsis in first instance addressed to Manuscript Reviews

S
Smith-Gordon

Independent science, technology, medicine publisher established 1988. Works internationally, mainly at the postdoctoral level in life sciences: books, journals, newsletters.

Editor(s): E Smith-Gordon
Address: 13 Shalcomb Street, London SW10 0HZ
Telephone: 020 7351 7042
Fax: 020 7351 1250
Email: publisher@smithgordon.com
Unsolicited Manuscripts: Life sciences only, and at author's risk

Colin Smythe Ltd

Primarily publishers of Irish literature and criticism as well as acting as agent for authors and/or their literary estates.

Editor(s): Colin Smythe
Address: PO Box 6, Gerrards Cross, Bucks SL9 8XA
Telephone: 01753 886000
Fax: 01753 886469
Website: www.colinsmythe.co.uk
Imprints: Van Duren, Dolmen Press
Payment Details: Royalties
Unsolicited Manuscripts: No

Snapshot Press

Specialises in haiku and related poetry, publishing individual collections, an annual haiku calendar, and two internationally acclaimed journals, Snapshots (haiku) and Tangled Hair (tanka). It also publishes an annual anthology featuring the best English-language haiku and senryu published in the UK and Ireland during the previous year. The inaugural edition, The New Haiku, was published in 1999. Snapshot Press also publish the winning entries to the Snapshots Collection Competition - an annual competition for unpublished collections of haiku, senryu and/or tanka. (send SAE for details - Closing date 31st July).

Editor(s): John Barlow
Address: PO Box 35, Sefton Park, Liverpool LI7 3EG
Email: jb@snapshotpress.freeserve.co.uk
Website: www.mccoy.co.uk/snapshots
Payment Details: Royalties
Unsolicited Manuscripts: Yes, for journals and competitions. Other material solicited

Social Affairs Unit

The SAU is an independent research and educational trust committed to the promotion of lively and wide-ranging debate on social affairs. Current areas of work include consumer affairs, corporate governance, the critical appraisal of welfare and public spending and problems of freedom and personal responsibility.

Editor(s): Digby Anderson, Michael Mosbacher
Address: 5/6 Morley House, 314-322 Regent Street, London W1R 5AB
Telephone: 020 7637 4356 (0161 9417728)
Fax: 020 7436 8530
Email: mosbacher@socialaffairsunit.org.uk
Website: www.socailaffairsunit.org.uk
Payment Details: Negotiable, £150 max
Unsolicited Manuscripts: No

S
Social Work Monographs

Publish up to 10 new titles each year. A complete checklist containing over 100 titles is available on subjects such as family and child care, child abuse, care of the elderly, mental health, people with disabilities, theory and research and social work with offenders.

Editor(s): A McDonald
Address: School of Social Work, Elizabeth Fry Building, University of East Anglia, Norwich NR4 7TJ
Telephone: 01603 592087
Fax: 01603 593552
Email: j.hancock@uea

Society For General Microbiology

Publisher of three learned scientific journals - Microbiology (monthly), Journal Of General Virology (monthly) and International Journal Of Systematic and Evolutionary Microbiology (bi-monthly). Also publishes the magazine Microbiology Today, and with Cambridge University Press, the SGM Symposium Series of books on current topics in microbiology. SGM is a limited company and registered charity.

Address: Marlborough House, Basingstoke Road, Spencers Wood, Reading RG7 1AG
Telephone: 0118 988 1800
Fax: 0118 988 5656
Website: www.sgm.ac.uk
Payment Details: No payments are made
Unsolicited Manuscripts: Scientific research papers are subject to peer review

Society For Promoting Christian Knowledge (SPCK)

Publishes for the Christian book market. There are books covering all the following areas: prayer and meditation; biography and letters; personal growth and relationships; counselling; healing and pastoral care; church, mission and ministry; social and ethical issues; theology and religious studies; science and religion; biblical studies; church history; liturgical studies and worship resources. SPCK aims to cover a broad spectrum of religious viewpoints, and fulfils its mission through helping people to understand and develop their personal faith. Founded in 1698, it comprises a chain of bookshops and a Worldwide branch, which supports the work of churches around the globe.

Editor(s): Simon Kingston (SPCK), Joanna Moriarty (Sheldon Press), Alison Barr (Triangle & Azure)
Address: SPCK, Holy Trinity Church, Marylebone Road, London NW1 4DU
Telephone: 020 7643 0382
Fax: 020 7643 0391
Email: spck@spck.org.uk
Website: www.spck.org.uk
Imprints: SPCK, Triangle, Azure, Sheldon Press
Parent Company: SPCK
Payment Details: Individual agreement
Unsolicited Manuscripts: To imprint editor

Society For Underwater Technology

Multi-disciplinary international learned society dedicated to the active promotion of the development, dissemination and exchange of ideas, information and technology arising from or related to the underwater environment. Publishes a quarterly learned journal, newsletters and conference proceedings.

Editor(s): Dr D Brown, Dr P C Collar
Address: 80 Coleman Street, London EC2R 5BJ
Telephone: 020 7382 2601
Fax: 020 738 2684
Email: daniel@sutpubs.demon.co.uk
Website: www.sut.org.uk

S

Society Of Dyers And Colourists

Professional organisation specialising in all aspects of the science and technology of colour and coloration. It publishes a series of books dealing with dyes and pigments, and with the coloration of various substrates, especially textiles.

Address: PO Box 244, Perkin House, 82 Grattan Road, Bradford BD1 2JB
Telephone: 01274 725138
Fax: 01274 392888
Website: www.sdc.org.uk

Society Of Metaphysicians Ltd

Neometaphysics: new fundamental science and its applications. Includes paraphysics, parapsychology, psychic science, estoteric and mystical studies. Evaluation of consciousness: in terms of empathy. Neometaphysics (fundamental laws) and politics... and religion... and the physical sciences. World unity and environmental matters. Journal The NeoMetaphysical Digest invites short articles.

Editor(s): John J Williamson, Alan J Mayne, Eleanor Swift
Address: Archers Court, Stonestile Lane, The Ridge, Hastings, East Sussex TN35 4PG
Telephone: 01424 751577 Freephone: 0800 1958 796
Fax: Same as phone
Email: newmeta@btinternet.com
Website: www.metaphysicians.org.uk; www.newmeta.btinternet.com
Imprints: MRG (Metaphysical Research Group)
Payment Details: By mutual agreement
Unsolicited Manuscripts: Yes

Sort Of Books

Sort Of Books, as the name suggests, are open to a wide range of books - fiction, travel, biography, popular culture. The list was launched in 1999.

Editor(s): Natania Jansz, Mark Ellingham
Address: PO Box 18678, London NW3 2FL
Telephone: 020 7431 1925
Fax: 020 7431 1925
Email: nat@kenbury.demon.co.uk
Unsolicited Manuscripts: Letter first please

Southgate Publishers

Educational publisher. Books for primary teachers especially in the curriculum areas of environmental education, mathematics, personal and social education, music and dance, and assembly books. Publishes with the Campaign for Learning - books related to lifelong learning, including workforce training materials.

Address: The Square, Sandford, Crediton, Devon EX17 4LW
Telephone: 01363 776888
Fax: 01363 776889
Email: dj@southgatepublishers.co.uk
Website: www.southgatepublishers.co.uk
Imprints: Mosaic Educational Publications
Parent Company: Southgate Publishers Ltd
Unsolicited Manuscripts: No - write first with synopsis, or telephone

S

SPA Books Ltd

History - military and Scottish; art and crafts; biographies. Classic writings in travel, philosophy and other literature.

Editor(s): Steven Apps
Address: PO Box 47, Stevenage, Herts SG2 8UH
Imprints: Strong Oak Press
Unsolicited Manuscripts: No - synopsis please in first instance

Spellmount Limited

Publishers of high-quality history and military history books. All historical periods are covered but with particular emphasis on the Napoleonic period, World War 1 and World War 2. Autobiographies are not considered.

Editor(s): Jamie Wilson
Address: The Old Rectory, Staplehurst, Kent TN12 0AZ
Telephone: 01580 893730
Fax: 01580 893731
Email: enquiries@spellmount.com
Website: www.spellmount.com
Imprints: Spellmount
Payment Details: By negotiation
Unsolicited Manuscripts: Synopsis with return postage please

Spokesman Books

Economics. Politics. International Affairs. Industrial Relations. Labour History. Trade Unionism. Disarmament. Peace.

Editor(s): Ken Coates, Tony Simpson
Address: Russell House, Bulwell Lane, Nottingham NG6 0BT
Telephone: 0115 9708318
Fax: 0115 9420433
Email: elfeuro@compuserve.com
Website: www.spokesmanbooks.com
Imprints: Spokesman, European Labour Forum, Socialist Renewal, The Spokesman Journal
Parent Company: Bertrand Russell Peace Foundation Ltd
Unsolicited Manuscripts: No

Spon Press

Spon Press publish highly authoritative books covering all aspects of construction, building, civil engineering, architecture, planning, landscape and environmental and public health engineering. Our titles, written by acknowledged experts, provide the latest information for academics and professionals.

Editor(s): Richard Whitby - Civil Engineering, Tony Moore - Building and Construction, Caroline Mallinder - Architecture, Landscape
Address: 11 New Fettter Lane, London EC4P 4EE
Telephone: 020 7842 2001
Fax: 020 7842 2300
Website: www.sponpress.com
Parent Company: Taylor & Francis Group
Unsolicited Manuscripts: Yes

S

Square One Publications

Autobiographies - military memoirs a speciality, but others considered. All manuscripts read and comments given.

Editor(s): Mary Wilkinson
Address: The Tudor House, 16 Church Street, Upton-on-Severn Worcs WR8 0HT
Telephone: 01684 594522/593704
Email: marywilk@tinyonline.co.uk
Imprints: Square One Publications
Payment Details: Arranged individually
Unsolicited Manuscripts: Yes

St Pauls Publishing

Theology, ethics, spirituality, biography, education, general books of Roman Catholic and Christian interest. No children's or poetry. Founded 1948.

Editor(s): Andrew Pudussery
Address: 187 Battersea Bridge Road, London SW11 3AS
Telephone: 020 7978 4300
Fax: 020 7978 4370
Email: editions@stpauls.org.uk
Unsolicited Manuscripts: Synopsis and sample chapter preferred

ST Publishing

Independent publisher specialising in youth culture, music and football. ST Publishing focuses on youth cults and music, Low Life is dedicated to pulp fiction related to youth cults, and Terrace Banter is a football imprint dedicated to the fans.

Editor(s): George Marshall
Address: PO Box 12, Lockerbie DG11 3BW
Email: stpbooks@aol.com
Website: http://www.stpublishing.co.uk
Imprints: ST Publishing, Low Life, Terrace Banter
Parent Company: ST Publishing
Payment Details: Advance plus royalties twice-yearly
Unsolicited Manuscripts: Synopsis and sample chapter preferred

Stacey International

Illustrated non-fiction, encyclopaedic books on regions and countries, Islamic and Arab subjects, world affairs, business guides, travel, art, dictionaries, archeaology, geology, botany, flora and fauna.

Editor(s): Max Scott
Address: 128 Kensington Church Street, London W8 4BH
Telephone: 020 7221 7166
Fax: 020 7792 9288
Imprints: Stacey International, Stacey London, Royal Genealogies
Parent Company: Stacey Arts Ltd

S

Stagecoach: Education

Straightforward, comprehensive easy to use photocopiable, structured photocopiable worksheets designed to be used in stages for children aged 3-6 years. Removable worksheets are simply designed, but become progressively more advanced as new skills are learned. Exercises are easily adapted for specific topic work, may be used to promote art and craft activities, and can be used in conjunction with any reading or writing scheme. Project packs are also available.

Editor(s): R L Day
Address: Carriers Crossing, Woodford Road, Stratford-Sub-Castle, Salisbury SP4 6AE
Telephone: 01722 782369
Imprints: Stagecoach, Stage 1, Stage 2, Stage 3, Stage 4 (6 packs per stage)
Parent Company: Stagecoach
Unsolicited Manuscripts: No

Stainer & Bell Ltd

Publisher of sheet music, hymnody and books related to music and hymnody.

Editor(s): Nicholas Williams
Address: PO Box 110, Victoria House, 23 Gruneisen Road, Finchley, London N3 1DZ
Telephone: 020 8343 3303
Fax: 020 8343 3024
Email: post@stainer.co.uk
Website: http:www.stainer.co.uk
Imprints: Gallard, Augener, Joseph Williams, Weekes
Unsolicited Manuscripts: Yes

Harold Starke Publishers Ltd

Publishers of illustrated works of reference including medicine, natural history and 'lifestyle' subjects.

Editor(s): Naomi Galinski
Address: Pixey Green, Stradbroke, Eye, Suffolk IP21 5NG
Telephone: 01379 388334
Fax: 01379 388335
Unsolicited Manuscripts: No

The Steel Construction Institute

Develops and promotes the effective use of steel in construction. It is an independent, membership-based organisation. SCI's research and development activities cover many aspects of steel construction including multi-storey construction, industrial buildings, light gauge steel framing systems, development of design guidance on the use of stainless steel, fire engineering, bridge and civil engineering, offshore engineering, environmental studies, and development of structural analysis systems and information technology.

Address: Silwood Park, Ascot, Berks SL5 7QN
Telephone: 01344 623345
Fax: 01344 622944
Email: library@steel-sci.com
Website: www.steel-sci.org

S

Stenlake Publishing

Photographic local history books; transport history books; maritime history books and industrial history books.

Editor(s): Oliver Van Helden, David Pettigrew
Address: 54-58 Mill Square, Catrine, Ayrshire, KA5 6RD
Telephone: 01290 551122 (Sales), 01290 552233 (Editorial)
Fax: 01290 551122
Email: enquiries@stenlake.co.uk
Website: www.stenlake.co.uk
Payment Details: By negotiation
Unsolicited Manuscripts: No, but freelance writers with experience of above fields always sought

Stobart Davies Ltd

Wood and wood related crafts.

Editor(s): Brian Davies
Address: Priory House, 2 Priory Street, Hertford SG14 1RN
Telephone: 01992 501518
Fax: 01992 501519
Email: sales@stobart-davies.com
Website: www.stobart-davies.com
Unsolicited Manuscripts: Yes

Arthur H Stockwell Ltd

Book publishers - all types of work considered.

Editor(s): B Nott
Address: Elms Court, Torrs Park, Ilfracombe EX34 8BA
Telephone: 01271 862557
Fax: 01271 862988
Email: stockpub@aol.com

Stokesby House

Textbooks for secondary schools and colleges - biology, human biology and environmental studies.

Address: Stokesby, Norfolk NR29 3ET
Telephone: 01493 750645
Fax: 01493 750146
Email: stokesbyhouse@btinternet.com
Unsolicited Manuscripts: No

Storysack Ltd

Publisher of children's storybooks and manuals for use with Storysacks. Also supplier of ready-made Storysacks and Storysack accessories. Scripts for children's short story/picture books and illustrations are invited.

Editor(s): Leslie Howard, Neil Griffiths
Address: Resource House, Kay Street, Bury BL9 6BU
Telephone: 0161 763 6232
Fax: 0161 763 5366
Email: storysack@cs.com
Website: www.storysack.com
Unsolicited Manuscripts: Yes

S

STRI (the Sports Turf Research Institute)

Publishers of specialist titles relating to the maintenance, management and construction of natural turf playing surfaces including golf courses, sports pitches, bowling greens, lawn tennis courts, racecourses etc. Also a quarterly 36-page full colour magazine International Turfgrass Bulletin; an annual Journal Of Turfgrass Science and an on-line trade directory, STRI-Green Pages. We sell our titles, plus 200 other publishers' related titles, via our specialist mail order service Turfgrass Titles of the World. Books can be ordered on-line via our website bookshop www.turfgrassbooks.com.

Editor(s): Dr Gordon McKillop, Anne Wilson
Address: St Ives Estate, Bingley, West Yorkshire BD16 1AU
Telephone: 01274 565131
Fax: 01274 561891
Email: anne.wilson@stri.co.uk, info@stri.co.uk
Website: www.stri.co.uk
Parent Company: STRI
Payment Details: On request
Unsolicited Manuscripts: Yes, by prior arrangement; we do publish other author's titles.

Stride

We expect poetry to show an engagement with the knowledge of contemporary poetics: we are not interested in rhyming doggerel, light verse or the merely confessional. We are interested in linguistically innovative work, and work in more traditional (whether formal or free) genres that reinvent the way we see the world. We are also interested in books of interviews for our Stride Conversation Pieces series; and documents (theses; essays; unedited interviews) for our Research Documents series. These should be in the field of arts, music (particularly jazz and 'out-rock') or literature.

Editor(s): Rupert Loydell
Address: 11 Sylvan Road, Exeter, Devon EX4 6EW
Email: Editor@stridebooks.co.uk
Website: www.stridebooks.co.uk
Imprints: Stride Research Documents, Stride Conversation Pieces, Stride
Parent Company: Stride Publications
Payment Details: Free copies / Royalties
Unsolicited Manuscripts: Yes, with SAE. No e-mail submissions.

Summersdale Publishers Ltd

Fiction and non-fiction publishing house. Specialist areas: travel literature; international fiction; biography and history; humour and gift books. No poetry or children's literature. Founded 1990.

Editor(s): Elizabeth Kershaw
Address: 46 West Street, Chichester, West Sussex PO19 1RP
Telephone: 01243 771107
Fax: 01243 786300
Email: liz@summersdale.com
Website: www.summersdale.com
Payment Details: Advances and royalties paid
Unsolicited Manuscripts: Yes

Supportive Learning Publications

Educational publishers specialising in the following: work books for children; photocopiable worksheet packs for schools; English as a second language for children and adults. Subjects covered include English, maths, science, history, geography, technology, art, craft, music, early learning etc. We also publish material specifically written for reluctant readers, produced as short plays or sketches with, usually, a comedy/adventure theme. The reading age of these plays is approximately 9 years but with an interest level of 7 to 14 years.

Editor(s): Phil Roberts
Address: 23 West View, Chirk, Wrexham LL14 5HL
Telephone: 01691 774778
Fax: 01691 774849
Email: slpuk.demon.co.uk
Website: www.slpuk.demon.co.uk
Payment Details: Negotiable
Unsolicited Manuscripts: Yes

S

Sussex Publications

Audio-visual materials only. No interest in books unless they are texts to accompany audiotapes, videotapes, slide sets, tape slide sets, computer programs, CD-ROMs and microfilms. All subjects covered.

Address: 4 Foscote Mews, London W9 2HH
Telephone: 020 7266 2202
Fax: 020 7266 2314
Email: microworld@ndirect.co.uk
Website: www.microworld.ndirect.co.uk
Imprints: Sussex Tapes, Sussex Video. Associates: Audio-Forum - The Language Source, World Microfilms, Pidgeon Audio-Visual
Unsolicited Manuscripts: N/A

Ta Ha Publishers Ltd

Books on Islam and Muslim world, and children's books.

Editor(s): A Clarke, A Thomson, A Siddiqui
Address: 1 Wynne Road, London SW9 0BB
Telephone: 020 7737 7266
Fax: 020 7737 7267
Email: sale@taha.co.uk
Website: http://www.taha.co.uk
Unsolicited Manuscripts: Yes synopses only with SAE

Taigh Na Teud Music Publishers

Publish Scottish traditional music and song with a specialisation in Highland and Gaelic material. Also some Gaelic non-music items.

Editor(s): Christine Martin (music), Alasdair Martin (Gaelic)
Address: 13 Breacais Ard, Isle of Skye IV42 8PY
Telephone: 01471 822 528
Fax: 01471 822 811
Email: editors@scotlandsmusic.com
Website: www.scotlandsmusic.com
Imprints: Taigh Na Teud
Payment Details: Royalties paid 6-monthly in arrears - 10% retail
Unsolicited Manuscripts: Contemporary tunes in the Highland idiom

Take That Ltd

Financial markets, personal finance, computing, Internet, gambling.

Editor(s): C Brown
Address: PO Box 200, Harrogate HG1 2YR
Fax: 01423 526035
Email: sales@takethat.co.uk
Website: www.takethat.co.uk
Imprints: Take That Books, Net.Works, Cardoza, TTL
Parent Company: Take That Ltd
Payment Details: 10%, no advances
Unsolicited Manuscripts: Yes

T

Tamarind Ltd

Children's full colour picture books which give a high positive profile to black children. Multicultural Picture Books 2-12 (ages).

Editor(s): Ms S Sideri, Ms V Wilkins
Address: PO Box 52, Northwood, Middlesex HA6 1UN
Telephone: 020 8866 8808
Fax: 020 8866 5627
Email: TamrindLTD@aol.com
Unsolicited Manuscripts: Yes

Tango Books

Publishers and distributors of children's novelty books: pop-ups, lift-the-flap, touch-and-feel, books and packages. Most for children 0-11. Fiction and non-fiction.

Editor(s): Sheri Safran (for submissions)
Address: Penthouse Studio
Telephone: 020 8746 1171
Fax: 020 8746 1170
Email: sales@tangobooks.co.uk
Website: www.tangobooks.co.uk
Imprints: Tango Books, Somerville, Vander Meer, Soundprints, I Kids
Parent Company: Sadie Fields Productions Ltd
Payment Details: Advance and royalties
Unsolicited Manuscripts: Yes

Tarquin Publications

Mathematics, paper engineering, patterns, things involving paper cutting, folding or models. Fundamental science treated in a three-dimensional way.

Editor(s): Gerald Jenkins
Address: Stradbroke, Diss, Norfolk IP21 5JP
Telephone: 01379 384218
Fax: 01379 384289
Website: www.tarquin-books.demon.co.uk
Imprints: Tarquin
Payment Details: Royalties and advance paid
Unsolicited Manuscripts: No - send a brief description in a letter

Tate Publishing

Publishers for the Tate Gallery in London, Liverpool and St Ives. As well as producing art books and exhibition catalogues we have a wide range of posters, postcards and stationery products.

Editor(s): Nicola Bion, John Jervis, Mary Richards, Judith Severne
Address: Tate Publishing, Millbank, London SW1P 4RG
Telephone: 020 7887 8869
Fax: 020 7887 8878
Email: tgpl@tate.org.uk
Website: www.tate.org.uk
Imprints: Tate Publishing
Parent Company: Tate Enterprises Ltd
Unsolicited Manuscripts: No

T

Taylor Graham Publishing

Publishers of academic books and journals, in areas of information technology, information management, librarianship, and education themes in general.

Address: 48 Regent Street, Cambridge CB2 1FD

The Templar Company Plc

Children's picture books and novelties. Children's trade non-fiction; particularly natural history and early learning first concepts.

Editor(s): Dugald Steer, Sue Harris
Address: Pippbrook Mill, London Road, Dorking, Surrey RH4 1JE
Telephone: 01306 876361
Imprints: Templar Publishing
Payment Details: Advances and royalties for author and artist ideas taken up
Unsolicited Manuscripts: Yes

Tempus Publishing Ltd

History publishers with special interests in local and regional history. Large series of regional books containing old photographs (the Archive Photographs series), including books on town history, transport, sport and other regional history including oral history. Also some early history and archaeology books and general world history.

Editor(s): David Buxton (topographical, regional and oral history), Campbell McCutcheon (transport and industrial history), Peter Kemmis-Betty (early history and archaeology), Jonathan Reeve (general history), James Howarth (sport history)
Address: The Mill, Brimscombe Port, Brimscombe, Stroud GL5 2QG
Telephone: 01453 883300
Fax: 01453 883233
Email: tempusuk@tempus-publishing
Parent Company: Tempus Publishing Group
Payment Details: Royalty in most cases
Unsolicited Manuscripts: Yes, to the relevant listed editor

Tern Press

Artists, printmakers, printers, type designers, Nicholas and Mary Parry have continued their work with a love of literature since Art College. In 1972, they acquired their own presses and have now produced 150 editions of books, in which technique and materials reflect their chosen subjects. Natural history, early british, biblical, war, poetry. Grey's Elegy, Alice in Wonderland and Alice Through The Looking Glass. All illustrated.

Editor(s): Nicholas Parry, Bill Griffiths, John Porter, Meirion Pennar, Norman Jeffares, Professor Eric Robinson, Yann Lovelock, David Powell
Address: The Tern Press, St Mary's Cottage, 20 Great Hales SP, Market Drayton, Shropshire TF9 1JN
Telephone: 01630 652153
Unsolicited Manuscripts: Will be looked at and considered

Textile & Art Publications Ltd

Textile & Art Publications brings together a specialist group of individuals with many years' experience in the art world and in the production, publishing, distribution and marketing of international art books, often linked to exhibitions. We have unique access to many major private collections and a reputation for producing generously-illustrated books to the highest academic, design and production standards, concentrating on a limited number of major titles each year. The company is building a varied list of books, covering Oriental, Islamic, Pre-Colombian and Medieval art; and has also produced international language co-editions of its titles for other publishers.

Editor(s): Michael Franses
Address: 12 Queen Street, Mayfair, London W1X 7PL
Telephone: 01749 850856
Fax: 020 7409 2596
Email: post@textile-art.com
Website: www.textile-art.com
Imprints: Textile & Art Publications

T
Thames & Hudson Ltd

Thames & Hudson, which celebrated its 50th anniversary in 1999, is one of the world's best-known publishers of illustrated books. Concentrating on books of high textual and visual quality for an international audience, its programme of more than 150 titles per year focuses on the arts of all kinds, archaeology, architecture and design, graphics, history, mythology, photography, popular culture and travel and topography.

Editor(s): Editorial Head: Jamie Camplin
Address: 181a High Holborn, London WC1V 7QX
Telephone: 020 7845 5000
Fax: 020 7845 5056
Email: h.farr@thameshudson.co.uk
Website: www.thamesandhudson.com
Imprints: Thames & Hudson
Payment Details: Royalties paid twice-yearly
Unsolicited Manuscripts: Send preliminary letter and outline before manuscripts

Thames Publishing

Thames: books about English classical music and musicians, particularly of earlier part of 20th century. Autolycus: backlist only of poetry (no new publications).

Editor(s): Proprietor: E. Betty Bishop
Address: 14 Barlby Road, London W10 6AR
Telephone: 020 8969 3579
Fax: Same as phone
Imprints: Thames, Autolycus
Unsolicited Manuscripts: No

The Perseus Press

Launched in the autumn of 2001, The Perseus Press is a new UK imprint made up of select quality non-fiction titles. This radical and exciting list encompasses history, science, business and current affairs.

Address: PO Box 317, Oxford, OX2 9RU
Telephone: 01865 860960
Fax: 01865 862763
Email: info@theperseuspress.com
Unsolicited Manuscripts: No

Third Age Press

An independent publishing company which recognises that the period of life after full-time employment and family responsibility can be a time of fulfillment and continuing development. The books encourage older people to make the best of the rest of their lives, but are also relevant to those working with older people or teaching students of gerontology or geriatrics. To date topics covered have included the following: writing and recording life stories, memory, health, alternative therapies, changes and challenges in later life, walking through Europe, the history of the old-age pension, sharing a house and running a care home. Through its Perspectives series, Third Age Press also produces self-published memoirs.

Editor(s): Dianne Norton
Address: 6 Parkside Gardens, London SW19 5EY
Telephone: 020 8947 0401
Fax: 020 8944 9316
Email: dnort@globalnet.co.uk
Website: www.thirdagepress.co.uk
Imprints: Third Age Press
Unsolicited Manuscripts: Yes if within areas detailed

T
Thistle Press

Scottish regional travel guides; local history; archaeology and geology with Scottish content; general Scottish interest; academic books on the environmental sciences. Member of Scottish Publishers Association.

Editor(s): Keith Nicholson, Angela Nicholson
Address: West Bank, Western Road, Insch, Aberdeenshire AB52 6JR
Telephone: 01464 821 053
Fax: Same as phone
Website: www.thistlepress.co.uk
Payment Details: Annual royalties as per contract
Unsolicited Manuscripts: Yes

Thoemmes Press

Thoemmes Press publishes primary sources and reference works in the History of Ideas for the global academic community. We have an exciting core programme of Biographical Dictionaries in Management and European Philosophy and more traditional product lines which make available long out-of-print and rare materials. Subjects include: Ancient Philosophy, 17th, 18th, 19th Century Philosophy, Idealism, Logic Scottish enlightenment, Aesthetics, Theology, Social and Political Thought, History of Economics, Business and Management history, Philosophy and History of Science, Development of Psychology, Irish Studies and the History of American Thought. Thoemmes Press offers a focussed service publishing single and multi-volume hardbound products to libraries and individual academics around the world.

Editor(s): Philip du Barry, Kirsten Robertson
Address: Thoemmes Press, 11 Great George Street, Bristol BS1 5RR
Telephone: 0117 9291377
Fax: 0117 9221918
Email: info@thoemmes.com
Website: www.thoemmes.com
Imprints: Overstone - Historical Sources in Economic Thought, Nico Editions - Classic Works on the History of the Book
Unsolicited Manuscripts: No, but unsolicited proposals are welcome

Thomas Cook Publishing

Produce a wide range of travel-related books, maps and timetables. Publications in the Thomas Cook Publishing portfolio include: European and Overseas Timetables - updated monthly; Travellers Guides (54-book series); European and South Asian phrasebooks; World Atlas Of Travel; Golden Age Of Travel; Greek Island Hopping 2001; Your Passport To Safer Travel; Rail Maps of Great Britain and Ireland and Europe; Hot Spots Guides (25-book series); Signpost Guides; Independent Traveller's Guides; Classic Short Breaks; Welcome Guides; Time for food (20 titles).

Editor(s): Donald Greig
Address: PO Box 227 Thorpe Wood, Peterborough PE3 6PU
Telephone: 01733 503571
Fax: 01733 503596
Website: www.thomascook.com
Parent Company: Thomas Cook Group
Unsolicited Manuscripts: Yes

F.A. Thorpe (Publishing)

Large print publishers.

Address: The Green, Bradgate Road, Anstey, Leicester LE7 3ZN
Telephone: 0116 234 0081
Fax: same as phone
Website: www.ulverscroft.co.uk
Imprints: Charnwood Hardcover, Ulverscroft Hardcover, Linford Softcover
Unsolicited Manuscripts: No

T

Thoth Publications

Publishers of metaphysical, western mystery tradition, and esoteric works, with each manuscript given care and attention by those with the knowledge within the particular field.

Editor(s): Tom Clarke
Address: 64 Leopold Street, Loughborough LE11 5DN
Telephone: 01509 210626
Fax: 01592 238034
Email: enquiries@thoth.co.uk
Website: www.thoth.co.uk

Timber Press

Timber Press is a leading publisher of books on gardening, horticulture and botany. Specialises in authoritative treatments of particular plant groups written by internationally renowned authors. Whether you are a keen gardener or a professional grower, Timber Press can help to inform you about the different genera, propagation and cultivation of many plants, trees and shrubs.

Editor(s): Neal Maillet
Address: 2 Station Road, Swavesey, Cambridge CB4 5QJ
Telephone: 01954 232959
Fax: 01954 206040
Website: www.timberpress.com
Imprints: Amadeus Press
Parent Company: Timber Press, Portland, Oregon USA

Titan Books

Founded 1981. Now a leader in the publication of graphic novels and film and television tie-ins. Publishes comic books/graphic novels, film and television titles about 70-80 titles a year.

Titles include Batman, Superman, Star Trek, Star Wars, The Simpsons and Farscape.

No unsolicited manuscripts or email submissions. Author guidelines available.

Editor(s): Nick Landau - Managing Director; Katy Wild - Editorial Director; David Barraclough - Editorial Manager; Simon Furman - Senior Editor; Adam Newell - Editor; Jo Boycett - Editorial Assistant
Address: 144 Southwark Street, London SE1 0UP
Telephone: 020 7620 0200
Fax: 020 7620 0032
Email: editorial@titanemail.com
Imprints: Titan Books
Parent Company: Titan Publishing Group Limited
Payment Details: Royalties paid twice yearly
Unsolicited Manuscripts: No

Tobin Music

The Tobin System of Musical Education gives a new dimension to all musical theory and simple composition and is applied to various instruments. This method uses many psychological and innovative means to explain many seemingly complex concepts so that even the youngest understand. All the senses are employed and colour and pattern help to elucidate and substantiate all conventional notation.

Available books on composition, scales and key signatures, pitch and rhythm, pre-school/infant, junior school classroom teaching, classical guitar, recorder and piano tutors. CD ROM demonstrating the complete system.

Editor(s): Chris Dell
Address: The Old Malthouse, Knight Street, Sawbridgeworth, Herts CM21 9AX
Telephone: 01279 726625
Email: candidatobin@candidatobin.co.uk
Website: http://www.candidatobin.co.uk
Parent Company: Helicon Print
Unsolicited Manuscripts: No

T

Topaz Publications

Publishers of legal texts in relation to Irish law only.

Editor(s): Davida Murdoch
Address: 10 Haddington Lawn, Glenageary, Co Dublin, Ireland
Telephone: 00353 1 2800460
Fax: Same as phone
Unsolicited Manuscripts: No

Trematon Press

Publish equestrian books, specialising in side-saddle riding.

Editor(s): Elizabeth Turner
Address: Trematon Hall, Saltash, Cornwall PL12 4RU
Telephone: 01752 842351
Fax: 01752 848920
Unsolicited Manuscripts: Yes

Trentham Book Ltd

Books for professional use by teachers and lecturers and other practitioners in education, social work and law. Not books for classroom use; not children's books, reminiscence, biography, fiction or poetry. No packs or other non-book material.

Editor(s): Gillian Klein
Address: Westview House, 734 London Road, Oakhill, Stoke on Trent ST4 5NP
Telephone: 01782 745567/844699
Fax: 01782 745553
Email: tb@trentham-books.co.uk
Website: www.trentham-books.co.uk
Imprints: Trentham
Payment Details: Annual royalty calculated 31st August and payable within six weeks thereafter
Unsolicited Manuscripts: Yes

Triangle Books

Publishers of Christian books, particularly in the areas of prayer, spirituality and personal growth. We also publish books on mission and the church in the modern world, as well as stories of faith in action. Triangle books are aimed at a popular Christian readership.

Editor(s): Alison Barr
Address: Holy Trinity Church, Marylebone Road, London NW1 4DU
Telephone: 020 7643 0382
Fax: 020 7643 0391
Email: abarr@spck.org.uk
Website: www.spck.org.uk
Parent Company: SPCK
Payment Details: By negotiation
Unsolicited Manuscripts: Send synopsis and sample chapter

Triumph Books

We specialise in books on American sports and sports people, especially golf, American football, baseball, and ice hockey. Our new imprint Triumph Entertainment is dedicated to producing 'instant' pictorials on pop culture, games/collectables and current events including: Britney Spears, NSYNC, Christina Aguilera, Eminem, The Beatles...

Editor(s): Tom Bast
Address: c/o Roundhouse Publishing Ltd, Millstone, Limers Lane, Northam, Devon, EX39 2RG
Telephone: 01237 474474
Fax: 01237 474 774
Email: round.house@fsbdial.co.uk
Website: www.roundhouse.net
Imprints: Triumph Entertainment
Payment Details: Royalties twice yearly
Unsolicited Manuscripts: No

T

Triumph House

Triumph House publishes Christian poetry books on various themes. It also produces a quarterly magazine, Triumph Herald, featuring items such as personal testimonies, Bible stories, prayers and general Christian arts news. Includes a section for young Christians to share their poetry along with a few crossword puzzles and word searches. A year's subscription to the magazine (four issues) is £15 in the UK and £21 for overseas. The Spotlight Poets imprint also publishes books of poetry containing twelve authors with each one having ten pages of the book dedicated to them and their work. The poems can be on a variety of subjects and themes. Please write or telephone for an information pack on any of the above. You can also contact us by email, but please be sure to include your postal address.

Editor(s): Managing Editor: Sarah Andrew; Editor: Neil Day
Address: Remus House, Coltsfoot Drive, Woodston, Peterborough PE2 9JX
Telephone: 01733 898102
Fax: 01733 313524
Email: triumphhouse@forwardpress.co.uk
Website: www.forwardpress.co.uk
Imprints: Spotlight Poets
Parent Company: Forward Press Ltd
Payment Details: Small payment for magazine material published, plus Top 100 Poets of the Year competition for anthologies: with a £3,000 first prize
Unsolicited Manuscripts: Send covering letter with sample poems only

Twelveheads Press

Twelveheads Press ahs been publishing good books about transport and industrial history, mainly in Cornwall and the south west of England, since 1977.

Editor(s): Michael Messenger, Alan Kittridge
Address: Chy Mengleth, Twelveheads, Truro, Cornwall TR4 8SN
Telephone: 01209 820978
Fax: 0870 056 7465
Email: mjm@twelveheads.com
Website: www.twelveheads.com
Imprints: Twelveheads Press
Payment Details: Royalties half-yearly
Unsolicited Manuscripts: No, already write with proposals beforehand

Two-Can Publishing Ltd

Two-Can Publishing is a leading provider of educational books and multimedia products aimed at children, parents and teachers. Established in 1987, Two-Can trades throughout the world, with a particular focus in North America and in Spanish and French language markets. Key partners include Scholastic, Worlds Book, Golden Books, Grolier and Egmont. Publishing infrastructures have been established in the UK, where Two-Can products are sold to schools, book clubs, traditional book shops and multiple chains and supermarkets, and recently in the USA.

Two-Can's key brands are interfact, covering a range of products that combine book and multimedia elements, and Make it Work!, practical and inspirational material for the teaching of science, history and geography.

Editor(s): Managing Director: Mr Ian Grant
Address: 43-45 Dorset Street, London W1H 4AB
Telephone: 020 7664 1654
Fax: 020 7224 7005
Email: ian_g@two-canpublishing.com

UCL Press

Social sciences, politics and international relations, media and culture studies, geography, archaeology, history and criminology.

Editor(s): Caroline Wintersgill, Luciana O'Flaherty, Kate Brewin
Address: 1 Gunpowder Square, London EC4A 3DE
Parent Company: Taylor & Francis Group
Unsolicited Manuscripts: No

U
UKCHR - United Kingdom Council For Human Rights

Monitor human rights in the United Kingdom, where there has been a radical restructuring of society. This process continues under New Labour. Publish leaflets and booklets on human rights issues, and a reference book on race, poverty and health: Of Germs, Genes and Genocide.

Address: Flat No 7, Sunley House, 10 Gunthorpe Street, London E1 7RW
Telephone: 020 7377 2932
Fax: 0870 055 3979
Email: ukchr@ukcouncilhumanrights.co.uk
Website: www.ukcouncilhumanrights.co.uk/

University Of Exeter Press

An established scholarly publisher. Around 25 titles a year in the arts and humanities, including European studies, medieval studies, history, classical studies, film history, theatre studies, linguistics, and landscape studies.

Editor(s): Simon Baker
Address: Reed Hall, Streatham Drive, Exeter EX4 4QR
Telephone: 01392 263066
Fax: 01392 263064
Email: uep@ex.ac.uk
Website: www.ex.ac.uk/uep/
Unsolicited Manuscripts: No

University Of Hertfordshire Press

Best known as a publisher of books on Gypsies and Travellers (history, sociology, literature etc) including the English language editions of the international publishing programme known as the Interface Collection. Also publishes serious academic books on parapsychology including the highly respected Guidelines series (volumes to date include psychic testing and ESP), regional and local history, astronomy (in the series Building Blocks Of Modern Astronomy) and most recently on literature and drama commencing with three volumes of Shakespearean studies by Professor Graham Holderness. The Press has recently appointed distributors in the UK and North America, is expanding its publishing programme, and welcomes approaches from potential authors in the areas within which it specialises.

Editor(s): W A Forster
Address: Learning and Information Services, University of Hertfordshire, College Lane, Hatfield AL10 9AD
Telephone: 01707 284681
Fax: 01707 284666
Email: uhpress@herts.ac.uk
Website: www.herts.ac.uk/uhpress/
Imprints: University of Hertfordshire Press and Hertfordshire Publications
Parent Company: University of Hertfordshire
Unsolicited Manuscripts: To the Editor

University Of London Careers Service

Specialising in Careers publications. Books written by Careers Advisors working in the Higher Education sector and mainly aimed at graduates and undergraduates although the underlying principles tend to be applicable to everyone.

Address: 49-51 Gordon Square, London WC1H 0PQ
Telephone: 020 7554 4521
Fax: 020 7383 5876
Email: milkround@careers.lon.ac.uk
Website: www.careers.lon.ac.uk
Parent Company: University of London
Unsolicited Manuscripts: No

U
University Of Wales Press

The University of Wales Press was established in 1922 and is wholly owned by the University and is one of the largest universities in Britain. The Press now concentrates on four main subject areas:

History
Political philosophy and religous studies
European Studies
Welsh and Celtic Studies

Each year the Press publishes nearly sixty new titles in addition to reprints, new editions and journal issues.

Editor(s): Commissioning Editors: Susan Jenkins, Duncan Campbell, Editorial Manager: Ceinwen Jones, Production Manager: Liz Powell
Address: 6 Gwennyth Street, Cathays, Cardiff CF24 4YD
Telephone: 029 2023 1919
Fax: 029 2023 0908
Email: press@press.wales.ac.uk
Website: www.wales.ac.uk/press
Imprints: Gwasg Prifysgol Cymru, University of Wales Press
Parent Company: University of Wales
Payment Details: Negotiable
Unsolicited Manuscripts: No

Usborne Publishing

Children's books. Usborne books are accessible, fun, visually exciting and inviting and start at a point which naturally engages a child's interest. As a result, Usborne books have been chosen by teachers, parents and carers for over twenty years to help children develop a love of reading and thirst for knowledge.

Editor(s): Managing Director: Peter Usborne, Publishing Director: Jenny Tyler
Address: 83-85 Saffron Hill, London EC1N 8RT
Telephone: 020 7430 2800
Fax: 020 7430 1562
Email: mail@usborne.co.uk
Website: www.usborne.com
Unsolicited Manuscripts: No, all titles created in-house

V & A Publications

V & A Publications publish a broad range of titles on the decorative arts. The objective is to produce books which have an international appeal, and are of high quality design. Subjects include fashion, glass, ceramics, paintings, photography. We also publish accompanying books for V & A major exhibitions.

Editor(s): Miranda Harrison
Address: VHA Publications, 160 Brompton Road, London SW3 1HW
Telephone: 020 7942 2966
Fax: 020 7942 2977
Email: j.smith@vam.ac.uk
Website: www.vam.ac.uk
Imprints: V & A

Vallentine Mitchell

International publisher of books of Jewish interest for both scholar and general reader. Published subjects include Jewish history, culture, and heritage, modern Jewish thought, biography and reference, holocaust testimonies.

Editor(s): Sally Green
Address: Crown House, 47 Chase Side, Southgate, London, N14 5BP
Telephone: 020 8920 2100
Fax: 020 8447 8548
Email: info@vmbooks.com
Website: www.vmbooks.com
Imprints: Vallentine Mitchell
Parent Company: Frank Cass & Co Ltd
Payment Details: Royalties
Unsolicited Manuscripts: Yes

V

Veloce Publishing Ltd

Automotive (car and motorcycle) histories, full-colour automotive books, practical and technical automotive manuals and books.

Editor(s): Rod Grainger
Address: 33 Trinity Street, Dorchester, Dorset DT1 1TT
Telephone: 01305 260068
Fax: 01305 268864
Email: info@veloce.co.uk
Website: www.veloce.co.uk
Imprints: Veloce
Payment Details: Royalty basis
Unsolicited Manuscripts: Yes

Vennel Press

Small press specialising in contemporary Scottish poetry, and, in its Au Quai imprint, poetry in translation.

Editor(s): Richard Price, Leona Medlin
Address: 8 Richmond Road, Staines, Middlesex TW18 2AB
Email: vennel@hotmail.com
Imprints: Au Quai
Parent Company: Vennel Press
Payment Details: Negotiable
Unsolicited Manuscripts: No

Venton Educational Ltd

Poetry, Careers, West Country, Maritime, Motoring and Travelogues.

Editor(s): Mr C Venton
Address: 57 Seend Cleeve, Seend Melksham, Wiltshire SN12 6PX
Telephone: 01380 828654
Fax: Same as phone
Email: K_and_A2000@tinyonline.co.uk
Imprints: White Horse Library and Uffington Books
Parent Company: Colin Venton Ltd
Payment Details: By arrangement
Unsolicited Manuscripts: Yes

Veritas Foundation Publication Centre

Poland, Eastern Europe, religion, Catholicism and Christianity, prayer books, memoirs and history.

Editor(s): Thomas Wachowiak
Address: 63 Jeddo Road, London W12 9EE
Telephone: 020 8749 4957
Fax: 020 8749 4965
Email: thomas@veritas.knsc.co.uk
Payment Details: Author to cover all costs
Unsolicited Manuscripts: No

V
Verso Ltd

Verso is a radical publisher, publishing about 40 titles a year. Titles are predominantly in the areas of politics, history, cultural studies and philosophy. Verso publish a number of trade titles but the bulk of the list is academically orientated.

Editor(s): Robin Blackburn, Sebastian Budgen
Address: 6 Meard Street, London W1V 3HR
Telephone: 020 7437 3546
Fax: 020 7734 0059
Website: www.versobooks.com
Payment Details: Advances given, standard royalties
Unsolicited Manuscripts: Yes

VERTIC (Verification Research, Training And Information Centre)

VERTIC is the Verification Research, Training and Information Centre, an independent, non-profit making, non-governmental organisation. Its mission is to promote effective and efficient verification as a means of ensuring confidence in the implementation of international agreements and intra-national agreements with international involvement. VERTIC aims to acheive its mission through research, training dissemination of information, and interaction with the relevant political, diplomatic, technical, scientific and non-governmental communties.

Editor(s): Dr Trevor Findlay
Address: Baird House, 15/17 St Cross Street, London EC1N 8UW
Telephone: 020 7440 6960
Fax: 020 7242 3266
Email: info@vertic.org
Website: www.vertic.org
Unsolicited Manuscripts: Yes

Verulam Publishing Ltd

Publishers and distributors. Subjects covering include: business, computers, cookery, english, finance, gift books, health, history, language learning (textbooks, audio, video), new age and mysticism, parenting, quilting, self-help, sport and fitness, theatre and performing arts and travel.

Editor(s): David Collins
Address: 152a Park Street Lane, Park Street, St Albans AL2 2AU
Telephone: 01727 872770
Fax: 01727 873866
Email: sales@verulampub.demon.co.uk
Imprints: Take That Books, Rutledge Hill Press, Stoddart Publishing, Covos-day Books, Cumberland House Publishing, Carton Publishing Group
Unsolicited Manuscripts: No

V
Virgin Books

Publish a wide range of books for the general consumer market, but do not publish any poetry, children's books or general fiction. Specialise in non-fiction books about popular culture, especially music, TV, sport, reference and in certain genres of fiction published strictly within imprint guidelines.

Virgin Publishing Non-fiction (All published under Virgin imprint)

Non-fiction books for the general reader, specialising in popular culture, especially music, travel, TV, film and sport. Unsolicited manuscripts are not accepted. Unsolicited submissions of a synopsis and some sample text are accepted, but only within the subject areas indicated. Authors are advised to request and read the company's house style sheet before submitting proposals.

Editorial Director: Humphrey Price (general non-fiction); Senior Editor: Rod Green (film, TV and radio tie-ins, celeb humour, pop culture); Editors: David Gould (popular reference); Jonathan Taylor (sport); Melissa Harrison (popular culture, music, biography). Editorial Director: Carolyn Thorne (lifestyle, health, music, media, pop culture (illustrated only); Editors: Ian Gittins, Stuart Slater (music - reference, bios, criticism, illustrated). Senior Editor: Kerri Sharp; Editors: James Marriot, Kathleen Bryson (sexuality, true crime film).

Virgin Publishing Fiction (Virgin imprint unless otherwise stated)

Unsolicited manuscripts not accepted. Unsolicited submissions of a synopsis and some sample text are accepted, but only for the imprints and series listed. Virgin do not publish one-off stand-alone novels. Authors' guidelines available for each imprint; submissions accepted only from authors who have read and followed the relevant guidelines. There are sometimes new series in development - authors should watch the press for announcements.

Editorial Director: Humphrey Price; Senior Editor: Kerri Sharp (erotic fiction by women - Black Lace); Editors: James Marriot (erotic fiction - Nexus); Kathleen Bryson (gay and lesbian erotica - Idol and Sapphire imprints).

Address: Thames Wharf Studios, Rainville Road, London W6 9HT
Telephone: 020 7386 3300
Fax: 020 7386 3360
Email: <name>@virgin-pub.co.uk
Imprints: Virgin
Payment Details: Usually by royalties on sales, but we'll consider other arrangements
Unsolicited Manuscripts: No

Volcano Press Ltd

Islam in Britain, Europe and the USA. Women's studies, preferably Muslim women and human rights issues.

Editor(s): A Hussain
Address: PO Box 139, Leicester LE2 2YH
Telephone: 0116 2706714
Fax: Same as phone
Email: asaf@volcano.u-net.com
Payment Details: Yearly 5-10% royalties
Unsolicited Manuscripts: No

Walden Publishing Ltd/World Of Information

Publisher of country business and economic information. Five annual reviews: Middle East, Africa, Asia and Pacific, Americas, Europe. Regional development series: The OAU Report (35 years in the service of Africa); The "Nations of the World"; The ADB Report (Sustaining Africa's growth); The OAS Report (50 years of the OAS); World Travel & Tourism (5 regional volumes).

Editor(s): Philip Alexander
Address: 2 Market Street, Saffron Waldon, Essex CB10 1HZ
Telephone: 01799 521150
Fax: 01799 524805
Email: info@worldinformation.com
Website: www//worldinformation.com
Unsolicited Manuscripts: No

W
Walk & Write Ltd

'We hike the paths and trails of the world for others to enjoy'. Authors, printer and publishers of local and national guides (walk guides). And international publishers of : Nottingham Heritage Series, Derbyshire Heritage Series.

Editor(s): John N. Merrill
Address: Unit 1, Molyneux Business Park, Whitworth Road, Darley Dale, Matlock, Derbyshire DE4 2HJ
Telephone: 01629 735911
Fax: Same as phone
Email: marathonhiker@aol.com
Website: www.countrywalks.com
Parent Company: Happy Walking Ltd
Payment Details: Agreement is royalty, 5% up to and after 500 copies sold, 10% after 1,000 copies sold
Unsolicited Manuscripts: Yes

Walkways/Quercus

Walkways publishes books of walks, especially long-distance footpaths, with the emphasis on the western Midlands. Quercus publishes general interest books about the western Midlands region, including history, mysteries, landscape and geography, biographies and natural history.

Editor(s): John Roberts
Address: 67 Cliffe Way, Warwick CV34 5JG
Telephone: 01926 776363
Fax: Same as phone
Imprints: Walkways, Quercus
Payment Details: 10% royalty on retail price
Unsolicited Manuscripts: No, approach first

Wallflower Press

Independent publisher specialising in film studies, media, cultural studies, and related subjects. Around 20 books a year produced, both academic and of general interest. Books distributed through North America by Columbia University Press.

Editor(s): Yoram Allon
Address: 16 Chalk Farm Road, Camden Lock, London NW1 8AG
Telephone: 0207 431 6622
Fax: 020 7485 0101
Email: info@wallflowerpress.co.uk
Website: www.wallflowerpress.co.uk
Parent Company: Wallflower Publishing Ltd
Payment Details: Royalties paid twice-yearly
Unsolicited Manuscripts: Synopses or sample chapters welcome

Waterside Press

Law publisher with leading edge in criminal justice, youth justice, prisons, policing, family matters, mediation, conflict resolution, restorative justice, relationships, women's legal rights, domestic violence, victims, community programmes, justice and the arts. Independently owned and managed.

Editor(s): Bryan Gibson
Address: Domum Road, Winchester SO23 9NN
Telephone: 01256 882250
Fax: 01962 855567 or 01256 882250
Email: watersidepress@compuserve.com
Website: www.watersidepress.co.uk
Imprints: Waterside Press
Payment Details: Royalty basis; occasionally advances, but not usually
Unsolicited Manuscripts: Please approach us first before submitting ms

W

Websters International Publishers Ltd

Publishers of high quality wine, cooking and travel books. Specialists in wine information in all formats.

Editor(s): Anne Lawrance, Susannah Webster, Fiona Holman
Address: Axe & Bottle Court, 70 Newcomen Street, London SE1 1YT
Telephone: 020 7940 4700
Fax: 020 7940 4701
Email: websters@websters.co.uk
Website: www.websters.co.uk and www.ozclarke.com
Unsolicited Manuscripts: No

Trust For Wessex Archaelogy Ltd

Publishes specialist and academic monographs on archaeological sites and surveys in the Wessex region.

Editor(s): Julie Gardiner
Address: Portway House, Old Sarum Park, Salisbury SP4 6EB
Telephone: 01722 326867
Fax: 01722 337562
Email: postmaster@wessexarch.co.uk
Unsolicited Manuscripts: No

White Cockade Publishing

Social and cultural history, oral history, architectural and design history, decorative arts; mainly nineteenth and twentieth century, and particular Scottish interest. Books to satisfy both the specialist and general reader.

Editor(s): Perilla Kinchin
Address: White Cockade Publishing, 71 Lonsdale Road, Oxford OX2 7ES
Telephone: 01865 510411
Fax: 01865 463644
Email: mail@whitecockade.co.uk
Website: whitecockade.co.uk
Unsolicited Manuscripts: Letter first, with s.a.e. please.

White Eagle Publishing Trust

A spiritual organisation with publishing trust set up 65 years ago. All books are produced within the organisation and all have spiritual teachings on various topics ie healing, death and dying, spiritual growth. 'Darkness will not touch you if you are radiating light' ... White Eagle.

Editor(s): Ylana Hayward, Colum Hayward, Jenny Dent, Jeremy Hayward
Address: New Lands, Brewells Lane, Liss, Hants GU33 7HY
Telephone: 0207 603 7914
Fax: 01730 892235
Email: info@whiteagle.org
Website: www.whiteagle.org
Unsolicited Manuscripts: No

W

White Row Press

Publisher of general Irish interest non-fiction, and (occasionally) prose. Good, well thought out ideas welcome. Enclose SAE.

Editor(s): Peter Carr
Address: 135 Cumberland Road, Dundonald, Belfast BT16 2BB
Telephone: 02890 482586
Email: whiterow@whiterow.freeserve.co.uk
Unsolicited Manuscripts: Yes if Irish interest non-fiction

Whittet Books

Whittet Books publishes reference books on natural history; including domesticated animals such as poultry; books on horses and donkeys.

Editor(s): A Whittet
Address: Hill Farm, Stonham Road, Cotton Stowmarket, Suffolk IP14 4RQ
Telephone: 01449 781877
Fax: 01449 781898
Email: Annabel@Whittet.dircon.co.uk
Parent Company: A Whittet & Co
Unsolicited Manuscripts: Yes

Whittles Publishing

Publisher of books in civil engineering and construction; surveying and photogrammetry and applied science. We also have a trade list specializing in maritime and nautical titles and nature writing.

Editor(s): Keith Whittles
Address: Roseleigh House, Harbour Road, Latheronwheel, Caithness KW5 6DW
Telephone: 01593 741240
Fax: 01593 741360
Email: whittl@globalnet.co.uk
Website: www.users.globalnet.co.uk/~whittl
Imprints: Whittles Publishing
Payment Details: Royalty payment will vary according to the project
Unsolicited Manuscripts: No

Whurr Publishers Ltd

Publishers of academic and professional books and journals in the professions allied to medicine.

Editor(s): Jim McCarthy
Address: 19b Compton Terrace, London N1 2UN
Telephone: 020 7359 5979
Fax: 020 7226 5290
Email: info@whurr.co.uk
Website: www.whurr.co.uk
Imprints: Cole & Whurr
Parent Company: none - independent
Payment Details: Royalties paid twice yearly.
Unsolicited Manuscripts: Yes

W
WI Books Ltd

WI Books is the publishing division of the National Federation of Women's Institutes. It publishes books for WI members on a range of subjects including cookery, crafts and gardening, often written by WI members who are already experts in their field.

Editor(s): Marketing Manager: Claire Bagnall
Address: 104 New King's Road, London SW6 4LY
Telephone: 020 7371 9300
Fax: 020 7736 3652
Email: c.bagnall@nfwi.org.uk
Website: http://www.womens-institute.org.uk
Parent Company: WI Enterprises, National Federation of Women's Institutes
Unsolicited Manuscripts: Yes

Wild Goose Publications

Religious books, tapes and songbooks. We also publish books on social, justice, peace and political issues.

Editor(s): Managing Editor: Sandra Kramer
Address: Unit 16, 6 Harmony Row, Glasgow G51 3BA
Telephone: 0141 440 0985
Fax: 0141 440 2338
Email: admin@ionabooks.com
Website: www.ionabooks.com
Parent Company: The Iona Community
Payment Details: Royalties every 6 months
Unsolicited Manuscripts: Synopsis and sample chapter only

Philip Wilson Publishing Limited

Quality publisher of books on the fine and decorative arts, from golf memorabilia to Vivienne Westwood creations.

Editor(s): Anne Jackson (commissioning); Caroline Venables (managing)
Address: 143-149 Portland Street, London W1N 5FB
Telephone: 020 7436 4485
Fax: 020 7436 4403
Email: pwp@monoclick.co.uk
Website: In preparation
Imprints: Philip Wilson
Unsolicited Manuscripts: No

Windhorse Publications

Books on Buddhism, meditation and related subjects.

Editor(s): Sara Hagel (Commissioning Editor)
Address: 11 Park Road, Moseley, Birmingham B13 8AB
Telephone: 0121 449 9696
Fax: 0121 449 9191
Email: sara-windhorse@compuserve.com
Website: www.fwbo.org/windhorse
Unsolicited Manuscripts: To Commissioning Editor

W

The Windrush Press

Publisher, established 1987, now part of the Orion Group. Military history, general history, 'ancient mysteries', Traveller's History series, non-fiction. Not fiction, travel writing or poetry.

Editor(s): Victoria Huxley
Address: Windrush House, 12 Adle Strop, Moreton in Marsh, Gloucestershire GL56 0YN
Telephone: 01608 658758
Fax: 01608 659345
Email: windrush@windrushpress.com
Website: www.windrushpress.com
Unsolicited Manuscripts: Yes, letter synopsis/sample only, SAE essential for return

Speechmark Publishing Ltd

Speechmark Publishing is a specialist publisher and producer of practical resources for professionals working with the special educational and therapeutic needs of people of all ages. We produce practical and accessible resources for speech and language, education, health, rehabilitation, elderly care, occupational therapy and all aspects of social care.

Editor(s): Commissioning Editor: Stephanie Martin; Editorial and Production Controller: Sarah Miles; Publishing Manager: Sue Christelow
Address: Telford Road, Bicester, Oxon OX26 4LQ
Telephone: 01869 244644
Fax: 01869 320040
Email: info@speechmark.net
Website: www.speechmark.net
Payment Details: Determined by contract
Unsolicited Manuscripts: Yes

Winslow Publishing

Interactive CD-ROM publisher, books on health, diet, cookery, crafts, and general well-being.

Address: 122a Cambridge Road, Southend on Sea, Essex SS1 1ER
Telephone: 01702 342698
Fax: 01702 347353
Email: crafthouse@clara.net
Website: www.crafthouse.uk.com
Imprints: Winslow, Crafthouse
Unsolicited Manuscripts: Yes

WIT Press

WIT Press a major publisher of engineering research. The company prides itself on producing books by leading researchers and scientists at the cutting edge of their specialities, thus enabling readers to remain at the forefront of scientific developments.

Our publications presently include monographs, edited volumes, books on disk and CD-Rom, and software, designed for a wide readership including undergraduate and graduate students, researchers, and engineers, scientists and managers within industry. Topics covered include: acoustics, architecture, bio-engineering, boundry elements, computing, earthquake engineering, environmental engineering, fluid mechanics, fracture mechanics, heat transfer, numerical methods, strucural engineering and transport engineering.

Editor(s): Director of Publishing: Lance Sucharov
Address: Ashurst Lodge, Ashurst, Southampton SO40 7AA
Telephone: 023 8029 3223
Fax: 023 8029 2853
Email: witpress@witpress.com
Website: www.witpress.com
Parent Company: Computational Mechanics Int.
Payment Details: Not disclosed
Unsolicited Manuscripts: Yes

W
Witan Books And Publishing Services

Founded in 1980 and guided by ecological and humanitarian principles. Publishes books on general subjects, especially biography, education, the environment, geography, history, politics, popular music and sport. Witan Publishing Services was developed as an offshoot to help writers get their work into print; it offers a comprehensive service including proofreading, editing, design and guidance to publication. Sample titles: Principles Of Open Learning; The Last Poet: The Story Of Eric Burdon; The Valiants' Years: The Story Of Port Vale; The Man Who Sank The Titanic?: The Life And Times Of Captain Edward J. Smith; The Mercia Manifesto: A Blueprint For The Future Inspired By The Past; The Potteries Derbies.

Editor(s): Jeff Kent
Address: Cherry Tree House, 8 Nelson Crescent, Cotes Heath, via Stafford ST21 6ST
Telephone: 01782 791673
Imprints: Witan Books
Parent Company: Witan Creations
Payment Details: Advances and royalties paid to authors
Unsolicited Manuscripts: Yes with SAE

Witherby And Co Ltd

Insurance publications: marine insurance, reinsurance, motor, liability, construction, offshore oil and gas, life assurance, captives, environmental, business interruption, aviation, insurance dictionaries, risk management. Shipping publications: surveying, safety, oil pollution, salvage, mooring, offshore engineering, the shipping of oil, gas and chemicals, marine survival and rescue, tanker structures, dictionaries.

Editor(s): Alan Witherby
Address: 32-36 Aylesbury Street, London EC1R 0ET
Telephone: 020 7251 5341
Fax: 020 7251 1296
Email: books@witherbys.co.uk
Website: www.witherbys.com
Payment Details: Royalties paid to authors
Unsolicited Manuscripts: Yes

The Women's Press

Literary fiction; crime fiction; health; women's studies; handbooks; literary criticism; psychology; therapy and self-help; the arts; politics; writing by black women and women of colour; disability issues and lesbian issues. All books must be women-centered and have a feminist message or theme.

Editor(s): Kirsty Dunseath, Charlotte Cole, Essie Cousins
Address: 34 Great Sutton Street, London EC1V 0LQ
Telephone: 020 7251 3007
Fax: 020 7608 1938
Website: www.the-womens-press.com
Imprints: Livewire Books for young women (12-16yrs)
Payment Details: Advance and royalties
Unsolicited Manuscripts: Yes, with return postage

Women's Sports Foundation

The only organisation in the UK solely committed to improving and promoting opportunities for women and girls in sport at every level.

Address: 305-315 Hither Green Lane, Lewisham, London SE13 6TJ
Telephone: 020 8697 5370
Fax: Same as phone
Email: info@wsf.u-net.com
Website: www.wsf.org.uk

W
The Woodfield Press

Publishers of Irish local history, womens' studies and biography. Established in 1995; ten books published to date.

Editor(s): Freelance, Publisher: Terri McDonnell
Address: 17 Jamestown Square, Inchicore, Dublin 8, Ireland
Telephone: 01454 7991
Fax: 01602 4875
Email: terri.mcdonnell@ireland.ie
Website: http://myhome.iolfree.ie/~woodfield
Imprints: The Woodfield Press
Payment Details: Royalty - 10-12% of net invoice value

Woodstock Books

Facsimile reprints of literary texts in series: Revolution And Romanticism 1789-1834, edited by Jonathan Wordsworth; Hibernia, edited by John Kelly; Decadents, Symbolists, Anti-Decadents, edited by Ian Small and R K R Thornton.

Editor(s): James Price
Address: Ilkley Road, Otley LS21 3JP
Telephone: 01943 467958
Fax: 01943 850057
Imprints: Woodstock Books
Unsolicited Manuscripts: No

W

Wordsworth Editions Ltd

Leading publisher of low-cost paperbacks. Series include Wordsworth Classics, Wordsworth Children's Library, Wordsworth Reference, Wordsworth Poetry Library, Wordsworth Classics Of World Literature, Wordsworth Military Library, Wordsworth Myth, Legend and Folklore, Wordsworth Interactive editions in CD ROM, study aids for schools. Wordsworth are primarily reprint publishers, but occasionally commission books, especially in the reference area.

Editor(s): Editorial Director: Laema Hartnoll
Address: Cumberland House Crib Steet, Ware Herts SG12 9ET
Telephone: 01920 465 167
Fax: 01920 462267
Email: editorial@wordsworth-editions.com
Imprints: As described
Unsolicited Manuscripts: No

Wrightson Biomedical Publishing Ltd

Publisher of books and journals in clinical medicine and biomedical science. Topics of particular interest: psychiatry, neuroscience, gastroenterology, dermatology, gerontology, cardiology. We are known for the high quality and speed of publication of our books, for attention to detail and friendly service.

Editor(s): Judy Wrightson
Address: Ash Barn House, Winchester Road, Stroud, Petersfield, Hants GU32 3PN
Telephone: 01730 265647
Fax: 01730 260368
Email: wrightson.biomed@virgin.net
Imprints: Wrightson Biomedical
Unsolicited Manuscripts: Yes

W

Writers And Readers Ltd

Philosophy, science, politics, religion, history, literature, music, psychiatry, women's studies, black studies, social science, biographies, novels, arts, media, theatre and US studies.

Editor(s): Vastiana Belfon
Address: 2a Britannia Row, London N1 8PA
Telephone: 020 7226 2522
Fax: 020 7359 1406
Email: begin@writersandreaders.com
Website: www.writersandreaders.com
Imprints: For Beginners, Black Butterfly Children's Books, Harlem River Press, Writers and Readers Inc (USA)
Payment Details: Negotiable
Unsolicited Manuscripts: No

Writers' Bookshop

Publishers of writers' aids. Annual directories such as the Small Press Guide and self-help titles such as Successful Writing by Teresa McCuaig, Poetry: How To Get Published, How To Get Paid by Kenneth C Steven, How To Write Non-Fiction Books by Gordon Wells, How To Write And Sell A Book Proposal by Stella Whitelaw and The Craft Of Writing Romance by Jean Saunders. Manuscript submissions and ideas in all areas of interest to writers are invited.

Editor(s): Ann Johnson Allen
Address: Remus House, Coltsfoot Drive, Woodston, Peterborough PE2 9JX
Telephone: 01733 898103
Fax: 01733 313524
Website: www.forwardpress.co.uk
Parent Company: Forward Press Ltd
Payment Details: 15% royalties
Unsolicited Manuscripts: Yes, please include postage for return

The X Press

Black interest popular novels, particularly reflecting contemporary ethnic experience: 20/20 - cult classic fiction; Nia - black literary fiction and non-fiction; Black Classics - reprints of American/African/British black classic novels.

Editor(s): Steve Pope, Doton Adebayo
Address: PO Box 25694, London, N17 6FP
Telephone: 020 8801 2100
Fax: 020 8885 1322
Email: vibes@xpress.co.uk
Website: www.xpress.co.uk
Imprints: 20/20, Nia, Black Classics
Parent Company: The X Press
Unsolicited Manuscripts: Yes

Yale University Press

Art, architecture, history and the humanities.

Editor(s): John Nicoll, Robert Baldock, Gillian Malpass
Address: 23 Pond Street, London NW3 2PN
Telephone: 020 7431 4422
Fax: 020 7431 3755
Email: sales@yaleup.co.uk
Imprints: Yale University Press, Pelican History of Art, Yale English Monarchs
Parent Company: Yale University Press, New Haven USA
Unsolicited Manuscripts: Yes

Roy Yates Books

Books for children in dual-language (bilingual) editions. Co-editions of established books translated into other languages. No original publishing undertaken.

Editor(s): Roy Yates
Address: Smallfields Cottage, Cox Green, Rudgwick, Horsham RH12 3DE
Imprints: Roy Yates Books, Ingham Yates
Unsolicited Manuscripts: No

Yes! Publications

Community publishing house based in Derry/Londonderry Northern Ireland. Established in 1986. Main publication is Fingerpost Community Magazine, the longest-surviving community magazine in Ireland. Explores issues of cultural identity through their publications.

Editor(s): Various
Address: 10-12 Bishop Street, Londonderry, Co Derry BT48 6PW
Telephone: 028 7126 1941
Fax: 028 7126 9332
Email: yes.pubs@business.ntl.com

Yore Publications

Specialist football book publisher, generally of an historical nature, from small paperbacks to substantial cased books. Currently the leading publisher of Football League club histories (over 20 to date) substantially written, illustrative and statistical. Also club (players) Who's Who books. Yore Publications is led by Dave Twydell, a member of the Football Writers' Association.

Editor(s): Dave Twydell
Address: 12 The Furrows, Harefield, Middlesex UB9 6AT
Telephone: 01895 823404
Fax: Same as phone
Email: yore.demon.co.uk
Website: www.yore.demon.co.uk/index.html
Imprints: Yore Publications
Payment Details: Varies
Unsolicited Manuscripts: No

Young Writers

Poetry written by young people aged between 8 and 18 years inclusive. Two series of books published per year: April - September 8 - 11 year olds, October - March 11 - 18 year olds. Poems usually submitted through schools, but individual entries are accepted. Poems can be written on any subject and in any style, but must not exceed 30 lines in length. If you choose to contact us by email, please include postal address. As well as regional anthologies, Young Writers also publishes two magazines: Scribbler! (8-11 yr olds) and Wordsmith !11-18). For further details, please send an SAE.

Editor(s): Managing Ed: Steve Twelvetree, Asst Managing Eds: Simon Harwin, Magazine Eds: Lucy Jeacock
Address: Remus House, Colstfoot Drive, Woodston, Peterborough PE2 9JX
Telephone: 01733 890066
Fax: 01733 313524
Email: youngwriters@forwardpress.co.uk
Website: www.youngwriters.co.uk
Parent Company: Forward Press Ltd
Payment Details: Prizes:- Per Series: 1 x £1000 5 x £250 10 x £100 awarded to schools. Per Book: 1 x £20 4 x £5 Book Tokens awarded to the writers of the five best poems. Prizes are also awarded for work featured in each magazine.
Unsolicited Manuscripts: Yes

Z
Zed Books Ltd

Radical independent publisher of scholarly books in development and environment, gender and women's studies, cultural studies, sociology, politics, economics, current affairs and international affairs. Zed's authors come from all over the world and we seek to make our books widely accessible throughout North and South.

Editor(s): Robert Molteno, Louise Murray
Address: Zed Books Ltd, 7 Cynthia Street, London N1 9JF
Telephone: 020 7837 0384
Fax: 020 7833 3960
Email: zed@zedbooks.demon.co.uk
Website: www.zedbooks.demon.co.uk
Imprints: Zed Books
Parent Company: Zed Books Ltd
Payment Details: By agreement
Unsolicited Manuscripts: No - please send outline proposal

Zero To Ten Limited

Children's publishers specialising in picture books.

Editor(s): Anna McQuinn
Address: 327 High Street, Slough, Berks SL1 1TX
Telephone: 01753 578499
Fax: 01753 578488
Email: tradesales@evansbrothers.co.uk
Parent Company: Evans Brothers Ltd
Unsolicited Manuscripts: No

Zymurgy Publishing

Publisher of mass market non-fiction in hard and paperback format.

Areas of particular interest include: mind, body and spirit, complementary medicine, popular science, biography and autobiography, photography and natural history.
Editor(s): Martin Ellis
Address: Hoults Estate, Walker Road, Newcastle-upon-Tyne, NE6 2HL
Telephone: 0191 2762425
Fax: 0191 2762425
Email: martin.ellis@ablibris
Unsolicited Manuscripts: No, please send synopsis

2003 Edition

Writers' Bookshop invites entries for the Guide to Book Publishers 2003

Entries or enquiries before 1 June 2002 to:
Editor, Guide to Book Publishers
Writers' Bookshop
Remus House
Coltsfoot Drive
Woodston
Peterborough
PE2 9JX